SAGE was founded in 1965 by Sara Miller McCune to support the dissemination of usable knowledge by publishing innovative and high-quality research and teaching content. Today, we publish over 900 journals, including those of more than 400 learned societies, more than 800 new books per year, and a growing range of library products including archives, data, case studies, reports, and video. SAGE remains majority-owned by our founder, and after Sara's lifetime will become owned by a charitable trust that secures our continued independence.

Los Angeles | London | New Delhi | Singapore | Washington DC | Melbourne

PSYCHOLOGICAL SKILLS TRAINING *for* HUMAN WELLNESS

PSYCHOLOGICAL SKILLS TRAINING *for* HUMAN WELLNESS

Agya Jit Singh
Ramneet Kaur

Los Angeles | London | New Delhi
Singapore | Washington DC | Melbourne

Copyright © Agya Jit Singh and Ramneet Kaur, 2021

All rights reserved. No part of this book may be reproduced or utilised in any form or by any means, electronic or mechanical, including photocopying, recording, or by any information storage or retrieval system, without permission in writing from the publisher.

First published in 2021 by

SAGE Publications India Pvt Ltd
B1/I-1 Mohan Cooperative Industrial Area
Mathura Road, New Delhi 110 044, India
www.sagepub.in

SAGE Publications Inc
2455 Teller Road
Thousand Oaks, California 91320, USA

SAGE Publications Ltd
1 Oliver's Yard, 55 City Road
London EC1Y 1SP, United Kingdom

SAGE Publications Asia-Pacific Pte Ltd
18 Cross Street #10-10/11/12
China Square Central
Singapore 048423

Published by Vivek Mehra for SAGE Publications India Pvt Ltd. Typeset in 10.5/13 pt Berkeley by AG Infographics, Delhi.

Library of Congress Control Number: 2020948292

ISBN: 978-93-5388-668-4 (HB)

SAGE Team: Rajesh Dey, Shipra Pant, Aishna Bhatt and Rajinder Kaur

To
our family members
by whose support we have been inspired
to write this book

Thank you for choosing a SAGE product!
If you have any comment, observation or feedback,
I would like to personally hear from you.

Please write to me at **contactceo@sagepub.in**

Vivek Mehra, Managing Director and CEO, SAGE India.

Bulk Sales

SAGE India offers special discounts
for purchase of books in bulk.
We also make available special imprints
and excerpts from our books on demand.

For orders and enquiries, write to us at

Marketing Department
SAGE Publications India Pvt Ltd
B1/I-1, Mohan Cooperative Industrial Area
Mathura Road, Post Bag 7
New Delhi 110044, India

E-mail us at **marketing@sagepub.in**

Subscribe to our mailing list
Write to **marketing@sagepub.in**

This book is also available as an e-book.

CONTENTS

Preface and Acknowledgements   ix

Introduction		1
Chapter 1	Human Wellness: Need of the Hour	20
Chapter 2	Managing Psychic Energy	41
Chapter 3	Mental Imagery: A Master Skill	60
Chapter 4	Motivation for Performance Enhancement	78
Chapter 5	Goal Setting: A Psychological Skill	100
Chapter 6	Emotional Arousal Regulation	120
Chapter 7	Stress Management Techniques	135
Chapter 8	Psycho-regulative Techniques	166
Chapter 9	Attention Skill and Concentration Ability	186
Chapter 10	Self-confidence as a Skill Area	204
Chapter 11	Understanding and Development of the Self	221
Chapter 12	Leadership and Communication Skills	242
Chapter 13	Decision-making and Problem-solving	263
Chapter 14	Implementation and Application of Psychological Skills Training Programme	279

References   300
About the Authors   307
Index   309

PREFACE AND ACKNOWLEDGEMENTS

Psychology involves not only the study of human behaviour but also helping a human being lead a stress-free life full of freedom, happiness and prosperity. Psychologists have devised some behavioural skills which make the life of an individual very useful, productive and effective. These psychological skills are meant for the welfare of human beings and their wellness. Every person should learn these skills to be successful in this fast-moving life, which is full of hustle and bustle. These skills need to be taught by the psychologists who are helping them face the rigours of life.

The present book *Psychological Skills Training for Human Wellness* has been written keeping in view the above-mentioned problems of the modern man. It will give educative information and knowledge to the readers about these psychological skills that are needed to be learnt in life. The skills which have been discussed in this book are psychic energy, imagery, motivation, goal setting, emotional arousal, psycho-regulative techniques, attention and concentration abilities, self-confidence, self-development, decision-making and problem-solving as well as leadership and communication. All these topics have been discussed comprehensively. In the end, the implications and practical applications of these skills have been narrated.

An attempt has been made to write this book in a very simple and comprehensive language and it is hoped that this book will be very useful to the general readers, professionals, research scholars, teachers and all those who are interested in knowing about the psychological skills and applying them in their lives.

The authors are thankful to all those experts and writers whose work have been consulted and quoted wherever required and referred with their courtesy to make this book more informative and valuable. They are also grateful to various sources from which some figures and useful material have been taken to seek help while writing the book. They also feel obliged to the reviewers of this book who have provided positive feedback and constructive suggestions for improving its quality as well. Last but not least, they will be failing in their duty if they do not acknowledge the helpful attitude and motivating behaviour of Mr Abhijit Baroi of SAGE. Without his help, this book would not have seen the light of the day.

The authors dedicate this book to the general readers for human well-being. It is also dedicated to the students and teachers whose love and affection the authors value the most and that act as a source of motivation and inspiration to them.

Introduction

Psychological skills are the behavioural devices that help human beings lead their life full of happiness, free of stress, enjoyable and healthy—both physically and mentally. These are the tactics and techniques of lifestyles that an individual would want to adopt in the journey of life. An individual has to learn these skills so that he/she may lead a healthy life. Psychologists are trying to devise these techniques and teaching them to human beings through counselling and other methods. The purpose is to make them physically and mentally fit as well as emotionally and socially adjusted so that they can develop a well-rounded personality. Learning these mental training skills involves psychological skills training (PST).

PST constitutes training the mind. Mental skills include learning diverse topics such as coping with the stress of life, keeping calm under difficult situations, resilience, persistence, self-motivation, self-confidence, strong moral character, leadership, time management and communication skills. Psychological skills also include stress management techniques, regulation of psychic energy, setting positive goals, emotional arousal control, applying mental imagery techniques and many more. All these skills have to be learnt, acquired and practised in daily life in order to make our life effective and productive.

PSYCHOLOGICAL SKILLS TRAINING (PST)

PST is the systematic and organized practice of strategies, techniques and methods designed to enhance an individual's performance by enhancing their behavioural skills. This includes teaching and learning of behavioural or psychological skills, such as managing stress and leading tension-free life, sustaining focus and handling emotions. These PST programmes should be conducted by a trained psychologist. PST is a scientific training process which can help in maintaining a balanced and calm state of mind under adverse competitive and stressful situations and can help in enhancing the performance of an individual.

PST is a kind of mental training for maintaining mental health to keep both the mind and the body fit in order to lead a healthy and productive life. It helps a man to be efficient in order to achieve success in day-to-day life. It is meant for the purpose of enhancing performance, increasing enjoyment and achieving greater self-satisfaction. Psychologists have devised some strategies and techniques which include behaviour modification, cognitive technique, rational emotive therapy, goal-setting skill, attention control, progressive relaxation exercises and systematic desensitization psychotherapy. Just like we need to regularly practise physical exercises daily to keep ourselves physically fit and to maintain physical health, we need to practice psychological skills such as focusing and sustaining concentration, regulating arousal levels, enhancing confidence and maintaining motivation need to be systematically practised. The basic psychological skills are given in Box I.1.

Box I.1: Psychological Skills

1. Psychic energy
2. Mental imagery
3. Motivation
4. Goal setting
5. Emotional arousal
6. Stress management
7. Attention and concentration skill
8. Skill of confidence
9. Self- regulation
10. Leadership and communication skill

All these above skills have been described in the following chapters, one by one in detail. All the above-given skills give a bird's-eye view of the psychological skills which are being used by the psychologists in the Western countries, especially in the USA. Of course, in India, these techniques are not being taught and applied either in the psychiatric clinics or schools, colleges and universities. But its use has started in sports institutions for the mental training of the Indian athletes for the enhancement of their sports performance.

PST involves providing training to individuals so that they can learn how to regulate their emotions under undesirable conditions and how to maintain their composure under adverse situations. During this kind of training, relaxation techniques are taught, and they help an individual in maintaining a balanced state of mind in the face of competition and can help in enhancing the performance of an individual. PST is of great significance in sports as the state of mind of the sportsperson influences their performance. If the sportsperson is trained to regulate their emotions during tough times, their performance can be improved. But it is also very important in many other areas of life, especially in professional life. Different training programmes can vary and have different skills to offer, but a majority of the programmes involve teaching some typical psychological skills.

PST is a programme that involves directions, practice and feedback in order to teach a new skill. The training is continued for some fixed time based on some predetermined criterion. Besides, there are many other skills such as communication, goal setting and planning, self-improvement, empathy, conflict resolution and time management. Their description is given below:

1. **Communication:** Communication skill is one of the psychological skills which is needed for everybody to become effective in their life. The process of communication involves (a) the decision to send a message, (b) encoding of the message, (c) sending the message, (d) the channel through which the message is sent, (e) decoding the message by the receiver and (f) an internal response to the message. Sending messages that are accurately decoded is a vital skill.

    Effective communication consists of both verbal and non-verbal communication, having body language and eye contact with others. Paying attention to what other people are trying to convey and comprehending their meaning is imperative. It is also very important to avoid communication gap as it can lead to very serious problems in life. Many people do not focus on the meaning of what other people are saying, and they act on their misunderstood notions and take wrong directions in their relations and also in their professional life. The lack of communication or miscommunication can be a big threat to the harmony and peace in life as well as it can harm the productivity of professional life. The communication training can help individuals to communicate effectively to have a happy, peaceful and productive life.

2. **Goal setting:** Learning how to set goals and how to achieve them motivates individuals and accelerates their performance during the high-level performance. Goal setting not only influences the performance but also brings positive changes in some psychological states such as anxiety, stress and confidence. Hence, it is an important technique which people with the help of a psychologist must regularly employ during the counselling period.

   Goal setting includes making a clear and defined action plan and a way to execute it to achieve the goal. 'Goal setting is defined as what an individual is trying to achieve and it is an objective of an action' (Locke et al., 1981). An individual can plan both short- and long-term goals for their performance. The goals can be either visualized or verbalized by the individuals. The writing of goals by individuals can help them to be more determined to achieve their goals. Weinberg (1988) showed that getting success in achieving goals leads to increased self-confidence (Hardy et al., 1996; Weinberg & Gould, 2003).

   Planning is very important for the accomplishment of the goals in life. Planning involves setting concrete goals and making efforts to achieve the goals. A strong commitment of a person plays a pertinent role in the planning and accomplishment of the goals.

3. **Self-improvement:** Employees at their workplace should grow and develop professionally. They should try to improve themselves by the training as well as by experience in their jobs. This will give them job satisfaction, which will lead them to success and happiness. They should consider their new task as challenging and

create will power to achieve it. Contentment is the basic requirement in one's life to accomplish something. It is only possible if they implement behavioural skills. Self-improvement training will give them objective feedback and critical analysis so that they can overcome their shortcomings and do better in the next task.

4. **Empathy:** Empathy is sensing the feelings of others. If we can put ourselves into other's shoes and look into the emotional behaviour of other people like our own, then we can understand other's feelings. Feelings and emotions are subjective experiences that everybody encounters. We should try to respect others' feelings, whether negative or positive ones. There may be differences with others, but still, we should try to adjust with them. It is only possible if we have the skill of empathy. We should believe in the dictum of 'forget and forgive'. Empathy is the ability to communicate with others positively, looking into their weaknesses and limitations healthily. In this way, we would be able to resolve our conflicts and find out the solutions. Empathy is a behavioural skill that can help us to maintain our peace of mind and can also make us more successful in our careers as interpersonal relationships affect the productivity of our work.

5. **Conflict resolution:** Whenever there is a dispute between two individuals or members of one group (Intra-group relationships), we should try to resolve the conflict by mutual consultation or arbitration. Disagreement can be removed if the proper environment can be created on both sides or if both parties are willing to resolve their differences mutually. If in any organization, disputes continue between employees on some issues, it will affect their performance, and the productivity will also suffer. It will also spoil their inter-personal relationships, which may affect their mental health. Conflicts are likely to occur among human beings due to their ego strength. However, it is essential to lead a healthy and prosperous life, so we should be able to resolve our conflicts as early as possible amicably.

6. **Time management:** Time management is a vital psychological skill which needs to be mastered by everybody. It is the acumen of a person to organize and execute one's work and complete it on time. This skill should be developed by each and everybody in our

lives. It is like setting a timetable for all the activities in our daily life. It will help us to save ourselves from the hustle and bustle of our fast life. When we are loaded with so many tasks, we are unable to decide which work should be done or which we should try to avoid. We should give preference to the task, which needs a priority and postpone the task, which is less important. This is a time management skill which we need to learn. We should be strict with the schedule which we have framed. In this way, we would be saved from the strains and stresses of organizational work due to overload.

Time management skill is a vital skill for the employees as they will learn to prioritize their work and will be able to produce more work. The pivotal skills learned through PST programme are highly effective in the workplace and will bring a positive change in terms of productivity in today's competitive world.

Behavioural Training

Behavioural training means learning and practising psychological skills and then developing these skills. The purpose of behavioural training is to inculcate good character and habits such as sociability, emotional maturity and making them smart. They also include social skills which help the persons how well they can get along with others. Developing social skills is very important in life in order to be effective and successful in professional life. Even sometimes, the employers organize a workshop at the workplace for their employees on how to develop social skills. This is called behavioural training. It will develop job satisfaction among employees and help them to achieve excellence in their work. It will bring more productivity as their performance will improve. For school students, developing social skills is an educative process that helps them to prepare for future life. The workplace should promote an environment in which employees can learn behavioural skills to enhance productivity.

The following figure shows the different behavioural skills which need to be developed. These skills revolve around our personality attributes behind behavioural competencies.

The behavioural skills are the personality characteristics which have to be developed among school students. These attributes include assertiveness, collaboration, creativity, dependability, diligence, friendliness, generosity, inquisitiveness, intellectual orientation, optimism, organization, self-discipline, stability and so on. These traits of personality are very important, which have to be inculcated among adolescents and school children. Here, the teachers can play a useful role as they are handling them and encountering them inside and outside the classroom in their schools.

Implementing Psychological Skills

The psychological skills can help us to do our best. Here is how to use them in one's life. Some of the methods for implementing psychological skills are given below.

1. **Imagery:** Imagery involves imagining an experience in mind. This experience makes use of our past memories. It is an internal experience and involves vividly recalling and reconstructing previous external events. Imagery is equalizing to a real sensory experience, which involves seeing, hearing, touching, smelling and touching as feelings, but the entire experience does not occur in real life but only in mind. Imagery is a mental experience which arises in the absence of the external stimuli. It is an internal experience and takes place when we experience the movement of our bodies within our minds.

   According to Richardson (1969), 'mental imagery involves quasi-sensory and quasi-perceptual experiences of which our mind is self-consciously aware, and which exists in our mind in the absence of those stimulus conditions that are known to produce their genuine sensory or perceptual counterparts'.

   Imagery involves more than just understanding experience in our mind's eye. Imagery involves senses such as visual, auditory and kinaesthetic. The kinaesthetic sense is the sensation of bodily physical position and bodily movement that arises from the stimulation of sensory nerve endings in muscles, tendons and joints.

Imagery is used by all of us to revive and relive experiences. Our mind has great potential to remember events and recreate pictures and feelings of them. Our thinking in mind can also go in future and can also imagine or picture events that have not yet occurred. Although imagery relies mainly on memory, our mind can build an image from several aspects of the memory. Mental imagery is essential to the way how our mind perceives different things. For example, an artist may sometimes envision a work of art before starting to create it. Mental imagery is critical to analyse problems and to enhance performance under situations that require physical or mental exercise.

Through imagery, we can prepare ourselves better for performance in future by recreating previous positive experiences or imagining pictures of new events. In the game of tennis, Chris Evert carefully envisioned every detail of a match, including her opponent's style, strategy and shot selection. She says, 'Before I play a match, I try to carefully rehearse what is likely to happen and how I will react in certain situations. I visualize myself playing typical points based on my opponent's style of playing. This helps me mentally prepare for a match, and I feel like I have already played the match before I even walk on the court.' Many athletes in other games also apply imagery as a mental exercise or as a mental rehearsal before they prepare themselves for the final competition.

PST techniques when used together rather than alone have shown to enhance performance; for example, 'mental imagery, when used in combination to goal setting and positive self-talk, has been shown to produce better results' (Porter, 2003). Imagery can be used to improve both physical and psychological skills, including the skills of self-confidence, manage activation and arousal regulation. For example, 'visualizing a successful performance under stressful circumstances, can improve self-confidence, and visualizing such a situation with positive responses and self-talk, is more likely to result in better performance' (Weinberg & Gould, 1999). Mental imagery simulates the actual situation of perfect performance, which in turn 'trains' the neuromuscular system. 'Physical performance improves because your mind cannot distinguish between a visualized and actual experience' (Porter, 2003). 'Mental imagery has also been found to improve mental rehearsal' (Hardy et al., 1996).

2. **Mental rehearsal:** 'Mental rehearsal is analogous to mental imagery. It is imperative to do mental rehearsal before practice or competition and it has been shown to improve performance in the absence of any physical activity' (Hardy et al., 1996). Mental rehearsal is an important psychological skill and can enhance the performance by the ability to envision the performance ahead of time in the mind. Studies have shown that mental rehearsal can help to maintain and sustain current levels of skill execution, though it will not increase the level of performance. Mental rehearsal, in some cases, helps to improve performance by regulating emotional arousal and increasing concentration at the assigned task.

3. **Self-talk:** Self-talk is an internal talk done by an individual when sitting in solitude. It is also called an autogenic discussion with the individual himself/herself. Self-talk entails talking to ourselves silently (Weinberg & Gould, 1999). Self-talk can improve cognitive and motivational functions (Hardy et al., 1996). Self-talk can increase self-confidence, helps in relaxing and arousal control and maintaining and increasing drive (Hardy et al., 1996). In a research study, the participants benefited from self-talk intervention programme as it increased their self-confidence and helped them in anxiety control and eventually enhanced their performance. (Hardy et al., 1996; Landin, 1994; Hamilton, Scott & MacDougall, 2007).

Self-talk involves goal achievement and builds self-confidence. Weinberg and Gould (1999) suggested that self-talk improves performance by positively concentrating on the goal and its desired outcome. Hatzigeorgiadis et al. (2007) have shown that positive self-talking techniques, that is, cognitive restructuring, countering and thought stopping tend to improve the performance more than the negative self-talk, because they enhance self-esteem, improve the confidence and attentional focus, while negative self-talk tends to make the individual nervous, increase the level of anxiety by being critical, and it has been associated with worse performances (Hardy et al., 1996; Weinberg & Gould, 1999).

Self-talk refers to statements that people make to their inner self, and they represent automatic verbalizations. Self-talk is talking to your own mind covertly. The impact of self-talk can be positive (e.g., I can do this) or negative (e.g., it is not possible) depending on what the individual is feeding the mind with. The positive self-talk, such as 'I can do it, I must do it and I will have to do it', can boost the morale of the individual and can lead to positive outcomes. However, while two persons might say the same phrase to themselves when fatigued (e.g., this is tough going on or I am tired too much), one may view the statement as an indication to give up the work, and the other might interpret it as a sign of doing more work and that the intensity he/she is working at is the appropriate level to keep going. Self-talk is sometimes referred to as private and silent speech, verbal rehearsal or inner dialogue.

Some early researches have examined and supported the use of mental skills which includes self-talk, mental imagery, relaxation and goal setting, but more recent research has been focused on self-talk alone. The results of the research have shown that the skill of self-talk can enhance performance.

4. **Mental toughness:** Developing the skill of mental toughness is also included in PST. The term 'mental toughness' is related to the concept of confidence which includes phrases such as 'a state of assurance' and a belief in one's powers. It is likely to maintain an elevated mental mindset. When we learn to keep the things within our control, we learn to control our mindset, which is a major step in building mental toughness.

   Mental toughness can be defined as 'the natural or developed psychological edge—that enables one to cope better than one's competitors with the demands of performance and to remain more determined, focused, confident and in control.' (Loehr, 1986). An essential attribute of mental toughness is an unshakable belief in one's ability to achieve competitive goals. So mental toughness is related to self-belief and self-confidence, which can be developed through training and which can be imparted by teachers and parents. It will help in enhancing mental toughness.

   Mental toughness includes attributes such as (a) emotional stability, (b) perspective, (c) readiness for change, (d) detachment,

(e) strength under stress, (f) preparation for challenges, (g) focus and (h) the right attitude toward setbacks.
5. **Relaxation:** It is the primary psychological skill technique that individuals use in order to cope with pressure. Hardy et al. (1996) says,

> For those persons who have difficulty in getting to sleep, relaxation must become an important daily aspect. The most common form of physical relaxation is Jacobson's progressive muscle relaxation (PMR) technique, a method that takes 10–15 minutes to complete. It has been used to enhance performance by reducing anxiety and enhancing self-efficacy. (Haney, 2004)

Another form of relaxation is transcendental meditation; this is best used anywhere up to half an hour before work to regain composure and control (Jones, 1993; Hardy et al., 1996). Relaxation also allows the mind to be more open to mental imagery, which in turn enhances performance further (Porter, 2003).

Basic Skills of PST

PST programme explains what is unique about the PST approach in helping the persons prepare mentally for their daily life. The basic skills of the PST programme are given below:

1. **Power of imagery:** Imagery is an essential psychological skill that helps to develop other skills among individuals. It can facilitate the learning of other techniques and strategies to improve upon the performance. Through the systematic practice of imagery, persons will be taught a powerful tool for improving performance and developing all other psychological skills.
2. **Managing psychic energy:** It is to help the people to learn how to manage their psychic energy and how to find the optimal energy zone, which helps them perform their best. When psychic energy gets too high, people become anxious or stressed.
3. **Managing stress:** Stress is a part of life, but too much stress leads to deterioration of physical and mental health. So the psychological treatment is how to help people manage stress—probably the most pervasive psychological problems in life.

4. **Problem of concentration and self-confidence:** Most of the people face this problem, as they cannot concentrate on their work and lack attentional skills. So psychologists and counsellors should help them improve their attentional skills so that they can concentrate on the task which they are performing. They should be taught this important skill. In this way, they will also develop their self-confidence and will be able to enhance their self-worth and self-concept.
5. **Goal-setting skills:** Through a unique goal-setting training programme, people should be made to learn how to set challenging and realistic performance goals that will improve performance by helping to develop optimal self-confidence.

These are vital skills for every person to possess and acknowledge how skilful they are in managing stress, concentrating under pressure and setting effective goals. In order to use these skills, they should first learn and then master these skills. Another psychological skill that comprises the PST programme consists of interpersonal skills, especially communication skills. These psychological skills are interrelated with each other, and the improvement of one skill helps the development of the other skills. It is quite obvious from the following figure:

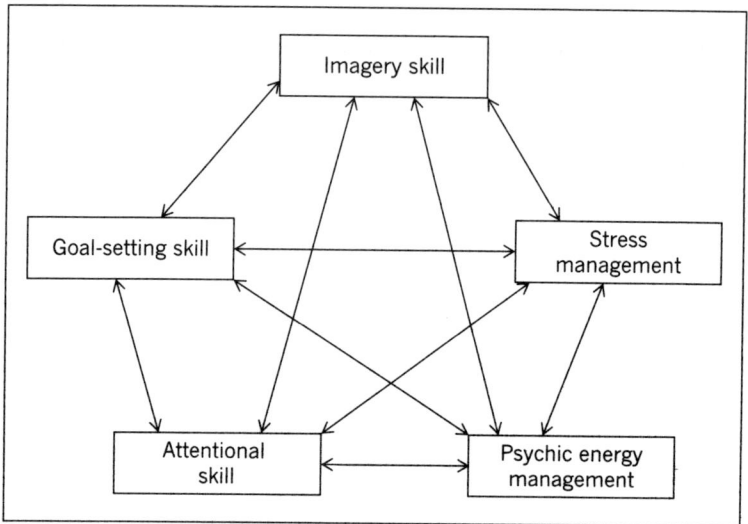

According to Orlick and Partington (1988), the psychological skills of successful performers are:

1. Developing competitive plans
2. Daily training goals
3. Simulations in practice
4. High confidence
5. Task-oriented thoughts
6. Positive imagery
7. Overcoming obstacles by planning

Vealey (1988) says, 'An educationally based psychological skill training programme enhances performance.' The basic PST methods include four techniques for developing skills, for example:

1. Arousal regulation/physical relaxation
2. Imagery
3. Goal setting
4. Attention/thought control

The basic methods for developing psychological skills have been given in Box I.2.

Box I.2: Methods for Developing Psychological Skills

Methods	Psychological skill
Physical practice	Imagery
Goal setting	Physical relaxation
Education	Thought/attention control

Source: Weinberg and Gould (1999).

'Psychological skills are learned and developed by using PST methods' (Hardy, et al., 1996; Weinberg & Gould, 1999; Porter, 2003). As with psychological skills, PST methods can be divided into two categories: foundation methods and specific PST methods. Foundation methods are the self-analysis of an individual, and the specific PST methods will be useful to them in developing the psychological skills that they are weak in and the actual practice of those methods (Hodge, 1994).

Goal setting, self-talk, mental imagery and mental rehearsal and relaxation are the four PST methods that Vealy (1988) identified as being the four most prominent PST methods. Each method enables an individual to work on developing more than one psychological skill, so that they are also working on improving and maintaining their strengths, such as commitment, concentration/attention and motivation as they build up their weak areas (Hardy et al., 1997; Weinberg & Gould, 1999).

The understanding of the physical and mental processes which influence performance will foster psychological skills. Three types of psychological skills that need to be developed are the foundation, performance and facilitative skills (Hodge, 1994). They are shown in the figure:

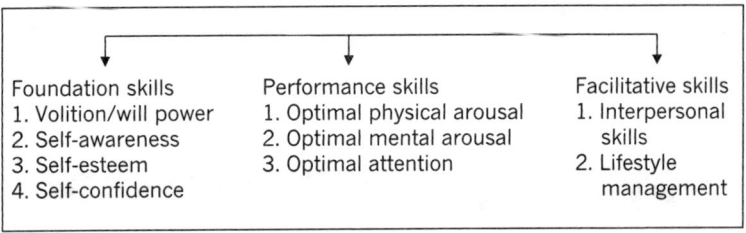

Foundation skills	Performance skills	Facilitative skills
1. Volition/will power	1. Optimal physical arousal	1. Interpersonal skills
2. Self-awareness	2. Optimal mental arousal	2. Lifestyle management
3. Self-esteem	3. Optimal attention	
4. Self-confidence		

Psychological skills developed in the PST programme are as follows:

1. **Foundation skills:** These are the basic psychological skills that form the 'foundation' for the rest of the psychological skills. Foundation skills include volition/will power, self-awareness, motivation, self-esteem and self-confidence.
2. **Performance skills:** Once the foundation skills have been developed, performance skills need to be inculcated. These are the psychological skills that are used during training. These are concentration/attention, coping with pressure (arousal regulation; Weinberg & Gould, 1999) and control activation (mental preparation and

readiness). They include optimal physical and mental arousal and attention.
3. **Facilitative skills:** Facilitative skills are necessary to be able to utilize performance skills effectively. These include communication, training motivation, team building, teamwork and team spirit, psychological rehabilitation from injury and retirement. Usually, they include interpersonal skills and lifestyle management.

According to Orlick (2000), the following points may be considered for developing psychological skills in life:

1. Choose and maintain a positive attitude
2. Maintain a high level of self-motivation
3. Set high and realistic goals
4. Deal effectively with people
5. Use positive self-talk
6. Use positive mental imagery
7. Manage anxiety effectively
8. Manage emotions effectively

1. **Positive attitude:** It is very essential to develop a positive attitude in life if we want to be successful and to enjoy life. Our life should be full of positivity. We should try to erase all the painful past experiences and start our life afresh with optimism and healthy habits.
2. **Self-motivation:** Maintaining and sustaining an intrinsic motivation is very much required in our life. Self-motivation means to motivate yourself internally. If you are moved to do some tasks without expecting any reward from any external agency, then it is self-motivation. Internal motivation is better workable than an external reward or incentive.
3. **Goal setting:** In fact, goal setting is an important psychological skill which has to be inculcated in all of us. Goal setting is not an easy task, but it is a complex activity. There are various factors which help us in setting the goals in our life. But we should be clear that we should set only those goals which are high, realistic and achievable.

4. **Effective dealing:** We should have a very cordial and affectionate relationship with other people who come into our contact. There should be no bitterness in our personal and social relationships. Our work dealings with other people should be very effective and efficacious.
5. **Self-talk:** The role of self-talk plays a very useful role in the behaviour modification of the people. Self-talk should be positive and suggestive. It works like autosuggestion to our mind. It is an inner and silent talk when you are saying something to your mind what you want to do in life.
6. **Mental imagery:** It is the master psychological skill. It has contributed a lot in achieving something in life. This skill has to be learnt for implementing in our day-to-day life. Its role has already been discussed previously.
7. **Anxiety reduction:** As we know that stress leads to anxiety which inhibits the performance of any task. There are various techniques for coping with anxiety-laden situations, and these techniques have to be learnt.
8. **Emotional arousal regulation:** Emotion is the affective domain of human behaviour, and it plays a significant role in the life of a man. For the benefit of human wellness, it is utmost essential that we are able to regulate and manage our emotions very effectively.

Three Phases of PST Programme

The following are the three phases of the PST programme. PST can be taught through three steps.

1. **Education phase:** First of all, individuals should recognize the importance of learning psychological skills and how they affect their work's and life's performance. They should be convinced that these skills are vital in their lives. Psychological skills can be learnt within a few days or in a couple of months. It depends upon the learner's capacity, ability and capability. Some are slow learners, whereas many are fast learners, for example, in teaching the skill of regulating arousal states, the cases of anxiety and finding out the relation of arousal and performance can be explained to learn to

find their optimal level of arousal. People should be made to learn how to transform tension or anxiety into positive energy. We have to educate them about each psychological skill so that they can:
   a. Recognize that these skills can indeed be learnt
   b. Understand how these skills affect the performance
   c. Learn how to develop these skills
2. **Acquisition phase:** This phase focuses on learning strategies and techniques of the different psychological skills. During this phase, first of all, both formal meetings are arranged for the learning of these skills; for example, when developing arousal regulation skills, training sessions might focus on positive coping statements to replace negative self-statements that surface under stressful conditions. In this phase, we have to help people acquire these skills through a structured and well-organized training programme, for example, how to use positive coping in actual settings and also to know failure anxiety (cognitive) and muscle tension (somatic anxiety).
3. **Practice phase:** During this phase, we have to practice these skills so that they are integrated into life situations. The only way these skills can become well-developed is to practice them until they become habitual and automatic. It has three primary objectives:
   a. To make the skills automatized through over learning
   b. To teach systematically to integrate psychological skills with physical skills
   c. To simulate skills, as one would want to apply to one's life situations

   During this phase, a person might progress by using imagery in a practice session as if it were a real-life situation.

Learning psychological skills should progress from practice and simulation to actual situations. The record should be maintained to provide feedback for improvement. These steps—educate, acquire and practice—are the same steps that we use to teach other skills. The strategies for acquiring these skills involve the following processes:

1. **Self-monitoring:** Once the skill has been introduced to persons, they are asked to keep a record of their progress in demonstrating the particular psychological skill being developed.

2. **Self-evaluation:** Here, the persons compare the information obtained from self-monitoring with the standards they have set for that particular skill.
3. **Self-reinforcement:** This is persons' response to the self-evaluation. Many of them may fail to reward themselves adequately for making progress towards their physical and psychological performance goals, but this is an important step in helping to develop psychological skills.

CONCLUSION

Psychological skills are the behavioural strategies through which a human being can act efficiently to perform their activities in their daily life. So learning psychological skills is a fundamental requirement in life in order to be a productive person. So teaching psychological skills has become a current topic for psychologists for discussion and research. So they are devising ways and methods to impart training to the people so that they can adopt these skills in their lives to lead a happy life. The psychological skills such as imagery, stress management, controlling emotional arousal, managing psychic energy and goal setting have to be taught, and people have to be trained in these areas to sustain their good mental health.

Psychological skills such as positive self-talk, mental rehearsal and relaxation exercises have proved to be a success in improving self-confidence, self-prestige, self-sufficiency and self-concept. Relaxation, especially in the form of transcendental meditation, serves to control one's anxiety and improve one's self-confidence, which will enhance one's performance. Hence, PST has attracted the attention of the psychologists who are working in this new area through which human life may be more comfortable and worth living. These skills have become very essential for human wellness.

PST should be conducted by a trained psychologist. PST is a scientific educative process which can help an individual in maintaining a balanced state of mind under stressful situations. PST involves providing training to individuals so that they can learn how to regulate their emotions under undesirable conditions with the help of relaxation techniques. PST is a programme that involves directions, practice and feedback in order to teach a new skill. These skills are communication, goal setting, self-improvement, empathy, conflict resolution and time management and so on.

Behavioural training means learning and practising psychological skills. The purpose of behavioural training is to inculcate good character and habits such as sociability, emotional maturity and making an individual smart. It also includes the inculcation of social skills to make the individuals socially smart. Social skills include the personality traits, which consist of many attributes such as assertiveness, collaboration, creativity, dependability, diligence, friendliness, generosity, inquisitiveness, intellectual orientation, optimism, organization, self-discipline and stability.

The skills which have to be implanted are imagery, mental rehearsal, self-talk, mental toughness and relaxation exercises. According to some psychologists, PST programme includes: (a) arousal regulation, (b) mental preparation (imagery), (c) confidence building, (d) goal setting/motivation, (e) attention/concentration skills. They have also suggested some methods for developing these skills. They have divided these skills into three main categories, for example, (a) foundation skills, (b) performance skills and (c) facilitative skills. Foundation skills include will power, self-awareness, motivation, self-esteem and self-confidence. Performance skills are concentration/attention, coping with pressure (arousal regulation), whereas facilitative skills include communication, training motivation, team building, teamwork and team spirit, psychological rehabilitation from injury and retirement. They also include interpersonal skills and lifestyle management.

There are three phases for developing the PST are (a) educative phase, (b) acquisition phase and (c) practice phase. The strategies for acquiring these skills involve (a) self-monitoring, (b) self-evaluation and (c) self-reinforcement. Now, in the following chapters, all the main as well as allied psychological skills will be discussed one by one. As these skills are meant for human wellness, so we shall have to know what we mean by human well-being and human wellness.

Human Wellness

Need of the Hour

INTRODUCTION

Psychological skills are concerned with human wellness. The main purpose of the training of psychological skills is to increase human well-being to make life more comfortable and help the man to be more happy, healthy and effective. So the concept of human wellness has acquired significance in the field of positive psychology in this current era when people are suffering from strains and stresses. Ever since more attention is being paid to 'quality of life', the concept of human wellness became more popular. However, less importance has been given to the conceptual development of the theory behind it, thus creating confusion among the terms such as psychological well-being, subjective wellness, quality of life, life satisfaction, happiness and mental health.

Quality of life or life satisfaction is a measure of an individual's perceived level of psychological wellness and happiness. It is sometimes used as a synonym for subjective or general well-being. Human wellness is related to the psychological well-being of an individual. The latter is concerned with the mental and emotional health of a man. It may be stated as the general feelings of enjoyment, happiness, contentment, job satisfaction and one's role at the workplace, sense of achievement, belongingness as well as there is no distress, dissatisfaction or worry and so on.

Human wellness is also related to self-concept and self-worth. This self-image or self-identity plays an important role in the psychological functioning of everyone. Self-worth has a feeling of self-prestige, self-esteem and self-sufficiency. But there are some investigations which find out the relationship between self-concept with psychological well-being and human wellness.

CONCEPT OF HUMAN WELLNESS

Human wellness or general well-being may be defined as the overall state of mental functioning of an individual who is well adjusted with their environment. The person has the general feeling of enjoyment, satisfaction with their experiences, job satisfaction and their role in the professional job as well as the sense of identification, and moreover, there has been no grief, fear, worry etc., in their personal and social life. Hence, the emphasis has been laid on the term 'subjective' or general wellness. Human wellness is not confined to physical, social, economic or spiritual wellness, but it is overall well-being. It also includes psychological and emotional wellness.

Most investigators engaged in research on subjective or human wellness conceptualize it as a multifaceted domain of interest, rather than as a unitary construct (Pavot and Diener, 2008). A representative definition is provided by Diener, Lucas and Smith (1999), that is, 'Subjective wellness is a broad category of phenomena that includes people's emotional responses, domain satisfaction and global judgments of life satisfaction.' In general, now, wellness in popular terminology is also known as well-being. The concept of wellness is a dimension of behaviour, that is, thoughts, feelings and attitudes, which can enhance a sense of subjective well-being and influence the individuals' attention to self-care and compliance with medical regiments.

Human wellness or emotional wellness depends on emotional intelligence (EI). If a person has a higher emotional quotient (EQ), they have good emotional health as well as they are an emotional well-being person. EI refers to the ability to perceive, recognize, manage and evaluate emotions for our welfare as well as for others welfare. Emotional intelligence quotient (EIQ) reveals how a person identifies, understands and controls their own emotions and intense feelings.

The good news is that EI can be acquired, learnt, developed and strengthened as it is not an inborn characteristic.

Besides EI, the concept of human wellness is also related to emotional maturity, social adjustment and mental toughness. It may also have a positive and high correlation with the quality of life, job satisfaction/general satisfaction level, sense of achievement, etc. On the other hand, human wellness has a negative relationship with some minor or major mental disorders, such as stress, anxiety, phobia, depression, paranoia or schizophrenia.

The contention about mental illness or mental health problem seems to have been replaced by psychological well-being or human wellness towards the last decade of the 20th century. We may expect greater attention at the beginning of 21st century, accepting the two-factor theory of mental health: (a) prevention of mental disorders and (b) preservation of mental health; but here, the presence of mental health does not necessarily mean the presence of human wellness only. According to Verma (1988), 'A person can have both conditions poor, both conditions good and, any one of them good, with all its accompanying results.' Many attempts have been made in the past to measure positive mental health, only one of which is the measure of subjective and a general sense of psychological well-being.

In recent years, many research studies have been conducted on human wellness (Diener & Diener, 1995). Human wellness has been considered in context to the experience of individuals (Campbell et al., 1976) which is their responses to their life, whether in terms of life satisfaction or positive emotional reactions. Diener and Diener (1995), however, contended that no attention was paid to whether the characteristics of psychological well-being and human wellness differ in various cultures.

MEANING OF WELLNESS

During the last two decades, 'positive psychology' has largely contributed to the notion of 'happiness', and psychologists have made attempts to conduct research work in this area. Such happiness is usually understood in terms of contentment or 'life-satisfaction'. Is positive psychology about wellness? Happiness is like a feeling of contentment for a short time. Wellness is a broader concept which includes happiness. Wellness is related to the overall state of mind of a person.

For defining human wellness, we will have to include all aspects of wellness and mental health. The following points of wellness should be considered:

1. **Intellectual wellness:** Wellness includes self-awareness of thoughts and mental functioning that may affect one's lifestyle. We may include skills such as problem-solving and decision-making, which ensure a healthy human wellness.
2. **Emotional wellness:** Emotional wellness means the awareness of one's feelings, emotions and attitudes as well as the ability to maintain emotional maturity. One should be able to change a negative emotion to positive one, so that one may apply the skill of problem-solving for resolving conflicts.
3. **Social wellness:** Social wellness ensures a supportive social environment which helps a healthy and wealthy lifestyle. If anybody is actively applying some social skills such as empathy and listening skills in the company of other people who are enjoying and nurturing friendships, then they will be in a state of happiness and ecstasy to maintain social wellness.
4. **Spiritual wellness:** If individuals have a feeling of spirituality and have imbibed healthy moral values for better living, and moreover, if they have an understanding of moral values and righteous purpose of life, then they will have spiritual wellness.
5. **Physical wellness:** Physical wellness is related with the physical health of an individual. One should try to take care of one's body by taking proper food, doing morning–evening physical exercises, taking adequate sleep, trying to avoid wrong habits such as use of wine, abuse of drugs, cigarettes or tobacco, etc. One should also find time for regular relaxation exercises to help the body and mind sound. Physical wellness is at the base level of the total wellness.

FACTORS OF HUMAN WELLNESS

Human wellness is a general term that has different connotations to different people. It is like self-realization, which is a feeling of accomplishment in life and brings peace and happiness to life. A person with 'wellness' is a happy and satisfied person. The factors that affect a person's wellness are given below. These factors were evolved by the author while working on a research project of 'Emotional Intelligence and Psychological Well-being' a few years back (Singh & Singh, 2012).

1. A feeling of need achievement
2. A feeling of utilizing one's abilities and capabilities to the fullest capacity
3. A feeling of social acceptance by others
4. A feeling of recognition of work by colleagues
5. Provision of opportunities for promotion
6. Adequate salary and wages

1. **Need achievement:** It is a very important factor in human wellness. It is related to achievement motivation. Every person has three main secondary needs, for example, security, affiliation and achievement. If these needs are not fulfilled, a person develops some personality malfunctioning. So for the development of personality, an individual should have the feelings of need achievement.
2. **Utilization of one's abilities and capacities:** Every man is born with some potentialities, which develop abilities, capacities and capabilities. For human wellness, it is very essential that these competencies must be developed to their maximum level, so that individuals may grow on the basis of their potential. Whatever levels of abilities are there, they must be utilized. If they remain unutilized, they may create havoc and crises in the life of a man.
3. **Social acceptance:** All individuals feel that they should be accepted by other people in their environment. They should get love and affection from others. Whatever they do, they should be appreciated and rewarded for their good work. If individuals are not socially accepted, they would develop an inferiority complex and possibly personality problems.

4. **Recognition of work:** It is also an important factor in human wellness. All children and even elderly persons want that their action must get applauded by others. They should be recognized in their group as an important member. In this way, they fulfil their need for affiliation or feeling of belongingness.
5. **Opportunity for promotion:** This is related to the need for status. It is very important for the growth of an individual. All persons have the feeling that they should be growing not only physically but also professionally and academically. Whether they are in a private or a public job or their own business or in some other profession, they should get an opportunity to show their worth, talent and skill to get a promotion.
6. **Salary and wages:** This factor of human wellness is related to the previous factor of opportunities for the promotion. Individuals must get sufficient salary and wages for doing any professional work, so that they may lead a happy and prosperous life.

There are various other factors that contribute to a person's wellness. The implication is that we all need an ultimate goal in our lives to be 'happy'. According to Ryff (1995), 'Wellness is a dynamic concept that includes personal, social, and psychological dimensions as well as health-related problems.' It focuses specifically on measuring multiple dimensions of human wellness. These dimensions include the following:

1. **Self-acceptance:** According to Ryff (1995), 'A person with high human wellness possesses a positive attitude toward the life as well as self and accepts many aspects of self, including good and bad qualities.' These type of people make peace with the past, enjoy their present life and plan about their rosy future. They believe in the forget and forgive policy. On the other hand, people with a low level of wellness feel dissatisfied with their own experiences of life. They are usually disappointed with what they have got in their past life and are also troubled about their certain personal limitations.
2. **Positive relations with others:** The second factor of human wellness is related to positive interpersonal relations. Ryff says, 'The person with high on this factor has positive, warm, satisfying and

trusting relationships with other people. He is usually concerned about the well-being of others and has pro-social and altruistic behaviour.' Individuals have positive relations with others and are capable of having a strong sense of empathy, affection and intimacy. They have the ability to give and take love as well as understand human relationships. On the other hand, individuals with negative relations with others do not have close, cordial and empathic relationships with others. Such individuals find it difficult to be free and frank and concerned about others. They remain in solitude and feel frustrated in interpersonal relationships and are not dynamic enough to make adjustments with others to maintain relations.
3. **A sense of autonomy:** Autonomy is the third factor of human wellness. According to Ryff (1995), individuals with a high sense of autonomy are self-determined and independent. They do not come under social pressures but to think and act in certain different ways. They try to regulate and manage their behaviour covertly and self-evaluate on the basis of personal standards and norms. On the other hand, individuals with a low sense of autonomy are concerned about others' expectations—suggestible to the opinions of other people in order to make important decisions in life. They try to conform to social pressures to think and act in certain ways. They do not seem to have a feeling of independence, but actually, they are dependent on others.
4. **Environmental mastery:** The fourth important factor of human wellness is environmental mastery. People with high environmental mastery have the ability in controlling the environment and make effective use of available opportunities. But on the other hand, persons with a low mastery of the environment feel incompetent in managing everyday affairs, and they are incapable of changing or improving the environment. They are unaware and oblivious of surrounding opportunities and do not have self-control over the outside environment.
5. **A sense of purpose in life:** The next factor of human wellness is a purpose in life. People with a high sense of purpose in life have higher goals in life to achieve and have a sense of belonging. They live in the present and enjoy it. They forget their past life and think

as well as plan for their future life. They have full conviction in themselves that gives purpose to their life. Moreover, they have higher goals and higher purposes for effective living. On the other hand, people with a low sense of purpose in life do not have any meaningful goals to achieve. Their life is purposeless, directionless and has no future. They have nothing to conceive that may bring colour in their life.

6. **Personal growth:** Another important factor in human wellness is personal growth. People with high personal growth have a feeling of continuous progress and perceive themselves as growing and developing. They welcome new ideas and are ready for new endeavours in life. They find improvement in their abilities and capabilities and behaviour over a passage of time. They have a dynamic personality. They keep on adjusting to the conditions that reflect more understanding of the self. But on the other hand, people with low personal growth have a sense of personal stagnation. They lack a sense of improvement and progress over the passage of time. They also feel tired, bored and uninterested with life and are unable of making changes to their life.

The concept of human wellness has faced some challenges and controversies. In the recent past, wellness had little effect on some people. Moreover, the criteria regarding wellness were diverse, extensive and value laden. Because the construct of human wellness in the past was non-existent, so non-theoretical concepts were frequently used, though they were limited in their definition of the construct.

HUMAN WELLNESS AND SELF-CONCEPT

Self-concept is a personality construct that refers to an individual's perception of 'oneself' in the context of a number of characteristics, for example, family, gender roles, racial identity, job involvement, nationality and many more. Self-concept is also called self-mirror, self-picture or self-sufficiency. It is different from self-consciousness, which is simply an individual's knowledge of one's self, knowledge about the good and bad points as well as the limitations. But it is also different from self-esteem, which is the purely evaluative aspect of self-concept.

Self-concept means how we are thinking, feeling and acting as well as how we try to assess ourselves. The term self-concept is a general term which is used to refer to how someone may think or perceive about oneself. It is a useful term for positive as well as humanistic behaviour.

Self-concept also comprises self-evaluation. The characteristics which are measured include the personality traits, skills, attitudes, knowledge and abilities, along with job requirement, hobbies, physical traits, etc. For example, the statement 'I am good' is self-evaluative that helps in the development of self-concept. However, the statement 'I am tired' would not be considered as a part of someone's self-concept since being tired is a temporary state, and it is more of a subjective statement. It is related to the physical and mental state of the organism.

Moreover, self-concept is not only concerned with the present, but it also consists of the past and future times. It is related to what has already gone, which is still in memory. Now, what you are planning about your future life also consists of your self-concept. Future selves represent individuals' ideas of what they would like to be or what they would like to become or what they aim to achieve in their future life. These aspirations and ambitions may function as incentives for future planning, and this also provides interpretive feedback for the present view of self.

The humanistic psychologists such as Carl Rogers, Abraham Maslow and many others who belonged to the humanistic school of psychology paved the way for this concept. According to Rogers (1961), everyone strives to become more like an 'ideal self'. There is always a discrepancy between the real self and the ideal self. The closer one is to their ideal self, the happier one will be. Rogers also gave the idea of unconditional positive regard (UPR), which is one factor in a person's happiness which often occurs in close or familial relationships and involves a consistent level of the ideal self.

Self-concept includes all our thoughts, ideas and judgments about ourselves. It shows how we perceive ourselves, whether good, bad or neutral. Self-concept does not necessarily reflect reality; a person can be smart, warm and successful but still have a negative self-concept or have a positive self-concept even though that person may be immoral or despised by others. A strong positive self-concept that is realistic and not too different from what we would ideally like to be is the goal of human beings, according to Rogers. The individual needs to receive positive regard from others as well as from the self. UPR by others facilitates self-regard and makes our self-concepts strong and positive. However, most of us grow up in such an environment where love is conditional.

According to Rogers, problems arise when people's behaviours do not conform to their self-concepts. If there is a discrepancy between what you do and what you think you are, you will experience anxiety. The wider the gap between our actions and our self-image, the greater the anxiety and tension. The healthy reaction to this disparity between our behaviours and our self-concept is to acknowledge the behaviour and feelings, rather than deny them.

Carl Rogers[1] believes that self-concept has different characteristics as shown in Box 1.1.

Box 1.1: Characteristics of Self-concept

1. The image you have of yourself (self-image)
2. How much value you place on yourself (self-esteem or self-worth)
3. What you wish you would really look like (ideal self)
4. Self-picture (what you see in yourself)

HUMAN WELLNESS AND SELF-ESTEEM

Self-esteem has been recognized widely as a key factor for mental well-being (Sonstroem, 1984). For example, it is strongly associated with such positive qualities as emotional stability, adjustment to life demands (coping with stress), happiness and life satisfaction (Diener & Diener, 1995). It means that human wellness and self-esteem are positively related to each other as self-esteem leads to human wellness

---

[1] https://www.simplypsychology.org/carl-rogers.html

and psychological well-being. People should have high self-esteem because it also enhances mental health.

On the other hand, low self-esteem often accompanies mental disorders such as depression, trait anxiety, neuroses, low assertiveness, feeling of hopelessness and helplessness and having suicidal tendencies (Brown, 1993). So a person with low self-esteem often has been identified as a case for psychotherapy (Rogers, 1951; Wylie, 1979). However, a person with high self-esteem is associated with many positive qualities (Wylie, 1989).

Self-esteem and more specifically self-perceptions as well as self-prestige are more closely related with each other as to how we choose to put our time and effort and whether we persist on or withdraw from the range of life activities (Harter, 1996). Our negative behaviour patterns such as smoking, alcohol and drug use and defective eating habits are associated with our wrong self-perceptions and also with low self-esteem.

Campbell (1984) contended that self-esteem is the first psychological principle of human nature, expressing how people put a large amount of their mental and physical energy in a lifelong struggle to know who they are or how they feel they should be. If psychologists want to understand individuals, their level of wellness and also how they function in different life situations, then they should try to know how individuals perceive themselves in general and in these specific life events.

Self-esteem and mental health are also related to each other. Self-esteem helps people to face life with more resilience, confidence, benevolence and optimism so that they can move forward and achieve the goal of self-realization. It permits oneself to be more liberal, ambitious and successful and also helps what one can experience emotionally, socially and spiritually. Hence, it is likely to preserve and enhance good mental health. Developing self-esteem will increase the capacity to be happy.

It is universally admitted that positive self-esteem can help develop the quality of treating other people with respect, benevolence and goodwill, thus enhancing good interpersonal relationships. According to Erich Fromm, who is a Neo-Freudian psychoanalyst, love for others and love for oneself are not integrated but can be replaced. But on the contrary, an attitude of love towards oneself (i.e., self-love) will be found in all of us. Self-esteem also helps develop creativity in the workplace, and it is an important condition for all types of professions.

'Self-esteem and self-concept are part of one's personality.' Personality can be stated as the distinctive and characteristic manifestation of thoughts, emotions and actions that describe an individual's interaction with the physical and social environment. To define operationally, personality characteristics are individual's unique style of living, that is, apperception, needs, cognition processes drives and ways of responding conflicts, integration of ego, super ego, thought processes, etc.

Self-esteem is also related to self-prestige. All of us have a concept of ourselves (self-concept). If we like our self-image or self-concept, then we have self-esteem. Of course, self-confidence is very much different from self-esteem. Self-confidence is the belief in our ability to perform a task. We can have self-confidence but not self-esteem and vice versa. In the real sense, both high self-confidence in our abilities and self-esteem are required in life.

MINDFULNESS IN HUMAN WELLNESS

Mindfulness is a new concept in the area of psychological well-being and human wellness. Mindfulness is the basic human ability to be aware of what we are, where we are and what we are going to do. Mindfulness is a quality that every human being should possess. It is not something that you just have to learn to get it, but it is a mental state of the organism which is achieved by focusing one's awareness on the present situation. So it is the quality or state of being conscious or aware of something.

Mindfulness also involves acceptance of all situations, which means that we should concentrate on our thoughts and feelings—without considering what is 'right' or what is 'wrong'. We should accept what is in our present and not regret what is not there, or you could not achieve in the past. It is a way of thinking or feeling in a given situation. When we apply mindfulness, our thoughts concentrate on what we are feeling in the present situation rather than thinking about the future. Mindfulness is a kind of technique that helps us to feel more aware of our present, focusing on and accepting ourselves—what we are actually as a real person.

While mindfulness may be innate or acquired, it can be cultivated through some therapeutic techniques, particularly through yoga and meditation. When we meditate, it brings about peace of mind as well as a calm and quiet state of mental functioning. When we are under the mindfulness state, we reduce stress, enhance performance, gain insight and awareness through introspecting and observing our own mind and increase our attention to ourselves and others' well-being, that is, for human wellness.

The concept of mindfulness is very simple. You focus your attention on your present experience, observe what is going on around you in your environment and also notice any thoughts, emotions and bodily sensations that come up. This sounds simple, but you will likely encounter obstacles along the way. You may feel restless, sleepy, bored or your mind may fill with doubts. The technique of mindfulness will help you to overcome these obstacles. In fact, it is as simple as learning or relearning an activity. Mindfulness infers to be more aware of what is going on at present here. It helps us to be not affected by our strong feelings of emotions and thoughts, which may cause stress, anxiety, negative feelings, frustration, resentment or self-doubt, etc.

Mindfulness is the psychological construct of bringing one's attention to situations voluntarily, which is occurring at the present moment without assessing. It can be developed through the practice of meditation and other relaxation procedures. While mindfulness has its roots in Eastern spiritual traditions such as Buddhism and yoga, it has been proved very much effective by Western psychologists. It is now a most valuable healing tool commonly used by clinicians and therapists. In recent years, the technique of mindfulness has entered the USA and other European countries in part through the work of Jon Kabat-Zinn and his mindfulness-based stress reduction programme. Initially, it was used for cancer patients suffering from chronic pain who were taught to meditate and feel their discomfort rather than ignore it. If it can be used for cancer patients, it can also be used for other types of patients.

On the basis of mindfulness, clinical psychologists and psychiatrists have developed a number of therapeutic techniques to help those people who are facing some psychological problems. Mindfulness technique has been applied to manage stress, control anxiety, reduce depression, and moreover, it has proved to be useful in the rehabilitation of drug addicts. Programmes based on the mindfulness model have been applied within schools, prisons, hospitals and many other centres. Clinical studies have shown that mindfulness technique has proved to be useful in maintaining physical as well as mental health among different patients and also among healthy people. It has been found that there is a positive relationship between mindfulness and psychological well-being as well as human wellness. The practice of mindfulness provides medical advantages to people with mental disorders, especially those suffering from a moderate level of psychosis. Moreover, mindfulness practice has also proved to be a preventive method for mental-health problems.

The following points are to be taken care of while applying the technique of mindfulness:

1. **Mindfulness is a comprehensive technique:** It is a quite comprehensive and useful technique for us because it is what we already know about it and how we already use it. It is possible that it may be called by many other names.
2. **Mindfulness develops the present qualities:** Mindfulness recognizes and cultivates the qualities which are usually present in us as human beings.
3. **Mindfulness has the potential:** This technique has the characteristics of being a transformative and social phenomenon. It has become a very useful technique in our modern society.
4. **Anyone can apply this technique:** Mindfulness technique is very simple and everyone can get benefit out of it and it is easy to learn.

So every person, whether a child or an adult, a boy or girl, a male or female, can use it for their benefit.

5. **It is a part of lifestyle:** Mindfulness is not just a practice or exercise, but it is a way of life. It brings awareness of our self and helps us to know what we do. It reduces mental and physical stress. It should become a part of the lifestyle.
6. **It is evidence-based:** Mindfulness has become a scientific technique because it has been empirically proved to be useful. We do not have to take it as granted, having blind faith in it. It has found to be beneficial for our health, happiness, work and social relationships.
7. **It brings innovation:** Mindfulness can help us to be an effective resilient to stressful life events and problems in life.

EMOTIONAL WELLNESS

According to the dictionary meaning, the word 'emotion' means the intense feelings of joy, sorrow, fear, hate, love, etc., and the word 'well' means (a) good or sound in body and mind, (b) proper, fitting or gratifying. The word 'ness' means (a) the fact of existing, (b) consciousness or existence of life. Combining these three words, emotional wellness is the state of consciously experiencing the existence of our feelings such as joy, sorrow, fear, hate and love at any given time. Emotional wellness consists of more than just the good or positive that emotions have to offer. Emotional wellness means managing your emotions, objectively and consciously.

A popular definition of 'emotional wellness' is offered by the Mental Health Foundation (World Health Organization, 2001). Accordingly, emotional wellness means 'a positive sense of well-being which enables an individual to be able to function in society and to meet the demands of everyday life; people in good mental health have the ability to recover effectively from illness, change or misfortune.' Many people equate emotional wellness to happiness. They think that in order to achieve emotional wellness, everybody should be happy, healthy and prosperous in their lives. People tend to associate emotional wellness to positive emotions or emotions that make you feel happy and good.

There is a positive relationship between emotional wellness and human wellness. Human wellness is different for each individual, but it has a holistic approach that affects the quality of life, leading to a balanced, healthy and happy life. Human wellness includes the mental, emotional and social wellness. Emotional wellness helps us to identify, recognize, understand and manage emotions for our benefit as well as for others' benefit and to channelize our emotions into socially acceptable behaviour patterns and healthy way of life that satisfy our personal and social needs.

Emotional wellness may also include contentment, enjoyment, self-sufficiency and self-assurance in life and the ability to cope with life's ups and downs, strains and stresses as well as storms and strives. Emotional wellness leads to developing satisfying interactional relationships with other people. It is also closely related to the social dimensions of life or the social adjustments of the individuals. Knowing our strengths and weaknesses, having autonomy, controlling anger effectively, managing strains and stresses of life events and solving mental conflict and dealing with interpersonal communication effectively and meaningfully with others all contribute to a positive state of emotional wellness.

Emotional wellness is a term that is being increasingly used in recent years. It is related to mental health and is concerned with such issues of mental disorders such as stress, anxiety and depression. Today, total health means that a person should be physically, mentally, emotionally and socially healthy. It means that people should be physically fit, mentally alert, emotionally balanced and socially adjusted in their life. So mental health is very much related to emotional health, as a mentally healthy person can be emotionally matured and balanced person. On the positive side, enhanced emotional wellness seems to contribute to increasing coping strategies, self-esteem, good performance and productivity at work, and even longevity of life (Fredrick & Thomson, 2002). Emotional wellness also consists of two aspects of personal and social wellness which can be assessed in terms of quality of life and by the evaluation of one's life in general (Kahneman & Angus, 2010). The following points should be considered:

1. **Emotional wellness is the key to a happy and healthy life:** It is essential that people should know the psychological skills which are required to face the emotional problems in life which will help them with a sound foundation of mental and emotional health. Emotional wellness is required, especially in the period of adolescence, which is the period of change and growth where the adolescents face many problems of strains and stresses and these skills will help them to overcome the situation of crisis.

   Emotional health has many facets. It is based on self-esteem, self-prestige, self-awareness and self-concept, that is, how one feels about oneself. It also depends on one's total behaviour that should be socially acceptable. The person who is emotionally healthy leads a life full of happiness and pleasurable. The characteristics of emotionally healthy people are given in Box 1.2.

   Box 1.2: Characteristics of Emotionally Healthy People
   1. They are dynamic and adaptable to change
   2. They can easily cope with stress and anxiety
   3. They have a positive self-concept and self-image
   4. They act independently to meet their own needs and demands

   Emotionally healthy individuals also have to face some psychological problems and hazards. But they know how to tackle those problems and find out their solutions easily in life. While doing so, they help others as well as themselves to get satisfaction and contentment in life.

2. **Good health leads to emotional wellness:** Wellness means leading a life full of happiness and bliss, which is a state of optimal wellness, that is, absence of stress anxiety and conflict in life. Having a lifestyle that nurtures wellness helps to prevent grief and distress or negative thought. The balanced and effective lifestyle teaches one how to manage stress, reduce tension, control anxiety and resolve conflict, which requires a conscious effort on the part of individuals. They make use of relaxation exercises, apply good coping strategies in order to learn some psychological skills and effective communication as well as modify behaviours to have a happier and healthier life. The concept of wellness also includes:

a. Maximum vigour and energy to enjoy life
   b. A feeling of satisfaction, contentment and happiness
   c. Increasing self-knowledge and developing abilities
   d. Cordial, affable and satisfying relationships
   e. A low level of vulnerability towards illness
   f. Commitment, control and challenge in your life

   Emotional wellness is achieved only when one is healthy in all areas of life, that is, physically, mentally, emotionally, socially and spiritually where mind, body and soul should be in a state of balance and work together or one is totally whole as a person.

3. **Total health includes emotional wellness:** There are many benefits of a healthy lifestyle. It is important to have good physical, mental, emotional and social health. There are a few suggestions, given below, which we should follow:

   a. **Synergy:** We should do regular physical exercises to maintain a positive and healthy physical health for sustaining our energy levels. Emotional wellness here means that we should feel energetic and healthy, rather than lethargic and fatigued.

   b. **Ageing factor:** Everybody feels ageing factor with signs and symptoms of early hair loss, memory loss, digestion problem, etc. But leading an emotionally healthy life will delay our ageing factor. We will not feel old so early in our life. On the other hand, a healthy and balanced lifestyle keeps us young.

   c. **Health:** A lifestyle with emotional wellness will keep us healthy. We will be less vulnerable to illness and disease, which may include cardiovascular disorders, diabetes, cancer, etc.

   d. **Unbiased mind:** When we are leading a healthy and happy life, we have poise and unbiased mind to perceive the environment independently. In this way, we will have a positive attitude in life and may be able to accomplish our daily tasks and achieve our goals easily. We will feel less fatigued, nervous and bored about situations and handle them comfortably.

   e. **Reducing illnesses:** When we are under a high level of stress, it puts a lot of strain on our body and mind. But when we are leading a lifestyle that promotes emotional wellness, minor physical disorders such as headache and backache may be controlled, and they may only occasionally occur.

So it is said that applying relaxing exercises, using stress management techniques and maintaining ourselves in good mental and physical health will definitely help us to have happier and freer lifestyles. It will increase our emotional wellness.
4. **Improving our children's emotional wellness:** Imparting emotional wellness should be a part of the functioning of all educational institutions. In present-day times, most children are mentally weak and emotionally imbalanced. They need to be educated on how to develop emotional wellness among the school students, especially adolescents. There are many factors such as poor working conditions at home, poverty, serious diseases and daily domestic quarrels among the members of the family, child abuse, death in the family, etc., which usually have a negative effect on the children's emotional health. Anyone of these factors can have a profound impact on the children's self-prestige and self-respect, which may affect their personality. So schools should prescribe a high quality and new type of academic and non-academic activities to ensure that the child is emotionally well-balanced and prepared for the challenges of life in this highly competitive society. We should help children to develop their emotional wellness.

A programme for developing EI and increasing EQ in the schools will be helpful. Opportunities should be provided to children to inculcate social skills such as participating in some co-curricular activities, handling conflict, mutual responsibility and maintaining relationships with their peer mates and age mates, which will enhance their capacity for preparing for their future life and also to develop life skills. So it is important for the schools to offer a curriculum that should clearly be useful for emotional and social learning and development as well as enhancing EI. The creation of a positive environment with effective care systems is the need of the hour. In this way, we may be able to help a child to develop emotional wellness.

CONCLUSION

The concept of human wellness has become very popular in the first decade of the 21st century. It is related to psychological well-being, quality of life, life satisfaction and happiness. It is the overall mental functioning of an individual as well as their adjustment to life. It consists of feelings of enjoyment, contentment, job achievement and belongingness. The concept of wellness is a dimension of behaviour, that is, thoughts, feelings and attitudes, which may enhance a sense of subjective well-being.

Human wellness or emotional wellness depends on EI. The concept of human wellness may also show some degree of positive and high relationship with life satisfaction, quality of life, feelings of achievement, etc. Human wellness is generally related to economic gains, but actually, it is related to mental satisfaction and peaceful state of mind, which is more stable and more productive.

The concept of wellness includes physical and mental health of an individual as well as it also includes moral and ethical values of a person. Human wellness includes (a) intellectual wellness, (b) emotional wellness, (c) social wellness, (d) spiritual wellness and (e) physical wellness. The factors of wellness are (a) feeling of need achievement, (b) feeling of utilizing one's abilities and capabilities to the fullest capacity, (c) feeling of social acceptance by others, (d) feeling of recognition of work by colleagues, (e) provision of opportunities for promotion and (f) adequate salary and wages.

Self-concept is a construct that refers to an individual's perception of 'self' in relation to many characteristics, for example, family, gender roles, racial identity, job involvement, nationality and many others. Carl Rogers believes that self-concept has different components, such as (a) self-image, (b) self-esteem or self-worth and (c) ideal self.

Mindfulness is a new concept in the area of psychological well-being and human wellness. Mindfulness is the basic human ability to be aware of what we are, where we are and what we are doing. Mindfulness also involves acceptance of the present situation, meaning thereby that we pay attention to our thoughts and feelings.

Emotional wellness means 'a positive sense of well-being which enables an individual to be able to function in society and to meet the demands of everyday life. People in good mental health have the ability to recover effectively from illness or misfortune.' Emotional wellness may also include contentment, enjoyment, self-sufficiency and self-assurance in life, and the ability to cope with life's ups and downs, strains and stresses as well as storms and strives.

To conclude, human wellness means the longevity of life with the absence of any kind of physical and mental illnesses and abnormities. The more we live healthily, the more happiness we derive from our prosperous life. It is only possible if we develop a healthy lifestyle by reducing our needs and leading a simple life with some higher goals to achieve. Human wellness consists of self-esteem, self-prestige, life satisfaction and quality of life. Human wellness depends on psychic energy, which is related to an individual's emotional life. In the next chapter, how to manage psychic energy will be discussed.

Managing Psychic Energy

INTRODUCTION

Human wellness depends on psychic energy. Every human being is born with psychic energy along with physical energy. The physical energy includes strength, speed power, agility, movability and other motor powers. A child is born with some potential, which is the ability, capacity, capability and aptitude besides emotional and motivational mechanism. This is the psychic energy of a person, which needs to be harnessed. The importance of managing physical and psychic energy has been recognized in these days. Physical energy is produced more efficiently by the proper exercise of the body and good nutrition, which increases the body's ability to release the energy stored as muscle glycogen, carbohydrate and fat. Psychic energy is produced more efficiently by the proper exercise of the mind and with realistic and constructive thoughts.

Physical energy influences psychic energy, that is, a fit body is an important part of a healthy mind, and physical fatigue can weaken the will of the mind. Psychic energy also influences physical energy, when the mind is energized, the body will follow, and when the mind is calm and in control, it can demand the same for the body. Hence, there is a need to strive to achieve a union of physical and psychic energy—an optimal psychophysical state. When people have low psychic energy, we try to find measures to psyche them up in order to motivate them. When they have too high psychic energy in the form of emotional upheaval or anger, we try to calm them. So first of all, we shall have to understand what is psychic energy.

CONCEPT OF PSYCHIC ENERGY

Psychic energy is said to be related to an individual's motivational level, optimum emotional arousal, mental toughness and activation. It is concerned with the arousal of the body and mind. Psychic energy is, in fact, the vigour, vitality and intensity of the body and mental power, which maintains and sustains motivation. It is distinguished from emotional arousal, which refers to the activation of the mind and body, which initiates any activity. Psychic energy may be either positive or negative and thus is associated with various emotional experiences such as excitement and happiness on the positive side and anxiety and anger on the negative side.

Psychic energy falls on a continuum. People have more or less of it at different times. Some tasks require relatively low psychic energy, like watching television. Other tasks require high psychic energy, like performing gymnastics in competition. When people go from low to high, they are getting psyched up, and when psychic energy is too high, they are psyched out. It is called the activation of the mind.

Psychic energy or activation level is very essential in all types of activities. It refers to a combination of physiological and muscular signs, which indicate that to what extent the individual is preparing themselves to perform vigorously. Activation is the readiness for action, which can be measured on a scale ranging from deepest sleep at one end to a highly excited state at the other. From a physiological point of view, the activation of an individual is marked by indices that the body is somehow preparing itself for action, including heightening of a muscle tone, changes in the optical system, increased heart rate and changes in respiration.

PSYCHIC ENERGY AND AROUSAL

Psychic energy is both physiological and psychological. It is related to emotional arousal and motivational aspects of behaviour. It is concerned with both the cognitive and affective domain. Arousal is a general combination of physical and mental activity in a person, varying on a continuum from deep sleep to intense arousal or from low to high excitement. The low arousal is the coma state of the organism, whereas high arousal is the intensity state of the mind, which is related to the higher level of motivation. It ranges from not at all aroused, that is, coma state to completely aroused state, that is, high intensity. According to Gould and Krane (2002), 'highly aroused individuals are mentally and physically activated; they experience increased heart rates, respiration and sweating.'

Arousal has typically been referred to as physical and mental activation or autonomic reactivity. Landers (1980) defined arousal as 'a motivational construct' that represents 'the intensity level of behaviour'. Landers and Boutcher (1986) viewed arousal as 'an energizing function that is responsible for harnessing of the body's resources for intense and vigorous activity'. Martens (1987) viewed arousal what he labelled as 'psychic energy'—as 'the vigor, vitality and intensity with which the mind functions'. Hence, arousal is viewed by Martens to be more than the physiological activation of the organism. It involves mental activation as well.

Psychologists have studied emotional arousal in terms of three components: physical, cognitive and behavioural. The three components appear to be interdependent. For example, physically, people who are better at detecting heartbeat changes will rate their subjective experiences of emotion at a cognitive level. They will feel more intense and are less able to detect physical changes. But these physical and cognitive components completely do not determine how emotion is expressed in the behavioural terms.

CONCEPT OF PSYCHOLOGICAL CAPITAL

At the end of the 20th century, a new approach in psychology emerged which became very popular, that is, the emergence of positive psychology. This branch of psychology has given birth to a new concept—positive organizational behaviour—which was researched by Luthans in 2004. It lays emphasis on some valid measures of positive psychological states that have an effect on the desired attitudes and behaviours of people.

Psychological capital is a newly developed concept devised by psychologists, which is defined as the extent to which an individual works in a positive psychological state. It refers to a number of resources a person can use to improve their work performance on the job and to seek their success. It includes four different resources: (a) hope, (b) self-efficacy (c) resilience and (d) optimism. The concept of psychological capital is strongly linked to increased well-being, work ethics and job satisfaction as well as human wellness.

The empirical research in the field of positive psychology suggests that the four psychological resources were determined to meet the positive organizational behaviour scientifically. Hope, efficacy, resilience and optimism were termed by Luthans and Youssef (2004) as psychological capital. The four constructs were empirically determined to be a core construct that had a stronger relationship with satisfaction and performance. The four components are defined as follows:

1. **Hope:** It is defined as a positive motivational state where two basic elements, namely a successful feeling of resources and means, interact. It is said that hope sustains life as there is no life without hope. Life continues until there is hope, which is also related to our physiological responses.
2. **Efficacy:** It is defined as people's confidence in their ability to achieve a specific goal in a specific situation at a specific time. Efficacy means an efficient and effective way of working pattern. Efficacy is related to self-belief when a person has this conviction that they will achieve their goals definitely, and there is no reason that they would not be able to reach the top of their accomplishment.
3. **Resilience:** It is defined as a positive way of coping with adversity or distress. In the organizational aspect, it is stated as an ability to recover from stress, conflict, failure as well as change or increase in responsibility. Resilience means that an individual has the capacity to overcome their strains and stress and face them boldly in life.
4. **Optimism:** It is related to hope, that is, a person in high spirits. Optimism reinforces efficacy and hope. Optimistic people are the

ones who change internal and external as well as personal and situational things into positive events. They have positive thinking and always have a positive attitude in their life.

MANAGING THE PSYCHIC ENERGY

People can learn to manage their psychic energy along with their physical energy. All of us learn to control and manage our psychic energy, to some extent, with the help of some techniques. So we have to teach to the people how to harness psychic energy to control their thoughts processes. People must learn to control and manage their thoughts. All our actions are representative of our inner thought and experience. In order to perform, first, we think, feel and then act. We plan, imagine and then decide in our minds what action will be taken.

Human energy, that is, psychic energy must not only be controlled, but it must be harnessed, explored and directed. We direct people to save physical and mental energy with necessary actions by directing their energy to run efficiently and skilfully. In the same way, psychic energy also needs to be directed because it can be constructive or destructive—positive or negative. People can be taught to direct their psychic energy by focusing on task-related matters and also avoid distractions, so that they may think of what can be done.

Psychic energy can be managed by persons through greater efforts and also by knowing how they react to various situations. Imagery skill can be applied to enhance psychic energy. In this way, they can exercise their energy in learning the psychological skills.

CHANGES DUE TO INCREASED PSYCHIC ENERGY

Three types of changes occur with the oncoming of increased psychic energy. They are physiological, psychological and behavioural changes, which are described below:

1. **Physiological:** They are related to bodily changes, for example, increased heart rate, high or low blood pressure, too much sweating, brain wave activity, pupil dilation, respiration, muscle tension,

oxygen uptake, high blood sugar level and increased adrenalin, decreased blood flow to the skin and frequent urination.
2. **Psychological:** They are concerned with stress, anxiety, worry, feeling emotionally exhausted, inability to make a decision, feeling confused, not able to concentrate, inability to sustain attention, not feeling in self-control and feeling differently.
3. **Behavioural:** Behavioural changes are likely to occur in the cognitive domain, for example, thinking, rapid talking, nail biting, foot-tapping, muscle twitching, increased blinking, yawning, trembling and broken voice.

PSYCHIC ENERGY AND PSYCHOLOGICAL STRESS

Psychic energy is closely associated with psychological stress. Psychological stress occurs when people perceive a threat in their lives when there is a substantial imbalance between what they perceive and what is being demanded of them. Psychological stress arises from non-coordination between perceived demand and perceived capability. When demands put on the people and their capabilities to respond to those demands are in balance, the optimal energy or flow state is more likely to occur. High stress is associated with high psychic energy, and low stress is associated with low psychic energy. In the optimal energy zone, the chances of performing optimally are maximized.

RELATIONSHIP BETWEEN SKILL AND CHALLENGE

Csikszentmihalyi (1990) investigated exactly what makes a task intrinsically motivating. He examined rock climbing, dancing, chess, music and amateur athletes—all activities that people do with great intensity but usually for little or no external reward or with no expected rewards (internal motivation). Through their research, Jackson and Csikszentmihalyi (1999) identified a number of common elements that make activities intrinsically interesting.

The most important part of Csikszentmihalyi's definition of flow is the balance between one's perceived skill and challenge. For the flow to occur, it is imperative that a person believes that they have the skills to successfully meet the physical, technical and mental challenges faced. The relationship between skill and challenge has been given in Box 2.1.

> **Box 2.1:** Relationship between Skill and Challenge
>
> 1. If the situation is of a high challenge, but the skill is at a low level, people will experience anxiety.
> 2. If the challenge is low and skill is also at a low level, the situation will be of apathy.
> 3. On the other hand, if the challenge is at a low level, but the skill is of high level, we find that the situation is of boredom.
> 4. But if both the skill and the challenge are of high level, there will be a flow state.

The flow state is achieved when both skill and challenge are high, for example, if an individual has a high skill level and the opponent also has the same which presents a high challenge, then the flow can be achieved. In this state, intrinsic motivation is also at the highest level, and maximum performance is achieved. But on the other hand, if an individual with less ability is matched against a high challenge, it will produce stress, anxiety and frustration. It means that if the task demands are higher than the capabilities, the individual becomes anxious and performs poorly. On the other side of the picture, combining low skills and low challenge results in apathy state whereas high skills and low challenge results in boredom; if skills are greater than the challenges of the task, the individual gets bored and performs badly.

PSYCHIC ENERGY: PERFORMANCE RELATIONSHIP

Now, the question arises as to what right amount of required psychic energy is for superior performance. The highest psychic energy is when you are extremely stressed, angered or grieved over some issue or event or when you are jubilant and enthused about some matter. You want to be energized, but you do not want to be over energized.

This principle states that as psychic energy increases from a very low level, performance improves until some point or zone at which the person performs at the best of their abilities, capacities and capabilities. Then, with further increases in psychic energy, performance deteriorates. It is quite evident from the following figure.

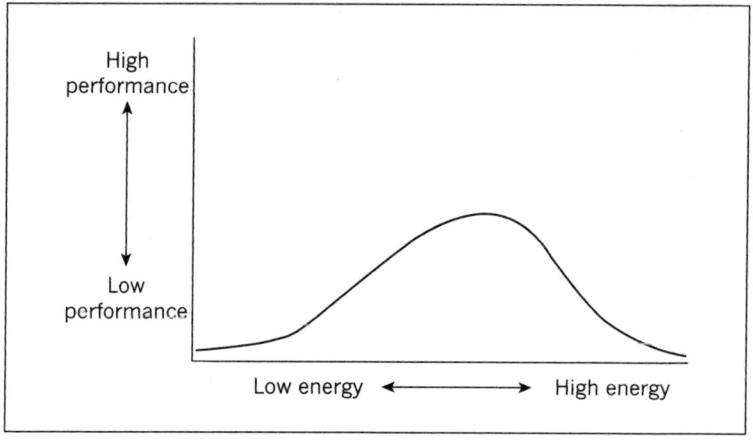

The inverted U-principle as given in the above figure indicates that the best performance occurs when persons have a moderate degree of psychic energy, regardless of whether this psychic energy is from a moderate level of excitement or stress. But research reports of the flow experience indicate that optimal performance occurs when people are very high in psychic energy and are stress free. Both situations are correct as people do not experience changes in psychic energy without assigning some causes to the changes. The change in psychic energy is assigned to some emotion or motivational source. Performance is determined by the level of psychic energy and also by the source of psychic energy.

Stress is an emotion—both positive and negative. It is a psychophysiological state, which is caused by the discrepancy between the perceived demands and the response capability of an organism to meet those demands. Stress may be eustress or de-stress according to some situations. Mostly, it is considered in negative terms, when we get some bad news, we are under stress, and we feel distressed and depressed. It is an aversive state, which we seek to avoid. Stress is known to hurt performance by creating unnecessary muscle tension, and attention becomes overly disruptive. Under high stress, people cannot concentrate intensely as concentration is required for the superior performance. When they are unable to concentrate, they have negative thoughts associated with the stress.

When people are in a flow state, their minds are fully focused on the task; when they worry, their attention is divided between the task and subject of their worry. The highest level of performance is achieved only when they are in stress. A free state exists between the two stress zones—anxiety and boredom. Worry and stress affect performance adversely. Scientific evidence shows that the best performances occur in a stress-free state.

Research shows that as positive psychic energy increases, performance improves, and no negative psychic energy affects performance. The more negative psychic energy individuals experience, the more their performance suffers. The best performance is in a state of maximum positive psychic energy with absolutely no negative psychic energy.

The ideal state of maximum positive psychic energy is sometimes achieved. People may have high positive psychic energy if the task is challenging, work is enjoyable, and the person has the determination to demonstrate competency as well as the perception of extrinsic rewards. But on the other hand, they may also experience negative psychic energy in the form of stress, anxiety, fear and anger. While positive psychic energy facilitates performance, negative psychic energy inhibits performance.

If only negative psychic energy exists, there would be no motivation to perform the task. When people perceive that there is no possible way that anything beneficial can come from participating in a contest and only negative consequences will result, they will not work unless the existing negative psychic energy is exceeded by more positive psychic energy.

It was assumed that some stress is good in motivating people up to the optimal level. Trying too hard is a common source of stress among many positively energized people. Thus, positive psychic energy can never be too high when the energy is directed to the task being performed. No research has shown that too much positive psychic energy is harmful to performance. The more positive psychic energy, the better it is.

FLOW: AN OPTIMUM PSYCHIC ENERGY

Csikszentmihalyi (1990) is credited with being the originator of the concept of the flow. In fact, it is a way of expressing a sense of the seemingly intrinsically joyful moment. People experience flow when they are engaged in an interesting activity for its own sake and no other external purpose or goal. Jackson (1995) says, 'Flow is a state of optimal experiencing involving total absorption in a task, and creating a state of consciousness where optimal levels of functioning often occur.' But in his original conceptualization of the flow construct, Csikszentmihalyi described flow as an end in itself, something that is to be enjoyed and appreciated.

'Flow' state is related to peak performance. Csikszentmihalyi (1985) who had worked in this area, extensively, has considered flow as the basis of intrinsically motivating experiences or self-rewarding activity. It is 'the state in which people are so involved in an activity that nothing else seems to matter' (Csikszentmihalyi, 1990). He investigated exactly what makes a task intrinsically motivating. One may be in the flow state but not necessarily by having achieved peak performance; however, when people experience peak performance, they appear to be in a flow state. Jackson and Roberts (1992) suggested that the flow state might be a precursor to or the psychological process underlying peak performance.

For intrinsic motivation, psychic energy is utmost essential, which activates the body for action and showing the peak performance. But it should be at the optimum level. Too much or too low psychic energy would affect the performance of people badly. Too much psychic energy may develop nervousness, anxiety, tension or any other emotional situation among them, which may inhibit in giving the desired results. On the other hand, too low psychic energy would create the state of apathy, which may develop the feelings of no interest. Hence, psychic energy should be brought to the optimum level with the help of some psycho-regulative technique when a person would be physically fit and mentally alert to participate in some tasks with high spirits. This state of mind is called 'flow'.

The flow state is achieved when people are totally involved in the activity; there is no space for self-praise or self-criticism. In the flow state, there is no stress, no anxiety and no boredom. The flow experience is so energizing that it is intrinsically motivated and rewarding. Flow is considered as the optimal energy zone when you want to help people reach to perform to the maximum.

Psychic energy is flexible and dynamic, and it goes on changing, so most of the people respond not only to their external environment but also to the internal situations, which they create through their thoughts. You may observe the changes in both positive and negative psychic energy among them.

Many factors can change psychic energy during a competition, for example, physical fatigue, mental fatigue, how well one is performing, how well the opponent is doing and receiving positive or negative feedback from others. For people to manage psychic energy successfully, they must become familiar with all these events that may cause positive and negative psychic energy to change. Then, they must have developed the psychological skills to keep their minds on the right track.

When people do some work and not expect any reward, recognition or any extrinsic motivation, it is because they are performing that activity due to their interest, and in that activity, they are intrinsically motivated. Due to their aptitude or internal urge to do so, they are doing it, and they are achieving their maximum output. An artist is performing their art because they have the talent. A painter who is busy in the job of painting without expecting any money or monetary reward from any agency satisfy the inner passion to do so. Similarly, a musician, dancer or any other actor who has the inborn ability to do something in life will continue their work and keep them absorbed in that activity. All these persons will be in a state of flow because of their optimum level of psychic energy.

Factors to Achieve the Flow

Some researches (Jackson, 1992; 1995) have found that some factors are the most important for getting into the flow. The following factors are considered the most important, which should be tried to understand for getting ourselves into the state of flow:

1. **Motivation to perform:** Motivation is very important to perform well and also for getting into the flow. When individuals are not motivated, it is not possible to achieve flow. The coordination between the challenge and skill may be the most important area which helps the individual to be motivated. High goals and a challenge are essential for achieving optimal motivation.
2. **Achieving an optimal arousal level before performing:** The feeling of relaxing, minimizing anxiety and enjoyment of the activity contributes to flow. Some individuals want to be relaxed before the activity, whereas others want to be more energized. However, some others try to find out a balance between calmness and arousal. For this, some mental exercises are required to be applied. A state of mental relaxation will bring confidence among us all.
3. **Concentration on the task:** Focusing and concentrating on the task is essential for maintaining proper attention. It will definitely bring the person into the state of flow. The positive result of concentration fully on the upcoming event will enable individuals to focus on their performance. Concentration on the task at hand is considered as one of the most important dimensions of the flow experience.
4. **Plans and preparation:** Planning for the activity is considered as one of the factors that influence the achievement of the flow state, along with confidence and a positive attitude. In the preparation of the activity, one should feel totally absorbed and ready before the task with the planning schedule as these are important components of planning and preparation.
5. **Physical preparation and readiness:** Having done the necessary preparation beforehand, you should work hard and feel that you are physically fit and ready as you are well prepared physically and mentally and able to have a good practice, and all these are necessary for getting into a flow state.

6. **Environmental conditions:** Some people can achieve a flow state by changing their own internal conditions, while many other persons are influenced by environmental situations that help them achieve a flow state. Such conditions give positive feedback from others, and optimal conditions may enhance the probability of the flow state.
7. **Confidence and positive feelings:** Confidence is one of the major factors in achieving a flow state. On the other hand, self-doubt, lack of confidences and putting pressure on oneself are perceived as factors that can disrupt the flow. Self-believe, positive feelings, avoiding negative thoughts and enjoyment in the work all help build confidence.
8. **Feeling good about performance:** Another factor for getting into the flow is feeling good about one's performance. In fact, getting feedback from others will give you a sense of satisfaction. Sometimes right, smooth and effortless things are usually related to getting into a flow state.
9. **Positive attitude:** It is the positive attitude which would give people self-confidence, develop positive thinking and sustain high motivation. Hence, the positive attitude will help them to achieve the flow. An individual should have self-talk in order to be positive with themselves, as it has to do with the feelings internally.

Factors Which Disrupt the Flow

Although it is important to understand how to enhance the likelihood of a flow state, it is equally important to understand what factors help in disrupting it (Jackson, 1995). The factors which disrupt the flow state are environmental and situational influences. The factors that prevent flow from occurring are:

1. Personal factors such as injury, fatigue and physical problems affect the flow state adversely.
2. Environmental or situational factors such as external stresses, unwanted crowd behaviour and uncontrollable conditions influence the event.

3. Factors such as lack of confidence or a negative mental state such as negative thinking, self-doubt and lack of control also work.
4. Behavioural aspects such as negative attitude, worrying about what others are doing and frustration may also affect.
5. Psychological factors such as lack of motivation to perform, setting unachievable goals, failures to achieve goals and lack of control, commitment and challenge and also low arousal may influence the flow state negatively.
6. No interactions with others, not performing well, lack of feelings of belongingness and negative talk within the group are some of the other factors which may also affect.
7. Performance going adversely, applying poor techniques and things not going as planned may disrupt the flow state.
8. Inability to maintain focus such as losing concentration, distraction, surprise results or interruption before or during a performance may prevent the flow state.
9. Negative mental attitude, for example, negative self-talk and self-critical attitude affect the flow state.

The state of flow does not just happen. But it depends on the mental and physical state of individuals and their environmental influences, which seem to interact to make it more or less likely that the flow will actually occur. It means that personal and environmental factors interact with each other to produce the flow state.

However, it is not easy to change the environment, but providing feedback to persons will maximize the possibility of them reaching and maintaining a flow state. Moreover, developing psychological skills such as emotional arousal regulation, stress management and thought control increases one's likelihood of experiencing the flow.

OPTIMAL PSYCHIC ENERGY ZONE

The optimal psychic energy zone is defined as a stress-free state of flow in which a person feels fully in control, concentration is intense and well-focused and the psychic energy level is high and positive. It is a zone in which people have very high psychic energy and less stress whatsoever. This zone is reached when they are in a state of flow.

Now, the question arises on how to help persons to reach the optimal psychic energy zone. Self-talk is one of the most useful techniques.

Psyching out: Being in the flow is being psyched up, and you cannot psych out someone unless they are first psyched up. Thus, psyching someone out is simply disrupting that person's state of flow.

Psyching out techniques are typically designed to get the other person to think about what they are or are not doing. It is an attempt to shift the attention of the person from the activity being performed to how the performer is doing the activity. Typically, persons psyche themselves out through their own analytical minds.

Psyching up: If disrupting the flow is psyching out, then psyching up is enhancing the likelihood of people experiencing the flow. Psyching up is no simple for putting people into the optimal energy zone. It is a long-term programme based on the same type of hard work required to develop the physical skills in order to perform well.

PSYCHOLOGICAL SKILLS TRAINING (PST) APPROACH TO MANAGE PSYCHIC ENERGY

A simple and an accurate tool for measuring positive and negative psychic energy does not exist. The problem in measuring psychic energy is complex. The best we can do in measuring this energy is to have each person indicate whether they are experiencing more or less psychic energy. To help people find their optimal psychic energy zone, there should be a method in which each of them makes comparison between their own psychic energy levels.

Procedures

The following points must be kept in view for helping people to find their optimal psychic energy zones.

1. They should have greater self-awareness regarding their psychic energy levels. They must become sensitive to their emotional states and perceive the psychic energy as they have during performance.

2. People need to initiate PST programme. They need to be educated about the programme through some questions as given in Box 2.2.

Box 2.2: Some Questions Regarding PST

1. What is psychic energy management?
2. What is the state of mind when they experience flow?
3. How positive psychic energy always facilitates performance and negative psychic energy always disrupts performance?
4. What are the principles for psyching up?
5. How to avoid being psyched out?
6. How to manage stress?

---

3. Develop a PST programme so that people can use it for changing their energy levels.
4. People may find a subjective scale useful that has been developed for rating psychic energy levels.
5. They should meet each one personally to implement the keeping of the programme and to set up a schedule.
6. They should reinforce the value of managing psychic energy by adopting the educative purpose.
7. Psychic energy undergoes a change as people respond to both their external and internal environment.
8. Self-talk may prove to be a well-advised means to increase psychic energy.
9. The PST approach in managing psychic energy is based on increased self-awareness combined with the acquisition of all the psychological skills.

The conclusion from the above discussion is shown in Box 2.3.

Box 2.3: Psychic Energy and PST

1. Psyching out someone is disrupting their flow.
2. Psyching up is achieved by increasing an individual's positive psychic energy.

---

3. The inverted U principle is widely held to be true. It states that performance improves as psychic energy increases to some optimal point but with further increment in psychic energy, performance decreases.
4. Psychic energy is both positive and negative. The positive psychic energy facilitates performance while negative psychic energy debilitates performance.
5. Negative psychic energy is stress. A person should be helped to acquire a state of mind where positive psychic energy is as high as possible, and negative psychic energy is non-existent.
6. One can hope that increased motivation may increase positive psychic energy.

NEED AND IMPORTANCE OF PSYCHIC ENERGY

Every individual has both physical and psychic energy. For the development of the personality of an individual, there is a need to harness and develop psychic energy. Of course, it is an innate and inborn power of an individual, but if they do not get the opportunity for its development, it will go waste and may not be utilized. If a child has an inborn talent or potential to become a painter, singer, dancer or an actor and if they do not get training or exposure to that environment where they may get an opportunity to grow and develop according to these abilities, they may use their talent in a wrong way and may become a naughty child. The importance of psychic energy can be seen in the following points:

1. Psychic energy is related to motivation. Motivation is very important to achieve success in life. Without motivation, nothing is possible in this life. If a person is in a flow state, that is, in the optimal psychic energy zone, they will be motivated. Then, they can accomplish anything which they desire.
2. Psychic energy is concerned with emotional arousal. Without emotions, an individual's life is just like a human machine. If an individual is having positive emotions, they are in a flow state and have an optimum level of psychic energy. Utilization of psychic energy is very much required in life to be successful.

3. Psychic energy also directs the good performance. It directs, controls and manages all types of activities. It helps in showing maximum performance.
4. Psychic energy leads to create interest and then increases the concentration ability of a person when they are in a flow state of mental functioning.
5. Psychic energy helps to develop a positive attitude and self-confidence in a person. Positive psychic energy is a sign of positive thinking, feelings and actions. It is very much required for psychological well-being as well as human wellness in these critical days.
6. There is a need to develop psychic energy, which may be possible through PST. Although it may not be possible to increase psychic energy, it can be developed and brought to the optimum level of psychic energy, which is possible through training.

CONCLUSION

Psychic energy is said to be related to an individual's motivational level, optimum emotional arousal, mental toughness and activation. It is concerned with the arousal of the body and mind. It is distinguished from emotional arousal, which refers to the activation of mind and body, which initiates any activity. Psychic energy or activation level is very essential in all types of activities. It refers to a combination of physiological and muscular signs, which indicate that to what extent the individual is preparing themselves to perform vigorously.

Psychic energy or arousal has typically been referred to as physiological activation or autonomic reactivity. Psychologists have studied emotional arousal in terms of three components: physical, cognitive and behavioural. Luthans and Youssef (2004) devised a theory which is called psychological capital in which they discussed the four constructs such as hope, efficacy, resilience and optimism.

Psychic energy must not only be controlled, but it must be harnessed, explored and directed. Three types of changes occur with the increased psychic energy, namely physiological, psychological and behavioural changes. Psychic energy is closely associated with psychological stress. Similarly, there is a relationship between skill and challenge. The flow state is achieved when both skill and challenge are high. Research shows that as positive psychic energy increases, performance improves and no negative psychic energy affects performance.

The flow is optimum psychic energy. Csikszentmihalyi (1990) is credited with being the originator of the concept of the flow. A person experiences flow when they are engaged in an interesting activity for its own sake and no other external purpose or goal. For intrinsic motivation, psychic energy is utmost essential, which activates the body for action and showing the peak performance. But it should be at the optimum level. There are many factors which help to achieve flow.

The optimal psychic energy zone is stated as a stress-free state of flow in which a person feels fully in control, concentration is intense and well-focused and the psychic energy level is high and positive. PST helps to achieve and manage psychic energy because there is a need to achieve it. Now, the psychologists have felt the importance of psychic energy for human wellness, which we can achieve through the PST programme.

The PST approach in managing psychic energy is based on increased self-awareness combined with the acquisition of all the psychological skills. Out of many psychological skills, imagery is considered as the master skill. How mental imagery plays an important role in human wellness, we shall have to understand the nature and concept of imagery as well as the practical exercises for practising this skill.

Mental Imagery
A Master Skill

INTRODUCTION

Every individual has psychic energy, positive as well as negative. If they harness psychic energy, it will be good for their human wellness. It can be practised through mental imagery exercises. Mental imagery is a basic psychological skill. Imagery is a mental skill which is related to the mental process of a person. It involves the cognitive domain of behaviour of an individual, for example, thinking, imagining, reasoning problem-solving and decision-making. There are three types of mental skills: (a) basic skills such as self-confidence, commitment and control, (b) psychosomatic skills such as stress response, relaxation and activation and (c) cognitive skills such as visualization, mental practice, focus, attention and concentration. Imagery is the cognitive skill, which is considered as the mastery skill.

Imagery is one of the important psychological skills. It occupies the top position. But it is a skill that a very few people try to apply as they have not learnt how to use it. Imagery can be a powerful help to our young people. They can imagine themselves achieving feats and removing hardships. The issue to the constructive use of imagery is how to harness this skill.

CONCEPT OF IMAGERY

Imagery means reliving an old experience in the mind. This process consists of recalling from memory lane some information, which has already been stored in the mind due to some past experiences. These old experiences, in fact, are recalled and reconstructed by our memory and then reconstructed by those previous and old experiences. Imagery is actually like that of simulated condition. It is similar to real sensory experiences and involves seeing, hearing, touching and feeling, but all these experiences happen in the mind.

According to Richardson (1969), 'Mental imagery refers to all those quasi-sensory and quasi-perceptual experiences of which we are self-consciously aware and which exists for us in the absence of those stimulus conditions that are known to produce their genuine sensory or perceptual counterparts.'

Imagery is an experience similar to a sensory one, which arises in the mind in the absence of some external stimuli. When you experience the movement pattern of your body within your mind, these experiences are essentially an outcome of your memory and become a part of imagery. They are experienced internally by clearly recalling and perhaps reconstructing previous external experiences.

Imagery is like visualizing an experience in your mind. Imagery may involve any one or all the sensory organs such as eyes, ears, nose, hands and tongue. Visual, auditory, taste, smelling and kinaesthetic or touching senses are most significant to everybody. The kinaesthetic sense is the sensation of bodily movement and presence of movement pattern that arises from the stimulation of sensory nerve endings in muscles, tendons and body joints.

We experience real things when we are attached to our emotional states. We can also experience these emotional experiences when we clearly imagine certain pleasant or unpleasant situations. We try to associate with these states of mind. This is an important dimension of imagery, which has made it a powerful tool for developing other psychological skills. As it is a mastery skill, other psychological skills are taught with the help of this skill.

In our life, all of us use imagery to create and recreate experiences. We can achieve these things because our mind can remember and retain those situations and recreate images of them later on. Our minds can also imagine pictures of these events. Although imagery depends mostly on memory, we can build an image from several other aspects of memory.

Through imagery, you can relive previous positive or negative experiences or imagine new events to prepare yourself mentally for performance in the future. Taking an example from the field of sports, specifically the game of tennis, the former Wimbledon champion Chris Evert carefully rehearsed every detail of a match, including her opponent's style, strategy and shot selection. She says, 'Before I play a match, I try to carefully rehearse what is likely to happen and how I will react in certain situations. I visualize myself playing typical points based on my opponent's style of playing. This helps me mentally prepare for a match, and I feel like I have already played the match before I even walk on the court.'

Imagery is a cognitive process or a 'mode of thought'. Here, the cognitive functioning of mind exists. It is a kind of visualization or mental rehearsal or practice. Mental practice is a term for a particular technique used by many people. Oxendine (1984) defines the mental practice as 'the introspective or covert rehearsal that takes place within the individual.' Many different kinds of processes can underlie this technique; for example, as Suinn and Clayton (1980) have pointed out, mentally practising a tennis serve could involve thinking, imagining an athlete hitting a perfect serve or visualizing a perfect serve you once hit.

This psychological skill is often being applied in the field of competitive sports as a part of psychotically training and mental preparation. Recently, coaches have begun to understand the potential of imagery for improving sports performance. In using imagery in sports, athletes 'think with the muscles'. Due to the effectiveness of imagery in improving sports performance, more and more athletes and coaches are including mental rehearsal in training. Imagery has also helped athletes with rehabilitation after injury. Many students also use imagery skill in rehearsing some points in their mind before the examination to know whether they have remembered those points, and they will be able to reproduce them in the examination.

Imagery rehearsal: Imagery has been utilized to achieve covert practice. Imagery rehearsal involves people imagining themselves successfully completing the task that is the focus of attention; for example, in sports, a tennis player learning a new serve may imagine the feel and look of the new skill before sleep (mental practice), or an elite diver may pause for a moment on the springboard, imagining themselves completing the dive they are about to attempt and then initiate the drive (psyching up).

In both cases, game skill is imaginably rehearsed in the absence of actual movement or activity of that game. In the first case, the goal is usually to reinforce the learning of a new technique or skill. In the second case, the goal is to enhance the performance of an already learned skill.

Imagery skills have usually been utilized in the sport contexts as components of the interventions, for example, relaxation, meditation and mind training. To study the relationship between imagery and human performance, it is important to understand the nature of imagery skill, which will enhance the general understanding of imagery and cognitive processes.

NEED AND IMPORTANCE OF IMAGERY

Imagery is imagining the old experiences in the mind in the absence of actual experiences. In fact, imagery experiences are mimicry of sensory or perceptual experiences. The individual perceives 'seeing' an image or 'feeling' the movements associated with mental rehearsal.

Imagery skill is being applied in the field of sports for enhancement of performance of athletes, and coaches have to learn this psychological skill in their training programme with the help of sports psychologists. But this skill is also required for all types of people, in fact for the whole mankind for their effective modern living. Imagery is a mental rehearsal for the activities to be initiated in future. As rehearsal is done by the actors before they perform at the platform at the final stage, so that they may show their best. Similarly, every individual is expected to do imagery exercises before they start any task in future. Students also rehearse in the mind what they have already learnt and recite in their mind those points of their lesson which they want to retain in their memory, so that they may be able to reproduce those points in their examinations. For this reason, imagery is considered as a basic skill because all other psychological skills are dependent upon it. For example, stress management, goal setting, attention and concentration are based upon imagery.

There are many advantages of imagery, which include improving concentration, building confidence, controlling emotional responses, acquiring and practising other skills and strategies for coping with stress, including the pain of injury. Besides these, there are many other uses of this skill, for example, enhancing motivation, preparing for lifetime competition, helping decision-making and solving problems.

Imagery is different from the dreaming or daydreaming as the latter experiences do not involve the conscious focus of awareness. Imagery takes place without known stimulus antecedents. No mountain or snow needs be present, but the skier can close eyes and imagine the experience of skiing on the snow of the mountain.

TYPES OF IMAGERY

There are two types of imagery: internal and external. We usually use imagery from an internal or external perspective, and which perspective should be used depends on the person and the situation. We can differentiate between internal and external imagery, such as:

1. **Internal imagery:** Internal imagery means imagining the execution of skill from your own internal mind as if you have a camera in your head. You can see only what you would have seen if you actually execute the particular skill. In the internal imagery, the images would emphasize the feel of the movement. It all happens with the physiological aspects of the organism. So it all depends upon the person's internal state of mind, which has a mirror. Through this mirror, you can perceive and imagine what you would like to think in your mind.
2. **External imagery:** Here, a person views themselves as if they are an external observer. It is as if they are watching themselves on videotape as some object. But there would be a little emphasis on the kinaesthetic feel of the movement. It all depends upon the external situation of the person. So it is external imagery.

Research studies have shown that internal imagery has proved to be a better technique than external imagery. Internal imagery facilitates to bring in the kinaesthetic sense, feel the movement and the approximate actual performance skills.

OBJECTIVES OF THE IMAGERY SKILL

The objectives of the imagery skill are:

1. To help people acquire or practice complex motor skills (motor imagery)
2. To rehearse the techniques which you would like to follow in a particular situation
3. To acquire and learn the psychological skills

APPLIED ISSUES FOR IMAGERY SKILL

Imagery interventions programme are very popular among applied psychologists. It is the applications of psychological intervention to life situations. Many imagery-based techniques have been utilized for skill acquisition and arousal regulation. For example:

1. **Skill acquisition:** Many studies (Feltz & Landers, 1983) suggest that learning a new skill can be assisted by the mental rehearsal of the skill. The more the number of cognitive aspects of the skill, the more facilitation in learning takes place by mental practice. In fact, some researches have suggested that 'tasks which emphasize kinaesthetic cues may not be mentally rehearsed'. But the evidence suggests that tasks that are primarily motoric in nature require a certain level of familiarity with the skill before mental practice can be effective. For cognitive tasks, mental rehearsal seems to help the learner in developing a conceptual orientation for understanding and organizing the task.
2. **Skill maintenance:** A few studies (Schmidt, 1982) have found that if a mental practice technique is used during learning, retention is usually better in skill maintenance. It would be interesting to

examine whether a skill, once learned, could be maintained for long periods of time by mental practice alone.
3. **Arousal regulation:** It is suggested that some people practice visualizing whatever provides them with a sense of relaxation. This strategy can be employed when they get nervous or worried about an upcoming event/performance in order to restore a sense of calm. Oxendine (1970) says that different tasks require different levels of optimal arousal. Techniques to increase one's arousal have been called 'preparatory arousal' techniques, and such techniques can enhance performance on certain tasks.

Imagery has been used to increase and decrease arousal. Studies have found that subjects reported increased arousal levels after imagining scenes that made them fearful or angry, but they showed no strength increases, after imagining a scene that made them feel calm, and subjects had significantly lower strength performance.

IMAGERY AS A TOOL

Imagery can be an effective tool for arousal regulation. It was suggested that emotive imagery is most effective when it is used as a cognitive coping strategy, and attention is directed towards utilizing the arousal to achieve goals. The following points may be considered:

1. **Planning for event management:** Another popular use of imagery techniques is to prepare persons cognitively for upcoming events or tasks. Visualization can be an aid in rehearsing such a plan prior to the actual situation. Mental practice findings regarding the effectiveness of imagery rehearsal in organizing tasks suggest that the approach to event planning has merit whether they can be taught to apply more effectively imagery techniques for cognitive planning.
2. **Stress management:** Psychologists suggest certain techniques change the negative emotions to positive ones with more appropriate cognitive strategies through the use of thought stopping or positive self-talk. One person imaginably rehearses the event and sees themselves coping successfully, using the techniques they

have practised. The goal of this intervention is for that person to develop and become familiar with a set of successful strategies for coping with stress. Smith (1980) has outlined a comprehensive cognitive-affective approach to stress management training, which is a useful guide for researchers. Imagery intervention is also one component of stress management technique.
3. **Self-image manipulation:** The images we hold of ourselves are one of our major sources of self-esteem. The fact that imagery can improve self-confidence has long been recognized by cognitive-behavioural therapists who ask persons to imagine more successful behaviour than they presently exhibit. These imaginable strategies include systematic desensitization, flooding coping imagery and implosion. Bandura (1977a) says that many psychological interventions achieve their effects through modifications of an individual's self-efficacy level. Such modifications can be achieved via both actual experience and through vicarious or even imagined experience.

    Rushall (1988) describes a successful application of covert modelling in sports setting to deal with lack of confidence. An intervention strategy is designed in which the person practises imagining themselves defeating specific higher rated opponents as well as the consequences of these victories (emotional responses).
4. **Injury and pain control:** Imagery-based techniques have been suggested by several authors for use in injury rehabilitation and healing and in controlling pain. Some authors have suggested the use of visualization for healing injuries, coping with pain and utilizing imagery following deep relaxation. A number of authors have described imagery methods that are applicable in helping injured persons. Hence, imagery can be used in many ways that go beyond simple practice of life skills.

PST THROUGH IMAGERY

Imagery can be used to help people to learn and acquire such psychological skills as controlling anxiety, improving attention skills and using goal-setting skills to develop and maintain an optimal level of self-confidence.

Imagery is important in the development of psychological skills. The self-awareness rather than sensory awareness is more emphasized for the development of psychological skills. The purpose of self-awareness training is to help people to know and feel emotional states they experience when doing something and to recall these experiences vividly.

For developing self-awareness, people are asked to recall the previous experiences, including anxiety and anger-provoking events to recall previous position experienced as well as those joyous moments of life. The PST programme uses imagery, first, to help them face their emotion, next, to help them acquire the basic skill of PST and, finally, to provide them with a way to practice these psychological skills in a self-simulated competitive situation.

FUNDAMENTALS OF IMAGERY TRAINING

Imagery is a skill acquired through practice like all other psychological techniques. First of all, we will have to understand the current imagery skill level. The following points should be considered.

1. **Vividness:** Good images use all our senses-organs to make the images as clear and vivid as possible. It is important to create or recreate images close to actual experience, which are perceptible in our mind. The closer images which are like the real thing, the better it is to transfer to the actual performance. One should also pay special attention to environmental situations such as the infrastructure of the facilities we have, the type of place and closeness of people around us. Then, we will also experience the thoughts and emotions of the actual situation. In this way, we may feel the emotions such as stress, frustration and anxiety and also have concentration, exhilaration or anger associated with our performance. All this will make the imagined task look more real and vivid.
2. **Controllability:** Another point for successful imagery is how to learn to manipulate our images so that we may do whatever we may like to do. Many of us may have difficulty in controlling our images. Having control over our image helps us to picture what

we want to achieve instead of making errors. We can practise by doing the controllability exercise.

PREPARING TO PRACTICE

Vividness and controllability are best practised under the following conditions:

1. Right setting of environment
2. Relaxed attention
3. Motivation to train
4. The right attitude or expectancy
5. Systematic practice

Their description is given below:

1. **Right setting:** Those highly skilled in the use of imagery such as yogis can practise and perform their skill in any environment. As people's imagery skills develop, they will learn to use imagery even when they are surrounded by all the distractions in their settings. They can let these distractions aware of their consciousness while they attend to their internal images.
2. **Relaxed attention:** Relaxation is an important part of imagery training. Before each imagery exercise, persons should try to be completely relaxed and do some relaxation exercises. They want to make their mind and muscles quiet, but at the same time, they should be attentive to what they are going to do. They should be in a state of relaxed attention. Relaxation is important if they have to do a lot of mental activity—analysing past mistakes, thinking about the day's events and so on. Relaxed attention releases imagery and tension suppresses it.

As long as the body is physically tensed, attention is distracted from what is going on inside you. So a quiet and calm state is required for imagery to have a greater effect on the nervous system. Imagery is the most effective when the brain waves are in the alpha phase, indicating a quiet and relaxed mind. Relaxation is very

much effective in imagery training. People will be more benefitted when practising imagery in a relaxed but attentive state.
3. **Motivation:** The best people are those who are intrinsically motivated, which keep them practising for months and even years in preparation for the big event. People must have that intrinsic type of motivation to develop both their physical and psychological skills. They should be motivated to practice the skills on a systematic basis.
4. **Expectation:** It is more successful when some people expect it to be helpful. Images are always more vivid and stable when people believe in them. Some of them are eager to use imagery but expect to achieve the results immediately. They can improve their imagery skills in a few weeks because these skills are usually quite underdeveloped. They must be realistic in their expectation of imagery.
5. **Practice:** Every person knows the importance of practice, but the quality of the practice is more important. Just going through the movements, when practising skills will not accomplish what they want and may even affect their performance adversely by introducing errors into the skill because they are not fully concentrating. So practice should be systematic and meaningful.

When to use imagery: Timing for the imagery is also very important. Although imagery can be practised at any time, there are some specific timings when it seems to be the most useful. One way to use imagery skill systematically is to execute it before and after morning or evening session. One should confine these sessions for about 10–15 minutes. To focus on concentration and get ready before practice, people should visualize the activities which they are expected to perform. After each practice session, they should assess the skills and strategies they work on and do self-assessment.

DEVELOPING AN IMAGERY TRAINING PROGRAMME

For developing an imagery training programme, we will have to devise such a programme which may prove to be very effective for imagery skill. To be effective, imagery should become a part of our daily routine life. It is important to initiate imagery programme to the needs, abilities and interests of every one of us. The imagery programme should be suitable for our daily training programme. The guidelines for implementing a successful imagery training programme are given below:

1. **Proper setting:** People who are adept in the use of imagery can perform this technique almost everywhere and anywhere. For the new learners, it is beneficial to practice in a place which is quiet and has no distractions. Some people may like to practice imagery skill in their own bedrooms before going to sleep while some others in any room which is comfortable for them.
2. **Relaxed position:** Imagery practice is preceded by relaxation exercise, which is also very effective. Imagery can take place only when the person is in a complete state of relaxed position. Before each imagery session, relaxing exercise is done by using deep breathing, progressive relaxation technique or some other relaxation procedure such as Shavasana. Relaxation is important for two reasons: (a) it helps us to forget everyday anxieties, worries and tension and (b) it will help us to concentrate on the task at hand.
3. **Sustaining motivation:** Sometimes, the negative thinking and attitude lowers imagery effectiveness. But the fact is that imagery can improve the skills if you do it systematically. Some people are usually intrinsically motivated to practice the skill of imagery for months together. Such dedication, devotion and determination are needed to develop psychological skills such as imagery and others. We should remember that efforts made in a systematic imagery programme are rewarded in the future time.
4. **Vivid and controllable images:** We should try to use all our senses and feel the movements as if they are occurring. We should move and position our body as if we are actually performing the skills that will make imagery and feeling of movement more vivid and clear. Moreover, it is important to learn how to image with our eyes open as well as closed. Working on the controlled images with self-instruction will produce the desired outcome.
5. **Positive focus:** We should focus on positive outcomes using imagery to analyse errors, which would be beneficial to us because nobody is 100 per cent correct, and we all make mistakes every time we act. We should use imagery to prepare ourselves for effectively coping with the mistakes.

First of all, we should try to imagine and think of the correct response and try to imagine performing the skill correctly. The image of the correct response (along with the feeling of that response) should then be repeated several times, and this should immediately be proceeded by the actual physical practice. Imagining successful outcomes help the body and mind to execute skills.

6. **Videotapes:** We can take the help of videotapes if needed. Videotapes can provide the feedback—a picture of how we see performing at our best. Looking ourselves on videotape for the first time is quite interesting. A person observes their skills in the same relaxed state prescribed for imagery training. After watching the film for several minutes, they close their eyes and imagine the skill. So videotapes are very useful in imagery skill.
7. **Image execution and outcome:** Imagery should consist of both the execution and outcome of the skills. Many of us imagine the execution of the skill and not the outcome or vice versa. We need to be able to feel the movement and control the image so that we may see the desired results.
8. **Imagining in real time:** The time spent on imagining a particular skill should be recorded, and it should be equal to the time the skill actually takes place. Because some people are likely to image faster than the actual time as it takes to perform the skill; it is a good idea to time the skill.

IMAGERY TRAINING PROGRAMME (ITP)

Imagery is one of the important psychological skills. It is considered as a master skill. So all individuals should try to improve their imagery skill through practice. Imagery is the most effective skill when it is practised properly. The main purpose of ITP is to improve one's imagery vividness and controllability through the practice of certain imagery exercises. In ITP, the following steps should be followed:

1. The first step in this programme is to assess the status of an individual's imagery skills using a simple imagery test. The purpose of the test is to evaluate the vividness or intensity of their imagery with regard to visual, auditory and kinaesthetic senses as well as

the related emotional state for a series of life situations. This test will help you determine the type and quantity of imagery training needed by your client.
2. Second, it is important to know that imagery is more than just visualization. The more sensation one can stimulate through imagery, the more vivid or intense the images are. The greater awareness of the senses by individuals and emotions stimulated by their images, the greater capacity they have to use images for their advantage.
3. Third, while vividness is important, it is also essential that a person should have the ability and capacity to control their images. The productive images manipulate shapes and move the person towards a desired goal.
4. Finally, imagery control involves whether it is internal (seeing it through your eyes as you are doing the activity) or external (seeing it from the outside). The internal part is usually desired because it more closely approximates the way persons actually perform activities. But if an individual is having a problem doing a task, it may help to analyse the error by taking an external perspective.

USES OF IMAGERY

Imagery is a useful psychological skill. But people have been exercising imagery on some occasion, but seldom have they used it systematically. Imagery must be practised regularly and correctly as it is helpful to the persons to achieve success in their tasks. In order to understand human behaviour, we have to understand the imagery powers of human beings.

The primary uses of the imagery skills are:

1. Imagery helps in developing such psychological skills as psychic energy and stress management through the rehearsal of the techniques.
2. Imagery helps to focus attention and increases the capacity to concentrate.
3. It helps build self-confidence as people see themselves attaining their goals.

People can employ imagery in the following ways to improve other psychological skills:

1. **Improve concentration:** With the help of imagery skill, you can improve your concentration skill also. By imagining what you want to do and how you would like to react in certain situations, you can avoid distraction. You can imagine yourself in situations where you generally have your full concentration.
2. **Build confidence:** With the help of imagery skill, you can build up your confidence, which is also an important psychological skill. Imagining yourself performing well will help you feel that you may be able to perform well under adverse conditions.
3. **Control emotional responses:** Imagery helps you to control your emotional reactions in some unpleasant situations. You can visualize those situations in the past that have caused problems such as choking under pressure or getting angry. You can imagine yourself dealing with these events in a positive way, by taking a deep breath and focusing on your breath control as you try to concentrate on the task at hand.
4. **Practice skills:** Imagining is a way to practise movement patterns in visualization. You can practise skills to pinpoint your weaknesses and perceive correcting them. So the practice for imagery skill is required too much.
5. **Practice strategy:** Imagery can be used to practise and adopt some strategies for useful activities. There are different strategies and methods for practising imagery skill. So training to learn these strategies is essential.
6. **Coping with pain and injury:** Imagery is useful for coping with pain and injury. It can help speed up recovery of the injured person and help to rehabilitate earlier. But some people may imagine during practice and thereby facilitate recovery. It has been found in the clinical practice that imagery plays a useful role in early recovery and rehabilitation of the injured patients.

Mental imagery can help increase a variety of skills to improve performance and can facilitate the learning of new techniques and strategies. The positive reinforcement of behaviour strengthens the possibility of success. Imagery may be a technique to help persons to come out of the vicious cycle of experiencing negative reinforcement. It will help in developing self-confidence, self-prestige and self-esteem. It also tries to minimize anxiety and reduce stress. To imagine success by having some people vividly perceiving themselves doing well and mentally reinforcing themselves internally for having succeeded in some activities are the main advantages of imagery as a psychological skill.

PRACTICAL SUGGESTIONS FOR APPLYING IMAGERY

For applying the skill of imagery in our life, some suggestions (Box 3.1) may be followed.

Box 3.1: Practical Suggestions for Imagery Practices

1. Lie down comfortably on your bed or cushion with loose clothes in a calm and quiet environment.
2. Start taking deep breathing for two minutes and concentrate on any point on your forehead. This step will help you to come out from all the distractions, which are affecting you adversely.
3. Now come to the normal breathing for two minutes and enjoy the sensation which is taking place in your body.
4. Now, start imagining about any activity which you are likely to start. Think about what you want to do and make future planning about that task in which you are interested.
5. This is a visualization which you are doing in your mind, so it is a mental rehearsal. It may continue about 15–20 minutes while your eyes are closed.
6. When you are satisfied that everything has been thought about, you may open your eyes gently after putting both of your palms on your eyes so that you may not feel tired.

CONCLUSION

Imagery is a psychological skill, which is related to the mental process of a person. It involves the cognitive domain of behaviour of an individual. Imagery means reliving an old experience in the mind. This process consists of recalling some information from the memory, which has already been stored in the mind due to some past experiences. Imagery is an experience similar to a sensory one, which arises in the mind in the absence of some external stimuli.

Imagery is like visualizing an experience in your mind. Imagery may involve any one or all the sensory organs such as eyes, ears, nose, hands and tongue. We can experience these emotional experiences when we clearly imagine certain pleasant or unpleasant situations. Through imagery, we can relive previous positive or negative experiences or imagine new events to prepare ourselves mentally for performance in the future. It is a 'mode of thought' and a kind of visualization or mental rehearsal or practice.

Imagery rehearsal involves the person imagining themselves successfully completing the task that is the focus of attention. Imagery skill is applied in the field of sports for the enhancement of performance of athletes. But this skill is required for each and every person to lead an effective and successful life. This skill is important because it is meant for improving concentration, building confidence, controlling emotional responses, acquiring and practising other skills and strategies for coping with stress, besides enhancing motivation, preparing for lifetime competition, helping decision-making and problem-solving.

There are two types of imagery: internal and external. We usually use imagery from an internal or external perspective, that is, the person and the situation perspectives. But it has been proved that internal imagery is better as it makes it easier to bring in the kinaesthetic sense, feel the movement and approximate actual performance skills.

There are some applied issues in ITP, which is the applications of psychological intervention to life situations. Many imagery-based techniques have been utilized for skill acquisition, skill maintenance and arousal regulation. Imagery may be used as a tool for planning event management, stress reduction and self-image regulation as well as attention and pain control. Imagery can be used to help people acquire psychological skills such as controlling anxiety, improving attention skills and using goal-setting skills to develop and maintain an optimal self-confidence level.

The fundamentals of imagery training consist of vividness and controllability, which can best be practised with (a) right setting of environment, (b) relaxed attention, (c) motivation, (d) the right attitude and (e) systematic practice. For developing ITP, we will have to devise a programme, which may prove to be very effective for imagery skill. The guidelines for implementing a successful ITP are: (a) proper setting, (b) relaxed concentration, (c) sustaining motivation, (d) vivid and controllable images, (e) positive focus, (f) videotapes, (g) image execution and outcome and (h) image in real time.

Imagery is a useful psychological skill. For ITP, many practical suggestions have been given; if followed properly, we can make use of this technique in a scientific way to get many advantages in our life. The best use of this technique is that it helps in motivating an individual. So motivation is another psychological skill which needs to be studied in detail. The next chapter deals with the concept of motivation, motives and theories of motivation.

Motivation for Performance Enhancement

INTRODUCTION

After imagery, motivation is another important psychological skill which needs to probe into. Motivation is very essential for human wellness and the development of a human being. The study of motivation in psychology is crucial for understanding human behaviour because our behaviour is a motivated one. Human behaviour is originated from our needs, which are invariably directed towards certain motives that are closely related to the satisfaction of our physiological and psychological needs. In studying motivation, psychologists examine the internal needs and drives that direct an organism towards a goal or motive. Some of these result from a physiological imbalance that the organism acts to correct. Other kinds of motivation are learned and involve a desire for mastery, achievement and affiliation. Later on, a man is motivated by things such as money, prestige, power and the desire to be socially acceptable.

Motivation is crucial to a full understanding of human behaviour. Motivation is a basic but important psychological process in understanding human wellness. Motivation is a process that starts from the deprivation of our physiological and psychological needs that activates behaviour that is aimed at a goal or motive. Motivation is the result of the interaction of an individual and their environment. Certainly, there are individual differences in the fulfilment of the basic motivational needs.

NATURE OF MOTIVATION

Motivation is derived from the Latin word 'movere', which means to move. Anything that moves an individual to action may be described as motives, drives, urges, etc. Hence, without motivation, no behaviour or no performance is possible. Motivation provides driving force and direction to all types of behaviour. It is that force which impels or incites an individual's action and determines their direction of actions.

Human behaviour is motivated one. Motivation refers to the internal conditions or states that activate or energize the individual, which leads to goal-directed behaviour. Motivation is the direction, energy and intensity of behaviour. It works as a guide by maintaining and sustaining our behaviour. It answers the questions, 'why do we do what we do? Why do people behave as they do? Why do some people persist in a certain course of action? Why some people work harder than others?' The answers to these questions lie in the nature of motivation.

Motivation is defined as the mental readiness and willingness to put some efforts towards the achievement of certain goals with the capacity to satisfy some individual needs and motives. Motivation is the psychic energy, which incites you to explore your potential and reach up to your excellence or your top level. Motivated persons are usually under a state of stress. To overcome this stress, they exert a lot of efforts and work hard. If the efforts successfully lead to the satisfaction of the goal, stress is reduced. In fact, this stress-reduction effort must be directed towards the achievement of goals.

Hence, 'motivation deals with factors that direct a person towards the achievement of a specific goal.' Some situations are generally motivating to most people, while other situations are not. Hence, motivation may be defined 'as any general condition internal or external to an organism initiated by drives, needs and desires that lead to satisfying goal-directed behaviour.' Motivation or motivated behaviour may develop from physiological and psychological needs or more complex desires.

CHARACTERISTICS OF MOTIVATION

The characteristics of motivation are shown box 4.1.

> **Box 4.1**
>
> 1. Motivation provides energy.
> 2. Motivation is goal-directed.
> 3. Motivation gives concentrated attention.
> 4. Motivation is a selective behaviour.
> 5. Motivation is energy mobilizer
> 6. It helps to attain the achievement of goals.
> 7. Motivation creates interest.
> 8. It helps in character formation.

MOTIVES

The human behaviour is directed, controlled and modified through certain motives. An individual searches food because they are hungry. Their hunger is a motive which provides them with an incentive to search for food. Thus, we may call the motives as the raw materials of human nature. They are the determinants of human conduct and behaviour. When the individual gets any motive, they experience tension and become restless. Their activities are then initiated. The individual feels a push to behave in a certain direction. Almost all the activities of individuals are determined by the motives. Individuals feel a dynamic push to act when they receive motivation. They begin to act, and their activities continue until they achieve a goal.

Motives originate action and continue the activities until the goal is achieved. They direct the activities in a particular direction. Thus, we may define a motive 'as a tendency of an activity initiated by a need and drive and concluded by an adjustment.' For example, due to the physiological activities of our body, we feel hungry. When we feel hungry, we feel tense. To remove tension, we begin to act in such a manner and in such a direction that we are able to satisfy our hunger. Hence, our activity has been initiated by a motive that is hunger motive and is concluded when we have satisfied our hunger and thus has achieved an adjustment. So motive is a condition—physiological or psychological—within the organism that disposes it to act in certain ways.

Motives are specific conditions that direct an organism to a goal. Hence, psychologists say that people are motivated and directed to specific goals by specific motives. Some views regarding motives are as follows:

1. Motives arising out of natural urges are dynamic forces that affect thoughts, emotions and actions.
2. Motives are thoughts, feelings or conditions that cause an individual to act.
3. Motives are energies, selectors and directors of activity, which are closely related to interests and attitudes.
4. McGeoach defines a motive as, 'any condition of an individual which points or orients them towards the practice of a given task and which defines the adequacy of their activities and completion of the task.'
5. According to Woodworth, 'a motive is a state of an individual which disposes them of certain behaviour and for seeking certain goals.'
6. Guilford says, 'A motive is any particular factor or condition that tends to initiate and sustain activity.'

CHARACTERISTICS OF MOTIVATED BEHAVIOUR

Motivation is a broad term used to cover those internal conditions or states that activate or energize the organism that leads to goal-directed behaviour. The following are the characteristics of motivated behaviour:

1. Motives may be primarily inborn or acquired, but whatever may be their origin when aroused, they initiate activity directed towards goals.
2. The term 'motive' refers to something that can never be directly observed. We infer the existence of a motive from behaviour or knowledge of certain other factors. On the other hand, the existence of some motives may be inferred directly from knowledge of the physiological condition of the organism. Stomach contractions, chemical changes in the blood and taste sensitivity are physiologically related to the hunger drive.
3. The following points suggest that motivated behaviour is cyclical:

a. A motive or drive is aroused. Motives, sometimes, stem from physiological needs such as the need for food or water, while in other cases, motives stem from psychological needs such as the need for companionship or acquisition.
b. A feeling of deficiency leads the individual to a state of disequilibrium or tension. The individual feels tense and restless.
c. A sequence of behaviour occurs during which the organism seeks a means of satisfying the need or reducing the drive.
d. Organism selects the most suitable means and makes use of it.
e. Finally, some goal is reached whereby the drive is reduced or terminated. It satisfies its need, and the goal is achieved.
f. But motive, once achieved, is not achieved for all times. Hunger, once satisfied, can never be permanently satiated. After sometimes, it again arouses, and the same process of its gratification starts.
4. A motive operates to make both behaviour and experience in the organism selective. A child who has been deprived of some money will exert greater efforts to get money or other goal objects relevant to the aroused motive.
5. Motivated behaviour is relatively active and persistent. In general, we may say that the stronger the motive, the greater is the organism's activity and persistence towards goals related to this motive.
6. Motivated behaviour is homeostasis. In organism, certain mechanisms are built into the body that tends to preserve a constant physiological equilibrium. This process of maintaining internal physiological equilibrium is called as 'homeostasis'. When any need remains unsatisfied, the tension produced within the organism drives it to seek the need and hence to alleviate the tension. Hence, all behaviour may, at least, be regarded as homeostasis in nature.

FUNCTIONS OF MOTIVATED BEHAVIOUR

Psychologists have studied the motivated behaviour of individuals and found some functions which are given below:

1. **Motivated behaviour energizes the organism:** Motivation activates and energizes the behaviour of the organism and helps it to

arouse for action. Motives not only energize the behaviour, but they also maintain and sustain our interest for a longer period in the activity.
2. **Motivated behaviour is directed and regulated:** Motivated behaviour is often thought as guided, directed and goal oriented. The motivated behaviour moves in a specific and positive direction. The behaviour of the organism is purposive and persistent.
3. **Motivated behaviour is selective:** Motivated behaviour is selective towards a goal, which individuals set for themselves; for example, students who are motivated to get high scores in the examination take interest in their studies and work very hard to achieve the goal by selecting appropriate methods. The motive is accomplished by the achievement of the goal.
4. **Hope sustains life:** So it is another aspect of motivation. Hope leads to motivation. Hope is, therefore, a criterion for people to be motivated. It is the cause for the effect, and it is the motivating factor which puts fuel or psychic energy in the human machinery that drives the human engine. Without hope, no person could ever be motivated. Power is another ingredient in motivating behaviour.

Psychologists consider motivation to consist of two dimensions: (a) direction and (b) intensity. Motivation can be said to be simply the direction and intensity of one's efforts which can be described as given below:

1. The direction is positive or negative. But motivation goes in a positive direction and is concerned with choosing a goal-directed behaviour. The direction of the effort indicates whether an individual seeks out, approaches or is attracted to certain positive situations. A student may be attracted to achieve higher scores in their final examination.
2. On the other hand, the intensity of effort refers to how much effort a person puts forth in a particular situation. Intensity is concerned with how much intense your efforts are and how activated or energized the person is, that is, how much effort is being given to reach a certain goal. The intensity of efforts means working very hard to achieve the goal.

In fact, there is a close relationship between the direction and intensity of effort. If people want to achieve their desired goals, they should be more motivated to set higher and achievable goals and then to work hard towards the achievement of those goals, understanding one's needs, which are the basis of a person's goals among the most important aspects of motivation.

DIFFERENT CONCEPTS OF MOTIVATION

Psychologists consider motivation on the basis of one of the three orientations, which are as follows:

1. **Trait-oriented motivation:** According to this view, motivated behaviour is a part of one's personality trait. It is primarily a function of an individual's personal characteristics. Some people have personal attributes or personality characteristics that seem to predispose them to work hard to achieve success as they possess a high level of motivation. But on the other hand, there are some other people who seem to lack motivation due to their personal goals and desires as they do not possess those personality traits.
2. **State-oriented motivation:** This view is concerned with situational motivation. It contends that the motivation level is determined primarily by situational factors. We agree that the situation influences motivation as we are affected by the environment in which we live. A teacher who creates a healthy and conducive environment will naturally increase the motivation of the students to a great extent.
3. **Interactional-oriented motivation:** This view puts forth that motivation is not the result of only the trait factors such as personality characteristics, needs, goals and interests of the individuals and also not only situational factors, but it is better to understand how these two sets of factors interact. It is the interaction of personal factors (P) and situational factors (S), that is, P × S.

TYPES OF MOTIVES

Many psychologists distinguish between two types or categories of motives, that is, physiological and social.

1. **Physiological motives:** They originate in the physiological requirements and self-regulating processes of the organism. They are inborn or present at birth. Hunger, thirst, sex, suckling of the young, temperature regulation, that is, avoidance of extremes of heat and cold, sleep or need for rest, elimination, pain avoidance and respiration are the physiological motives. The criteria of these motives are:
   a. The motive must constitute a reaction to an organic demand.
   b. The reaction to the disturbed internal balance must constitute an aroused state of the organism.
   c. They must be universally available among all members of the same species in the manifestation of the motive.
   d. The motive must be unlearned.
2. **Social motives:** Many social motives are acquired in the course of being socialized in a given culture. They are formed relative to interpersonal relations, established social values and norms of institutions. The desires for promotion, status, membership and higher wages are all social motives. They also serve to energize and direct our behaviour. Such motives are learned in the process of interacting with other human beings in a given culture. The social motives may be reduced to four wishes or desires, that is, security, recognition, love and new experiences. Some psychologists think that acquisition, orderliness, achievement, autonomy, aggression, superiority and affiliation are some of the other social motives.

Social motives are internal conditions which direct people to establish and maintain a relationship with other people and establish feelings about themselves and others. These social motives emerge from the convergence of learned social needs. A social need is an aroused condition involving feeling about self, others and relationships. People have social needs for achievement, order and nurturance. These needs for achievement, affiliation and good feelings about one's self are affected by many factors, including socioeconomic status and race and experiences from birth onwards.

Hence, social motives are the forces that direct human behaviour towards certain patterns of relationships with other people. These motives are often referred to as acquired, implying that social motives are learned. Unlike the physiological motives, they have no basis in the organic functioning of the body. But they are influenced by cultural heritage and philosophy of life of the people. Of course, they are rooted in physiological motives and emerge out of them gradually with advancing age of the child. Social motives are the sources, which bind human beings and social progress depends on their proper development.

There is no universally accepted list of social motives. Murray (1938) proposed a list of human needs that form the basis of social motives, that is, achievement (to accomplish difficult tasks), affiliation (to gain affection from friends), autonomy (independence), exhibition (to make an impression on others), understanding (intellectually asking questions), dominance, order, play, nurturance, defence and others. He believed that complex human behaviour could best be understood by studying the interplay of these social motives within a particular individual.

INTRINSIC AND EXTRINSIC MOTIVATION

Psychologists have made distinction between two types of motivation, namely intrinsic (internal) and extrinsic motivation (external), which are detailed below:

1. **Intrinsic Motivation:** When we engage in a task without expecting any reward and work hard to get something in life due to our interest in the job, then it is called intrinsic motivation. Human beings engage in a wide range of activities that bring no tangible rewards. Psychologists call such behaviour performed for no apparent reward, except the pleasure of the activity itself, as intrinsically motivated behaviour. Some people perform tasks to get pleasure, achieve stimulation and a sense of accomplishment, competence and mastery. Intrinsic motivation means when people are interested, and they have fun to do even when they produce no external rewards. When an individual tries to enter an activity primarily for personal satisfaction and enjoyment, they are said

to be intrinsically motivated. The consequences of the behaviour are of lesser concern to them than the enjoyment they experience. For example, children typically report that fun is a more important reason for their involvement in sports.

Hence, intrinsic motivation is the one when an activity is performed for its own sake or the sake of enjoyment. We perform those activities primarily because of the pleasure they give, not because they lead to other external rewards. Intrinsic motivation is the desire to perform activities because they are rewarding by themselves. Athletes who take part in an activity due to their true love of that activity have intrinsic motivation. Hence, intrinsic motivation is thought to have a moving and sustaining effect on learning and performance and to be, therefore, more desirable as the extra new rewards maintain peak motivational levels for a shorter period of time.

For intrinsic motivation, psychic energy is utmost essential, which activates the body for action and for showing the peak performance. But it should be at the optimum level. Too much or too low psychic energy would affect the performance. Too much psychic energy may develop nervousness, anxiety, tension or any other emotional situation, which may inhibit an individual in giving the desired results. On the other hand, too low psychic energy would create the state of apathy, which may develop the feelings of disinterest in the activity.

2. **Extrinsic motivation:** On the other hand, extrinsic motivation means money, rewards, prizes and public recognition. It produces satisfaction independently of the behaviour that produces them. Whereas extrinsically motivated behaviour appears to be regulated by response-produced external events, intrinsically motivated behaviour comes from within, and the rewards are internal. External rewards can strengthen existing behaviour and provide people with the feedback of information about their performance. Positive results will probably increase feelings of self-worth and competence. An extrinsically motivated person responds to positive or reinforcing responses like rewards from the external environment (e.g., another person).

Extrinsic motivation is the promise of giving rewards in terms of trophies, medals and money for winning the events. It is external as it comes from the outside environment. It may come from other people through positive and negative reinforcement, which may be tangible rewards. When these reinforcements are received, they are known as extrinsic motivation. It is a kind of materialistic motivation which brings recognition, gain or glory. Extrinsic motivation sometimes helps in increasing the level of intrinsic motivation.

3. **Interaction of intrinsic and extrinsic motivation:** Intrinsic and extrinsic motivational forces may interact in very meaningful and complex ways. Receiving a commemorative medal for completing a task or any material reward may instil pride and satisfaction and thereby increase an individual's intrinsic motivation. But sometimes, externally provided rewards may have an undesirable impact upon intrinsic motivation. Intrinsic motivation for any activity may be reduced when an extrinsic goal is used as a means of initiating and sustaining activity. The individual who competes only to receive a medal may stop participating if these awards are no longer used as incentives. The term over-justification hypothesis is applied to explain the inhibiting effects of external rewards upon internal motivation. External awards, therefore, should be given cautiously to children. Symbolic rewards which have an informational value such as positive feedback and social approval should depend on desirable behaviour such as effort or creativity.

Now, here the main problem is whether extrinsic rewards will undermine intrinsic motivation. Of course, it seems that combining extrinsic and intrinsic motivation would help to induce more motivation because adding extrinsic rewards to an activity that is intrinsically motivating should increase motivation accordingly. Hence, it is imperative that an intrinsically oriented person must be given external rewards and extrinsically motivated in order to sustain their motivation in that activity. It should be remembered here that motivation should be at an optimum level, neither too high nor too low.

NEED HIERARCHY MODEL OF MOTIVATION

Motivation is the drive, energy or degree of activity that a person displays. Motivation is a psychophysiological process, originated by some need, which leads to some activity that will satisfy that need. Motivation generates a strong and continuous desire to do something. It is an urge from within and a clear picture of goals outside. A motive is a desire to which a goal has been connected. Anything that moves one to action is motive.

All human activities reflect human behaviour. The behaviour of all individuals is always dependent upon their motives. Psychologists have tried to understand all underlying motives of an individual's behaviour. There are diverse views regarding the complex process of motivation. They have tried to study them scientifically and have developed a large number of theories and models. There are many theories which discuss divergent opinions to explain the motivated behaviours of individuals. But out of all these theories, need hierarchy theory given by Maslow (1943) is the most well-known and is applicable in all walks of life.

Maslow (1943) founded the Humanistic School of Psychology and propounded his theory of need hierarchy. He assumes that human motives are arranged in a hierarchical order. The needs that have the greatest urgency at a given time dominate our behaviour and demand satisfaction. The individual feels driven by a high-priority need. When the need is satisfied, a higher-order need comes into the picture and demands satisfaction and so on to the top of the hierarchy of human needs.

Note: Abraham Harold Maslow (1 April 1908–8 June 1970) was a professor of psychology at Brandeis University, Brooklyn College, New School for Social Research and Columbia University.

According to him, there exists a hierarchy of five needs within every human being, which are given in Box 4.2.

Box 4.2: Hierarchy of Needs

1. Physiological, that is, bodily needs
2. Safety needs, that is, security and protection from physical and emotional arousal.
3. Social needs, that is, needs for love, belongingness, acceptance and friendship
4. Esteem needs, that is, self-respect, self-prestige, status and recognition
5. Self-actualization needs, that is, exploring the potential or the drive to become what one is capable of becoming

---

When one need is satisfied sequentially, the next need arises and becomes more dominant to be satisfied. All these needs are fulfilled one by one. If you are unable to achieve the first need, all the other needs remain unfulfilled and become redundant. The higher order of needs can only be fulfilled if the lower order of needs is fulfilled, otherwise not possible. So if you want to motivate someone, you need to understand where that person currently stands on the hierarchy of needs and focus on satisfying those needs at or above that level.

Physiological and safety needs are lower-order needs that are satisfied externally (by such things as money, prizes, wages, rewards, etc.). But on the other hand, needs for social, self-esteem and self-actualization are higher-order needs that are satisfied internally, which are essential for the development of the personality of an individual.

A. H. Maslow's (1908–1970) hierarchical needs model of human motivation is a contemporary humanistic perspective. There are two characteristics of this model: (a) his hierarchical conception of motivation and (ii) his efforts to develop a more valid and comprehensive psychology of motivation through the study of self-actualization: His model was fully expressed in his 1954 book *Motivation and Personality*.

According to Maslow, once a need is satisfied, it no longer remains a need and the person moves up to the next higher need in hierarchy. These needs, which he has identified, are useful in helping us to think about the goals. His model of hierarchy of needs is depicted in Figure 4.1.

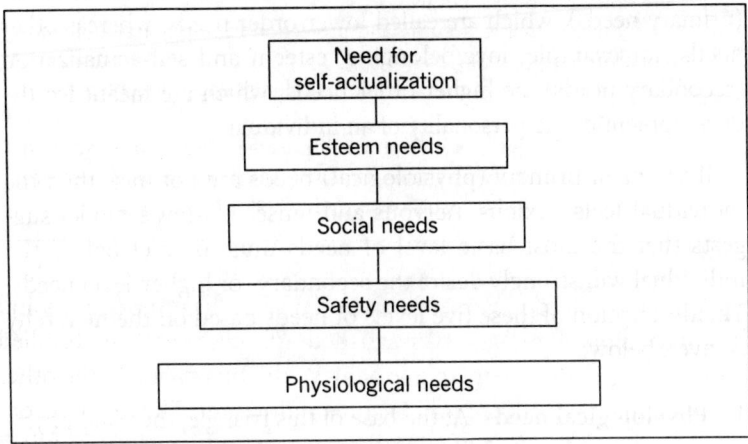

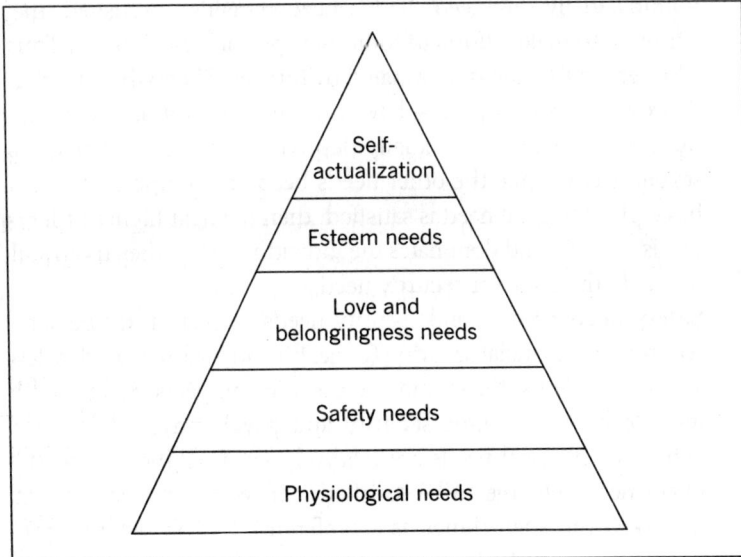

Figure 4.1 *Maslow's Model of Hierarchy of Needs*

Maslow's hierarchy of needs is often shown in the shape of a triangle, with the most fundamental levels of needs at the bottom and the need for self-actualization at the top. The most fundamental and basic four layers of the triangle contain what Maslow called 'deficiency needs', for example, esteem, friendship and love and security. Out of these needs, physiological and safety are related to our bodily needs (primary needs), which are called lower-order needs, whereas other needs, for example, love/belonging, esteem and self-actualization (secondary needs) are higher-order needs, which are meant for the development of the personality of an individual.

If the most primary (physiological) needs are not met, then the individual feels anxious, nervous and tense. Maslow's model suggests that the most basic level of needs must be met before the individual will strongly desire the secondary- or higher-level needs. The description of these five levels of needs based on the hierarchy is given below:

1. **Physiological needs:** At the base of this triangle, there are physiological needs which, are related to our body. The individual is dominated by this need. If this need remains unsatisfied, they continue to make efforts to fulfil their physiological needs. Thus, a hungry individual is dominated by hunger. Their whole thought process is pre-occupied solely with getting food and satisfying hunger. Similarly, the sexually deprived individual is driven by sexual desire while the other needs become unimportant. If this basic physiological need is satisfied, then the next higher order of needs emerges and dominates the individual. Then they try to seek to satisfy the safety or security need.
2. **Safety needs:** Safety and security needs consist of: (a) personal security, (b) financial security, (c) health and well-being, (d) safety against accidents/illness and their adverse impacts. Safety needs include both economic security and psychophysical security. When the physical needs are relatively satisfied, the individual's safety needs emerge to be satisfied. These safety needs present themselves in such things as a preference for job security, protecting the individual from an autocratic authority, keeping bank accounts, life insurance policies, accommodation or housing

problem and the like. The individual seeks security by building a home and finding a job with an assured future.
3. **Love and belonging needs:** These are also called social needs. After physiological and safety needs are fulfilled, the third phase of human needs is social needs, which involve feelings of love and belongingness. The need is especially strong in childhood. Every child wants love and affection from their parents, friends and teachers. Humans need is to have a sense of belonging and acceptance, from the group to which they belong, such as clubs, religious groups, professional organizations, sports teams, gangs or other social groups. They want acceptance and recognition from their family members, intimate partners, mentors, close colleagues, friends and so on. This need is also related to affiliation needs when an individual wants to be affiliated with their family, school or any other group. They need to love and be loved by others. This need for love and belongingness will emerge only and can be fulfilled if the physiological and security needs have already been fulfilled. These needs will only arise if the two lower-order needs are reasonably well satisfied.
4. **Esteem needs:** The fourth order of needs is esteem needs. These needs include the desire for self prestige and self-concept. In all of us, there is a desire for self-assurance, self-sufficiency and self-worth, leading to a feeling of independence and freedom. All human beings have a desire to be respected and to have self-esteem. Besides these, individuals also seek prestige, dominance, recognition and acceptance from others. The satisfaction of these needs will create feelings of worthiness, self-confidence and self-sufficiency. People with low self-esteem also need respect from others; otherwise, they will develop an inferiority complex. They may try hard to seek fame or glory, which again depends on other people. Bandura' theory of self-efficacy is also concerned with the esteem needs of individuals.
5. **Self-actualization:** Finally, if all the above needs are satisfied, the need for self-actualization emerges, which impels the individual to action to explore their potential. In Maslow's own words, 'A musician must make music, an artist must paint, and a poet must write if he is ultimately to be at peace with himself.' We may call this need 'self-actualization.'

'What a man can be, he must be.' This forms the basis of the perceived need for self-actualization. Every child is born with some potential. While growing up, if they achieve whatever they can, then they will be the most satisfied person. This level of need pertains to what a person has full potential and then trying to accomplish that potential. Maslow describes this need as the desire to become more and more what one is, to become something that one is capable of becoming. In fact, this is the need for self-actualization.

What Is Self-actualization?

Located at the peak of Abraham Maslow's need hierarchy model, he added three more needs to his theory of motivation, for example:

1. **Need for self-fulfilment:** This high-level need is the desire for self-fulfilment, that is, the tendency to become actualized according to one's potentiality. He assumed that people have an innate tendency to develop their potential and seek *beauty, truth and goodness*. In other words, they are innately motivated toward self-actualization, that is, self-fulfilment. Maslow believed that people are opening and trusting and can experience the world in truly healthy ways. Self-actualized people are those who have achieved their true nature and fulfilled their potential. Self-actualization, here, means the process of realizing one's uniquely human potential for good. The process of achieving everything that one is capable of achieving.

    Later on, Maslow added two additional types of needs to the basic theory of motivation. These were the needs for knowing and understanding (curiosity needs) and truth and beauty (aesthetic needs).
2. **Need for curiosity:** Maslow believes that children, creative people, explorers and ordinary matured individuals reveal that curiosity of the desire to learn, discover and explore the mysterious and unknown. This is a fundamental aspect of human nature.
3. **Aesthetic Needs:** The aesthetic needs are revealed in the deep-seated need for beauty expressed by some individuals. Maslow found that beauty was experienced as promoting a feeling of well-being and enhancement of the self-image.

Maslow's theory provides an interesting way to organize aspects of behaviour and their relative importance. But this theory may not be valid in all cultures. However, his theory deals with the fundamental importance of physiological needs in motivating behaviour. Unless people's basic physiological needs are met, they are not likely to be able to grow and develop physically, let alone develop or acquire social and aesthetic motives that might direct behaviour. Only if one's needs for food, shelter and physical safety are met, people can attend to developing a sense of self-respect or sense of beauty.

Maslow's theory of need hierarchy has received wide recognition but also invited a lot of criticism. Research does not validate the theory as Maslow did not provide any empirical evidence. There is no scientific support as the unsatisfied needs can motivate or that a satisfied need activates any activity, which will lead to a new need level.

EXISTENCE, RELATEDNESS AND GROWTH (ERG) THEORY OF MOTIVATION

Clayton Alderfer (1969) has modified Maslow's need hierarchy theory, which is called ERG theory. In fact, there are three groups of core needs. ERG means the following:

1. **Existence:** The existence group of needs is concerned with providing our basic core needs, which is related to the requirement of material existence. Physiological and safety needs are included in this group.
2. **Relatedness:** The second group of needs is those of relatedness, that is, social needs of love and affection from others. It is concerned with the desire that we have for maintaining important interpersonal relationships. These social and status needs require interaction with others. They are like social needs and esteem needs of Maslow's model.
3. **Growth:** Growth group of needs is related to higher-order needs. Alderfer thinks the growth needs as an intrinsic desire for personal development. These include the intrinsic motivation from Maslow's esteem needs and self-actualization categories.

Self-determination Theory of Motivation

Self-determination theory is a theory of motivation that deals with three universal internal psychological needs, that is, (a) competence, (b) autonomy and (c) relatedness. It was first described by Ryan and Deci in 2000. It is related to people's inherent growth tendencies and innate psychological needs. It is concerned with motivation without external influence. It is concerned with an individual's behaviour which is self-motivated and self-determined.

The concept of self-determination emerged from the research studies comparing the intrinsic and extrinsic motivation and especially the role of intrinsic motivation played in an individual's behaviour. It was in 2000 that this theory was formally propounded and accepted as a sound empirical theory of motivation.

E. L. Deci and R. Ryan later expanded on their early work differentiating between intrinsic and extrinsic motivation and proposed three main intrinsic needs involved in the self-determination of an individual. According to Deci and Ryan, the three psychological needs motivate the self to initiate behaviour that is essential for psychological health and well-being of an individual, which need to be nurtured in the context of the social environment. They identify three innate needs that, if satisfied, allow optimal functioning and growth in the behaviour. These needs are said to be universal, innate and psychological and include the need for (a) competence, (b) autonomy and (c) relatedness.

1. **Competence:** Competence is concerned with the outcome of the performance. It seeks to control the results, which are related to the mastery experience.
2. **Autonomy:** Autonomy means a feeling of independence. It is related to the desire to be the master of one's own life and act accordingly on the basis of one's own thinking in harmony with one's self.
3. **Relatedness:** It is a feeling of belongingness. It is concerned with the desire to interact with other people and have a feeling of relatedness.

This theory supports three basic psychological needs that must be satisfied to foster well-being, mental health and human wellness. These needs are universally applicable. But they are expressed differently based on time, gender, culture or experience. These needs are seen as globally essential, which are innate, not learnt, but applicable to humanity.

Deci and Ryan (2002) claim that there are three essential elements of the theory:

1. Humans are innately proactive and want to master their inner forces such as drives and emotions.
2. Humans have an innate tendency towards growth, development and integrated functioning.
3. Humans have optimal development and actions, but they cannot function automatically.

If this happens, there would be positive consequences, for example, psychological well-being and growth, but if not, there may be negative consequences. So this theory lays emphasis on humans' natural tendency toward positive motivation. However, this will not happen if the basic needs are not fulfilled. This theory is very much applicable to human wellness and quite useful for human growth and development. As motivation is one of the psychological skills, the model given by Ryan and Deci can be easily applied by the psychologists in this modern period.

CONCLUSION

Human behaviour is motivated one. So the study of motivation is crucial in the field of psychology. Motivation arises from the deprivation of physiological and psychological needs, drives and motives. Motivation is derived from the Latin word 'movere', which means to move. Anything which moves us to some activity or initiates any work is called motivation. Motivation provides driving force and direction to all types of behaviour. Motivation refers to the internal conditions or states that activate or energize the individual, which leads to goal-directed behaviour. It is the psychic energy, which induces you to explore your potential and reach up to your top or your maximum level according to your abilities, capacities and capabilities.

The human behaviour is directed, controlled and modified through certain motives. Motives originate action and continue the activities until the goal is achieved. Thus, a motive is a tendency of an activity initiated by a need and drive and concluded by an adjustment. So motive is a condition physiological and psychological within the organism that disposes it to act in certain ways.

Motives arising out of natural urges are dynamic forces that affect thoughts, emotions and actions. Moreover, they are energies, selectors and directors of activity, which are closely related to interest and attitudes. The functions of motivated behaviour include: (a) motivated behaviour energizes the organism, (b) motivated behaviour is directed and regulated and (c) motivated behaviour is selective.

The different concepts of motivation are (a) trait-oriented motivation, (b) state-oriented motivation and (c) interactional-oriented motivation. The trait-oriented motivated behaviour is primarily a function of an individual's characteristics, for example, personality traits. The state-oriented is concerned with situational motivation and contends that motivation level is determined primarily by situational factors. But the interactional-oriented motivation is how these two sets of factors interact. It is the interaction of personal factors and situational factors.

Many psychologists have distinguished between two types of motives, that is, physiological and social. Physiological motives originate in the physiological requirements and self-regulating processes of the organism. They are inborn or present at birth. Hunger, thirst, sex, suckling of the young, temperature regulation, that is, the avoidance of extremes of heat and cold, sleep or need for rest, elimination, pain avoidance and respiration are the physiological motives. Social motives are acquired in the course of being socialized in a given culture. They are formed relative to interpersonal relations, established social values and norms of institutions. The social motives may be security, recognition, love and new experiences. Some psychologists think that acquisition, orderliness, achievement, autonomy, aggression, superiority and affiliation are some of the other social motives.

Psychologists have made a distinction between two types of motivation, namely intrinsic (internal) and extrinsic motivation (external). Intrinsic motivation is one when an activity is performed for its own sake or the sake of enjoyment. When we engage in a task without expecting any reward and work hard to get something in life due to our interest in the job, then it is called intrinsic motivation. On the other hand, extrinsic motivation means money, rewards, prizes and public recognition. Extrinsic motivation is the promise of giving rewards in terms of trophies, medals and money for winning the events. It is external as it comes from the outside environment. It may come from other people through positive and negative reinforcement. It is a kind of materialistic motivation, which brings recognition, gain or glory.

There are many theories which discuss divergent opinions to explain the motivated behaviours of the individuals. Out of all these theories, need hierarchy theory given by Abraham Maslow (1943) is the most well-known, which is applicable in all walks of life. According to him, there exists a hierarchy of five needs within every human being, for example, (a) bodily needs, (b) safety needs, (c) social needs, (d) esteem needs and (e) self-actualization needs. It includes growth, achieving one's potential and self-fulfilment. Later on, he added three more needs on his list of five hierarchy needs which are (a) need for self-fulfilment, (b) need for curiosity and (c) aesthetic needs.

Clayton Alderfer has modified the Maslow's need hierarchy theory, which is called the ERG theory. In fact, there are three groups of core needs, that is, (a) existence, (b) relatedness and (c) growth. Self-determination theory of motivation was devised by Ryan and Deci in 2000, which discusses three universal, innate and psychological needs: (a) competence, (b) autonomy and (c) psychological relatedness.

Motivation teaches an individual how to set goals in life to achieve something. It means that motivation leads to the goal-setting process in the life of an individual. In fact, the motives are the goals. How to set these goals, we will study in the next chapter. We will also discuss the meaning, nature and concept of goal setting as well as the practical suggestion for setting the goals on life.

Goal Setting
A Psychological Skill

INTRODUCTION

Recently, psychologists have identified a number of psychological skills for helping people in achieving excellence and proficiency in their lives. Motivation is an important psychological skill, which we have already discussed in the previous chapter. Motivation and goal setting are related to each other. In this chapter, we will describe concept, types and styles of goal setting with its needs and importance. How to set the goals and the problems being faced and suggestions for guidance of designing the goals will also be narrated.

Goal setting is one of the important psychological skills for motivating us so that we may give our best in our tasks on some occasions. Goal setting not only gives motivation to individuals but also brings positive changes in some psychological parameters such as anxiety, stress and confidence. Hence, it is an important technique, which we must employ regularly during our tasks and other activities in our daily life. Of course, it also influences the performance of people.

There is an accepted belief that the people should themselves set their own goals, which will help them in enhancing their performance. But it has been observed that many of us set inappropriate and inadequate goals or do not set goals in a systematic way as we do not know how to set the goals. Moreover, the goal-setting technique is not always effectively employed by us, and if we happen to set so, we often do not go for the follow-up and evaluation programme, which are necessary for goal setting to be effective. For setting appropriate goals, we must understand the goal-setting procedure and many factors, which are involved in this programme.

DEFINING GOALS

According to Locke et al. (1981), a goal is defined as 'attaining a specific standard of proficiency on a task, usually within a specified time limit.' From a practical point of view, goals are set for achieving some standard whether it may be for increasing one's batting average in a cricket match or lowering one's time in the 800 metres race in athletics or increasing the weight gradually on the weight bar in the weight-lifting game or a student wants to increase their percentage score in his academic achievement. It also implies that such performance standards will be achieved within some specified time limit.

A goal is defined as 'an objective, a standard and an aim of some action or a level of performance or proficiency'. An objective is something to be maximized or continuously improved. The aims are as reaching a particular standard in an event or on a task.

According to Locke and Latham (1990), 'Goal setting is a theory of motivation that effectively energizes persons to become more productive and effective.' Goals set by people represent either intrinsic or extrinsic motivation, depending on whether or not the goals are internalized and personalized. Goals have two important properties:

1. A goal has a direction—positive or negative—and persons set their goals towards something.
2. A goal has some intensity of efforts made by individuals as the goal can be the most important in their life.

People should not only recognize and identify goals but also try to set the clear and achievable goals, which may provide the right direction and also make efforts of increased intensity in order to enhance motivation and also to achieve their goals.

Goals should be set realistically in terms of previous achievement, performance, commitment and progress, and then, we should apply specific strategies to achieve them. People need to be taught that goal setting is an important exercise, which should be learnt. They also need to be convinced of setting effective goals and designing a programme to achieve them.

TYPES OF GOALS

Psychologists such as Martens (1987) and Burton (1989a) have made specific distinctions between types of goals. They have made differences between outcome and performance goals. These types of goals have been discussed below:

1. **Outcome goals:** These goals represent standards of performance that focus on the results of a contest between two parties. They depend on the final results of the performance of the participants. Outcome goals lay emphasis on achieving a victory in a contest. They typically focus on an outcome or result in an event such as winning a match, earning a medal or scoring more points than an opponent or securing a good position in an examination or qualifying in a competitive examination. Thus, achieving these goals depends not only on your own efforts but on the strengths and weaknesses of other competitors.

   The outcome goals are meant for group achievement. When a business manager sets a target of profit for their company per year, they give target to their employees for working hard for the company in order to go for the achievement of the goal. In these days, all the private banks expect from their subordinate staff to collect so much money per month and ask on the last day of each month their progress report. Life Insurance Corporation of India gives incentives to the agents of the organization and expects them to complete their target per month or year.

2. **Performance goals:** People may also set performance goals. These goals are limited to specific behaviour. They focus on improvements in terms of one's own past performance and previous achievements, for example, improving one's timings in a race or securing more marks in the present examination as compared to last year examination scores. It means that the performance of the person is compared with their own previous performances. Achieving a performance goal does not depend on other people' behaviour but one's own behaviour. For this reason, performance goals tend to be more changeable, and they are within one's own control. They are linked with superior performance during the

competition as compared to outcome goals. Hence, the performance goals focus on achieving standards based on one's own previous performances, not the performances of others.

These goals are set to measure the performance of each individual separately. A teacher sets the goals of the academic achievement of their students on the basis of their past achievement level, abilities and capabilities. They go on raising their level of expectation step by step and motivates them to work very hard for the achievement of their goal. These are performance goals. Similarly, in the field of sports, a coach also tries to set the goals of their trainee athletes and measure their performance. After they have achieved that level, they go on increasing their target of achievement so that they may perform well and reach excellence according to their potential.

1. **Process goals:** Besides outcome and performance goals, Hardy et al. (1996) have included 'process goals', which specify the procedures in which the performer will engage during the performance. These types of goals are useful in changing behaviour and performance. They focus on specific behaviours exhibited throughout a performance. These goals need a proper and an effective technique for executing a specific task. If the person succeeds in setting process goals, then improved performance and outcome goals should be the result. Process goals may also be set with regard to acquiring certain knowledge and strategies about the tasks. These process goals are related to both outcome and performance goals. Certainly, goals should be set for acquiring psychological skills. These goals are usually concerned with habit formation or changing one's habits in one's daily life, for example, getting up early in the morning for late risers.
2. **Smart goals:** The smart goals are set by the people in the corporate world, especially by the businessmen or managers working in the industries. Here, the word 'smart' is used as a tool for planning and achieving our goals. So the smart goal means a goal which helps to guide for goal setting. In fact, 'smart' consists of five words, that is, specific, measurable, achievable, realistic and timely. Therefore, a smart goal includes all these characteristics

to help focus our efforts and increase the chances of achieving our goals. They are given below:

1. **Smart goals are specific:** They are well-defined, clear and unambiguous. Goals that are specific have significantly greater chances of being achieved.
2. **Smart goals are measurable:** They assess the progress towards the achievement of the goal. The smart goals must have characteristic for measuring progress in their achievement.
3. **Smart goals are achievable:** It means that they are attainable. Smart goals must be achievable and attainable. The achievability of the goal should make you feel challenged so that you may work very hard.
4. **Smart goals are realistic:** They are very much relevant for our life purpose. Smart goals must be realistic in that the goal can be realistically achieved given the available resources and time.
5. **Smart goals are timely:** The goals which are achieved within time budget with starting and target date are the smart goals. Smart goals must be time-bound so that it has a start and finish target date. If the goal is not time-constrained, there will be no sense of urgency and motivation to achieve the goal.

Smart goals are set up for success by making it specific, measurable, achievable, realistic and timely. The smart method gives you a sense of direction and helps you organize and reach your goals. The smart goals are applied by the personnel managers, organizational psychologists and human resource persons in the private and public sectors in many big organizations while preparing the blueprint of the different projects and setting the targets of starting and finishing the work. They well define the outlines of their projects, which are quite comprehensive for other employees in the organization. They set specific and achievable goals, whose progress can be easily be assessed periodically. They are quite realistic and within the well laid down time framework. The budget of the project is also prepared according to the guidelines given by the competent authority or managing director of the company as well as within the reach of the financial health of the organization.

NEED FOR GOAL SETTING

Psychologists have studied goal setting as a psychological skill in terms of motivational technique. It focuses on whether setting specific goals improves performance. Goal setting is a psychological skill that really works wonder. It is a powerful technique for enhancing performance. A systematic and organized goal-setting programme is needed, along with monitoring the progress to determine whether goal setting is effective or not. Hence, the need for the goal-setting programme cannot be overemphasized, and it needs to be implemented correctly. So the need for goal-setting has been felt due to the following reasons:

1. Goals pay more attention to important aspects of the task being performed.
2. Goals energize the performer's intensity of efforts and power by providing incentives.
3. Goals increase consistency and persistency of efforts while performing a task.
4. Goals motivate people to find out the most appropriate techniques for achieving them.

Psychologists have felt the need for setting goals as changes in performance occur due to the influence of many extraneous variables such as anxiety, lack of confidence and satisfaction and low motivation. It also depends upon the focusing of attention to important aspects of the task being performed, the energizing of effort, increase in consistency and persistency as well as the development of new techniques.

GOAL SETTING AND PERFORMANCE

It is very much important to learn that how goal-setting influences performance. So the psychologists should know how goal setting should be effective. When problems occur in a goal-setting programme, then people must try to assess the situation and overcome the obstacles on the way in order to make adjustments. Research has clearly shown that goal setting is a powerful technique for enhancing performance. But it is equally important for psychologists to understand how goal setting influences performance. Psychologists have given their own explanation.

According to Locke et al. (1981), there are five basic ways in which goal setting can influence performance. They contend that goals influence performance in some ways as shown in Box 5.1.

Box 5.1: Goal Setting and Performance

1. Goals focus the performer's attention to important aspects of the task.
2. Goals help the performer energize the effort.
3. Goals increase persistency of effort and also help prolong effort.
4. Goals often employ new learning strategies.
5. Indirect thought process affects the psychological state.

These five explanations are being discussed below to make people understand why goal setting is important so that its programme should be very effective:

1. **Focused attention:** Goal setting helps the person to focus their attention on the task in order to achieve the goal. So it increases attention and concentration. When people have no specific goal, their attention wanders from one place to another. Setting a specific goal causes them to focus their attention that is associated with that goal. Goals direct people's attention to important elements of the task being performed. In this way, performance is improved.
2. **Effort mobilization:** After focusing attention towards a particular goal, it is necessary for the person to mobilize the effort necessary to achieve that goal. Effort mobilization will have a positive effect on improved performance. Goal setting will have the effect of increasing people's effort during practice so that they can accomplish their goal. Goals mobilize the performer's efforts and give energy and persistence by providing incentives and hence improve their performance. After setting the goal, the person must put all their efforts into the task at hand to accomplish the goal.
3. **Persistence:** Another way that goal setting should be effective in influencing performance is through persistency of efforts. It is essential to focus attention and mobilize efforts for improving this

skill, but to be successful in a task, one must continue efforts for a long period of time. Persistence is the outcome of effective goal setting. After people want their goal should be achieved, they will have to persist in their efforts needed to accomplish it.
4. **Development of new learning strategies:** A goal-setting programme requires new strategies to be applied if the old ones are not effective. So a person has to learn new strategies to apply in their goal-setting programme. So there is a need for originating the development of new learning strategies. The setting of new goals not only nurture persistence, but it also encourages people to learn new and better strategies for accomplishing a task. Goals motivate them to find out the most appropriate strategies for achieving goals.
5. **Indirect thought process:** Indirect thought process is the new way of achieving a goal. This process proposes that goals influence performance indirectly by affecting a performer's psychological state, including factors such as confidence level, anxiety, satisfaction and success.

Burton (1983) focuses solely on how goal setting influences performance in an environment. Goals are linked to the levels of anxiety, motivation and confidence when they direct their attention only on the outcome of goals, which can lead to decreased confidence, increased anxiety and poor performance. But performance goals assist them in forming realistic expectations, which result in optimal levels of confidence, cognitive anxiety and motivation and ultimately enhanced performance.

Garland (1985) contends that goals influence one's performance through one's indirect thought process. He says that when an individual sets a task goal, it will affect his task by performance expectancy and values. Performance expectancy is an individual's self-efficacy or confidence, which helps in achieving a specific goal, that is, the more confidence one has about achieving a specific task goal, the better one will perform.

DESIGNING A GOAL-SETTING PROGRAMME

Goal setting is a powerful technique for enhancing performance and increasing motivation, but it must be implemented correctly. In order to be successful in implementing a goal-setting programme, it should be designed properly and effectively. Some psychologists have recommended three stages for the goal-setting programme, that are:

1. **Planning stage:** This is an initial stage of a goal-setting programme but a very important phase. Before people try to set goals, they should first spend considerable time planning them if goals are to be achieved effectively. Before discussing the goals, they must identify the individual and group needs. Following the need analysis, they must identify the group and individual goals. Hence, goal setting involves commitment and effort on the part of people. Hence, planning of the programme should be very much thought-provoking.
2. **Preparation stage:** This is the second stage of a goal-setting programme. Once people have considered the individual and group needs, they should prepare for their implementation. First of all, they should chalk out the schedule of the goal-setting meetings. The meetings may be formal or informal. At the first meeting, they should convey the information of the main agenda of goal setting, for example, the need for setting goals, areas in which to set goals, types of goals to set, the importance of performance goals and so on. Then, we may ask other members to think about their general and specific objectives as well as a specific individual and group goals.

   A few days after the first meeting, a second meeting should be called for the purpose of discussing some of the points. It is essential to examine group goals with respect to their importance and realistic nature. It is also desirable to examine possible strategies for achieving these goals. Goals should be realistic and achievable.
3. **Follow-up stage:** This is the final and evaluative stage. It is called the follow-up stage. Goal setting can only be effective if evaluative feedback is provided after follow-up. It is important to schedule meetings for goal evaluation throughout the session. To facilitate follow-up and evaluation, systematic ways of providing feedback should be developed. Here, the printed evaluation cards in terms of checklist or questionnaires should also be prepared and used to evaluate performance. The evaluation cards are completed

after the various tasks have been performed and when combined with other available data serve as feedback for follow-up meetings. We may help in the goal evaluation and follow-up process as follows:

a. **Find out the appropriate evaluation procedure:** It is better to identify the most effective procedure for monitoring evaluation and follow-up programme for goal setting. We should clarify the evaluation process by having to keep the record completed relating to one's goals. We should also call meetings for skills tests while others are being received feedback about their performance progress towards their goals.

b. **Provide support and encouragement:** Throughout the season, we need to ask participants about their goals and encourage them about their goals process—showing enthusiasm about the goal-setting process, supports them and motivates them to achieve their goals. So motivation is very important in this process.

c. **Plan for goal re-evaluation:** Goals must be modified as they should be challenging ones. It is necessary to re-evaluate goals intermittently. Modifying and re-establishing goals is a normal part of the process.

COMMON PROBLEMS IN SETTING GOALS

Goal setting is a complex psychological skill to design as many problems will be faced while designing and then in implementing the goal-setting programme. Here, some of the problems which are likely to occur while setting goal will be discussed as follows:

1. **Setting too many goals:** It will be wrong if one sets too many goals at one time in their goal-setting system. It is common for some people to set three or more specific goals. This may have adverse effects. They may have some individual goals which they cannot properly monitor as they find difficulty in keeping their record, and then, they may lose interest in this task of goal setting. A better way is to set goals on their importance basis and focus on accomplishing them one by one on a priority basis. When these goals have been achieved, they then should pay attention to the next most important goals.

2. **Failing to recognize individual differences:** As there are individual differences among human beings, not all people may be interested in setting goals. We should not force others to set goals. But rather we should try to motivate all other persons to the goal-setting programme and then work with them who may show interest. By the time, their success would encourage others to begin setting goals.
3. **Goals should not be too general:** It is not possible to set the specific goals most of the time, but we usually set goals that are too general. However, the emphasis should always be on to state-specific goals in behavioural terms. When setting the goals, the performer should be asked to apply specific characteristics of improved technique in the goal-setting programme. When setting goals, we should always ask whether we can make this goal measurable and specific.
4. **Try to use realistic goals:** A number of people, sometimes, fail to change the goals that have become unrealistic due to some reasons. Changing goals once they have been set will be a difficult task. We must recognize this problem and continually emphasize the feasibility of changing the goals if necessary. We should try to change unrealistic goals to realistic ones.
5. **Failing to set performance goals:** For most of us, outcome goals are the only worthy goals. This is psychologically unsound and illogical, but it is happening due to the tremendous pressure of winning rewards. Hence, failure to set performance goals occurs frequently with us. Performance goals should be emphasized throughout the teaching–learning process. Teachers should continuously put emphasis on the attainment of performance goals. For example, they must remind students that great performances will typically lead to the best possible outcome.
6. **Lack of evaluative feedback:** A lack of follow-up and evaluative feedback is one of the major problems in the goal-setting programme. A follow-up and feedback plan in goal setting has become very essential in these days, and then, it should also be examined critically. To implement goal setting without follow-up and evaluative feedback is simply a waste of time and effort.

7. **Time budgeting needed in a goal-setting programme:** Goal setting needs time to be implemented. It must be recognized that a good deal of commitment on us is needed. When planning a goal-setting programme, we should consider how much time is available to commit to goal setting. It is much better to devote half an hour per week to goal setting throughout the training session.
8. **Setting only technique related goals:** When setting goals, it is very easy to focus our attention on technique-related goals. But there are a number of other techniques on which one may work for goal setting.
9. **Setting only technique-related goals:** We should be committed to the programme of goal setting for which we need to create a supportive and congenial environment for goal setting by our positive attitude. We should also develop a communication style that includes good listening skill, a sincere orientation and a positive approach to life.
10. **Failing to modify goals:** Modifying goals, especially adjusting them, once they have been set may be difficult but not impossible. Because first, we should discuss the need to adjust goals upward and downward, and second, if goals have to be changed due to some reasons, we should make the adjustment part of the goals that are related with the original goal.

PRINCIPLES OF GOAL SETTING

Several principles of goal setting have been identified. The application of these principles provides a strong basis for designing a good goal-setting programme. Widmeyer and Ducharme (1997) suggest the following guidelines. Now, let us discuss each principle one by one:

1. **Set specific goals in behavioural terms:** We should set specific goals in terms of behavioural and measurable terms. Specific goals are more useful and effective in bringing behavioural changes as compared to the general goals. Hence, it is important that goals may be expressed in terms of specific and measurable behavioural terms in life situations. Goals such as 'do your best'

and 'show your maximum' are the general goals, which are not effective. But on the other hand, specific and measurable goals should be set. Specific goals direct the behaviour of persons more precisely, show explicit expectation and affect behaviour change better than general goals do.

2. **Set difficult but realistic goals:** We should set difficult but realistic goals. It should be remembered that difficult goals give better performance. Unrealistic goals will lead to unsuccessful, failure and frustration. Thus, it is recommended that difficult and realistic goals should be set so that they may challenge persons as they are easily achievable. Hence, goals should be challenging rather than easy ones because challenging goals are more motivating. Difficult and realistic goals are effectively achieved, as they prove to be a challenge to a participant. But on the other hand, if goals are not achieved, it may lead to frustration, reduced confidence and poor performance.

3. **Set short- and long-range goals:** Both types of short- and long-term goals should be set. One way to employ this principle is to think of a long-term goal at the top, but the short-term goals should connect to the top and bottom. Terry Orlick (1988) developed a sequence that links a person's long-term goals with a series of immediate short-term physical and psychological goals. However, many psychologists have suggested setting more short-range goals. Short-term goals are needed because they allow persons to know immediately some improvements in performance, which may give them feedback as well as it will enhance motivation. Moreover, without short-term goals, people may ignore their long-term goals. But the long-term goals should be very realistic, challenging and specific.

4. **Set performance goals as compared to outcome goals:** Performance goals should be given preference as compared to outcome goals as too much emphasis placed on outcome goals creates anxiety during the event, and the person spends too much time worrying. Hence, one should make efforts to achieve performance goals. Some researches (Burton, 1984, 1989) have found that outcome goals have proved to be less effective than performance goals because people have a commitment, challenge and control over performance goals.

5. **Write down the records of goal achievement:** It is a good practice to write down the record of achievement of goals, which have been set. Otherwise, it may be possible that with the passage of time, we may likely to forget what we have achieved early. It will also help us to make a comparison with the new records to find out whether we have made any progress or not and also achieving various performance standards. Several psychologists have suggested that once goals are set, they should be noted down in writing where they can be easily followed-up. Therefore, it is useful for people to record their goals in written form. It may be done on a daily or weekly basis.
6. **Set positive goals not negative ones:** It has been recommended that whenever possible, positive goals should be set and not the negative ones. The positive goal-setting procedure helps persons to focus on success instead of failure. It is better to identify behaviour to be expressed positively as opposed to behaviours that should not be expressed or in negative terms.
7. **Set target dates for attaining goals:** We should set target dates for goal achievement. It will help people to be motivated to achieve the goals in targeted time by considering the urgency of attaining their goals at the right time.
8. **Develop strategies for goal achievement:** We should devise strategies regarding the achievement of goals. Strategies should be very specific and indicate how much and how often they are to be implemented. People should be very flexible for their goal achievement in applying the strategies. Hence, the development of strategies for achieving goals is very important for any effective goal-setting programme.
9. **Provide feedback for goal evaluation:** It has been recommended that evaluation of the goal-setting programme is absolutely necessary if goals are meant for achieving good performance. Therefore, evaluative and positive feedback should be given regarding the performance in relation to their goals. Feedback regarding knowledge of results about progress in performance is absolutely necessary if goals are to be effectively achieved in bringing a behavioural change in performance. Goal evaluation strategies should be implemented at the end of the goal-setting programme.

It should be continuously applied. Feedback and goal evaluation are essential parts of reaching towards the goals.
10. **Provide social support for goals:** A goal-setting programme will not be successful if it is not given social and moral support. Therefore, efforts must be made to acquaint the individuals as to the importance of their social support in encouraging progress towards the goals. Other people can also be helpful for their social and moral support in the achievement of goals.
11. **Foster individual commitment for goal setting:** A person will not be able to achieve a goal without commitment and challenge for achieving it. They should have the commitment and self-control over the event by knowing progress and getting consistent feedback. They should not set his goal for himself directly or indirectly.
12. **Consider the personality traits of participants:** When helping people to set goals, it is important to consider their personality traits. Individuals' motivation and goal orientation as well as how they will proceed well with the functions of the goal-setting process influence the goals they set. People with good achievements will have high motivation to achieve success and will easily seek to adopt challenging but realistic goals.

STYLES OF GOAL SETTING

Psychologists have suggested the following styles of goal setting:

1. **Performance versus outcome goals:** We should set performance goals and not outcome goals because we may have more self-control over performance goals. The following points should be considered while setting performance goals:
   a. **Control of goals:** Performance goals are usually better than outcome goals because persons have greater self-control over their performances. In fact, performance goals are related to the specific behaviour to be achieved and are not dependent on the actions of others for someone to attain them. Outcome goals, especially winning, are only partially under the control of any one individual. The outcome of an event is dependent not only on the individual but also on the other people as well.

The outcome is also determined by many situational factors, such as the equipment and situation, the weather and luck. The setting of outcome goals causes many psychological problems for many persons. They know that society equates winning with good performance and rewards. By performing better, you would increase the likelihood of winning. It suggests that to increase persons' chances of winning, they can be the best. The outcome of winning may impair the ability of a person to perform well.

b. **Degree of control:** People should set performance goals that are 100 per cent under their control. They should set goals that are much under their control as possible.

c. **Self-worth and achievement:** When persons think that their self-confidence is based on the goal of winning, self-confidence is not stable. It causes a source of uncertainty, anxiety and frustration. The only criterion for evaluating their worth is that they are not able to separate their performances from the outcome.

d. **Why performance goals:** Some people have confidence in themselves that they will attain their goals. Confidence is the belief in winning and the expectation or belief that the performance of one's task will result in winning. Setting the performance goals as compared to outcome goals is the main principle of the goal-setting programme.

2. **Challenging versus non-challenging goals:** We should set challenging goals rather than non-challenging goals because challenging goals are more motivating. However, if goals are very much difficult, people may not commit themselves to achieve them. It has been found that challenging goals give better performance than non-challenging goals. But the goals should not be too difficult that people may fail to consider them seriously after many efforts because, in this way, they will lose their interest. Goals that are too difficult will lead individuals to conclude that they will face failures and threaten their self-worth.

3. **Realistic versus unrealistic goals:** We should also set realistic goals and not unrealistic goals. The goals which cannot be achieved should not be set. For setting realistic goals, people need to know what they are to set realistic goals. While it is not easy to set

realistic goals, it is easier to set them realistically at the outset than to adjust them later based on changing circumstances. Goals need to be adjusted if they are to remain realistic on the basis of their previous experience and their present health status.

4. **Specific versus general goals:** We should set specific rather than general goals because the formers direct our behaviour more precisely and effectively by specifying the criterion for success. Specific goals should be quantifiable and specify a time period or a precise event. One of the reasons for the systematic goal setting is still applied so frequently that it involves considerable work on your part and requires the ability to develop creative means to quantify the specific behaviour of people.

5. **Short-term versus long-term goals:** We should set short-term goals first because long-term goals cannot be easily achieved as they are very realistic, challenging or specific. Setting short-term goals rather than long-term goals is the main consideration of the goal-setting programme, which involves setting challenging, realistic and specific performance goals. We should first set short-term and, at a later stage, long-term goals.

   Although it is useful to have long-term objectives, goals should not be set many months ahead, which tend to be unrealistic, vague and too lengthy. There are many factors such as illness, injury, life crises, speed of learning, non-availability of facilities and equipment and bad weather, which may result in long-term goals being unachievable and ineffective. On the other hand, short-term goals are more effective because they are more motivated and provide immediate direction to actions.

   Short-term goals are more specific and challenging ones, which provide greater opportunity to reward success in moving toward long-term objectives. Also, they help us to identify specific problems that people may have to face in acquiring the skills needed to attain the goals.

6. **Individual versus team goals:** We should set individual goals rather than team goals. But we may use team goals when we want to motivate the group and also to work together more effectively. So it can be said that the emphasis in our goal-setting programme should be on individual goals rather than on team goals. Team

goals tend to be unclear, which may try to diffuse responsibility. In fact, in many cases, they are not goals at all but long-term objectives. Research has shown that team goals simply are not effective unless they are accompanied by individual goals that conform to the principles of good goal setting.

USES OF GOAL SETTING

An effective programme of goal setting is a highly useful technique of increasing self-confidence, improving self-image and becoming more competent because one has to work very hard to achieve the goals. This technique is used during the training period to help people develop both physical and psychological skills. Some persons often do not know how to set goals effectively, nor do they pursue goal setting systematically. According to Marten (1976), the following are the uses of setting goals:

1. Goals may increase as well as enhance performance.
2. Goals improve the quality of practices.
3. Goals try to make a clarification about expectations.
4. Goals help to relieve tiredness, boredom and fatigue by making learning more challenging, interesting and motivating.
5. Goals increase interest and intrinsic motivation for achieving them.
6. Goals enhance pride, satisfaction and self-confidence.

Those who are well versed at setting realistic goals (a) are less anxious, (b) concentrate better, (c) perform better, (d) are more satisfied with their participation and (d) are more self-confident.

GUIDELINES FOR GOAL SETTING

Many psychologists have devised a number of useful guidelines for initiating a goal-setting programme.

1. You should first set long-term goals, which are specific and challenging.
2. You should set long-term goals by first setting the short-term goals.

3. You may involve all members of the group in setting goals.
4. You should carefully monitor progress toward the goals-setting programme.
5. You may reward success in goals achievement.
6. You may inculcate efficacy concerning the goal achievement.

CONCLUSION

A goal is stated as an objective, a standard and an aim of some action or a level of performance. Goal setting is attaining a specific standard of proficiency on a task, usually within a specified time limit. Usually, goals are set for achieving some standards. People should not only identify goals but also try to set the realistic and achievable goals, which may provide the right direction and also make efforts of increased intensity in order to enhance motivation and also to achieve their goals.

There are many types of goals, for example, outcome goals, performance goals, process goals and smart goals. The outcome goals represent standards of performance that focus on the results of a contest between two parties. They depend on the final results of the performance of the participants. On the other hand, performance goals focus on improvements in terms of one's past performance and previous achievements. The process goals specify the procedures in which the performer will engage during the performance. They focus on specific behaviours exhibited throughout a performance. Smart goals are concerned with the goals set by the managers and directors of corporate industries for setting their organizational goals for the achievement of their targets within a specific time limit.

A systematic goal-setting programme is very much needed, and it requires to be implemented correctly. The goals influence performance because (a) goals pay more attention to important aspects of the task being performed, (b) goals energize performer's intensity of efforts and power by providing incentives, (c) goals increase consistency and persistency of efforts while performing a task, (d) goals motivate persons to find out the most appropriate techniques for achieving them, (e) goals often employ new learning strategies and (f) indirect thought process affects the psychological state.

In order to be successful in implementing the goal-setting programme, it should be designed properly and effectively. Some psychologists have recommended three stages for a goal-setting programme, namely (a) planning stage, (b) preparation stage and (c) follow-up stage. Before people try to set goals, they should first spend considerable time planning them if goals are to be achieved effectively. Once people have considered individual and group needs, they should prepare for their implementation. Goal setting can only be effective if evaluative feedback is provided after the follow-up.

Goal setting is a complex skill as many problems will be faced while designing and then in implementing the goal-setting programme. Some of the problems which are likely to occur while setting goal have been described. Several principles of goal setting have been identified and described. Psychologists have suggested a few styles of goal setting. Of course, some suggestions have been advanced to solve the problems, yet there may be some cases where the obstacles or hurdles occur on the way. Then, people may feel frustrated and face some emotional problems and have emotional arousal. In order to help them, they may be well acquainted with the phenomenon of the emotional state of the mind. The next chapter deals with emotional arousal regulation.

Emotional Arousal Regulation

INTRODUCTION

While setting the goals, some people face many psychological and emotional problems. For solving those problems and overcoming the hurdles, which occur in the way of setting goals, we should know what type of emotional arousal arises and how to control that phenomenon. The present chapter will discuss the concept of arousal effect of emotions on performance and practical implications for emotional arousal regulation.

Emotional arousal is necessary for peak performance in every field of life. Frustrations and disappointments are inevitable in all activities of competitive life. Anxiety, stress as well as joy and fun are a part of our busy life. Anger and fear also arise as people clash in competitive activities. General emotional excitement is a part of almost every situation in life. The cheering by other people, the music, the barking of the vendors in street and the partisan attitude of parents and friends all add to the euphoria of excitement and stimulate in most individuals in emotional responses. Many emotions are hereditary, while others are learned. Terms such as 'stress', 'anxiety' and 'tension' are used to represent emotional states. There are distinct differences in the pattern of responses invoked by each such state. Since emotions have such a strong effect on human behaviour, we are to understand how emotional stress affects our life performance.

Emotional arousal is non-directive generalized bodily activation, whereas stress and anxiety are unpleasant emotional states, and both of them describe the kind of negative emotional state, which may occur when emotional arousal levels are very high. Basically, some degree of uncertainty is there in increased arousal, but too much uncertainty may be producing anxiety. Thus, emotional arousal is a negative state of human behaviour.

CONCEPT OF AROUSAL

Before considering how arousal is related to our life performance, it is necessary to clarify the meaning of the word 'arousal'. Arousal is a combination of both physical and mental activity in a person, varying on a scale of the continuum from a state of no feeling (apathy) to intense feeling (excitement). It refers to the direction and intensity dimensions of behaviour at a particular moment in life. The direction may be in a positive or negative way. Sometimes, emotional arousal may be positively oriented when there is an intense feeling of love, affection, enjoyment, happiness and success. On the other hand, the negative arousal may be in the moment of sadness, fear, anger, jealousy, worry and dejection.

This intensity of emotional arousal falls along a continuum scale from low to high level. The low arousal is the coma state of the organism, whereas high arousal is the intensity state of the body and mind. It ranges from no arousal to completely highly aroused state, that is, the disturbed state of mind (Gould & Krane, 2002). Highly aroused individuals are mentally and physically too much upset and highly activated, and they face some physiological changes, for example, increased heart rate, fast respiration, too much sweating and high blood pressure. Arousal is associated with either pleasant or unpleasant events. You might be highly aroused on getting the good news of a promotion, or failures, in some matter, might equally arouse you.

Arousal has typically been referred to as physiological activation in the autonomic nervous system. Landers (1980) defined arousal as 'a motivational construct' that represents 'the intensity level of behaviour'. Martens (1987) viewed arousal what he labelled as 'psychic energy'—as 'the vigor, vitality and intensity with which the mind functions'. Hence, arousal is viewed by Martens as being more than physiological activation of the organism. It involves mental activation as well.

Hence, arousal is defined as the general physiological and psychological activation of both body and mind. Arousal has been considered in terms of physiological indexes such as heart rate, respiration and blood pressure, but it also represents a cognitive intensity of behaviour. The environmental stimuli place a person in a state of arousal and their homeostasis is disturbed. Emotions, as a consequence or in anticipation of experiences, are accompanied by internal chemical and physiological changes and sometimes by outward behaviour.

The term 'arousal' is used synonymously with the term 'activation', and both these terms refer to the intensity level of behaviour (Duffy, 1957). Both these terms also refer to a non-directive generalized bodily activation or arousal dimension. Conceptually, Duffy (1962) argues that any given point on this continuum from deep sleep to agitated state of mind is determined by 'the extent of release of potential energy, stored in the tissues of the organism, as shown in activity or response.' Here, arousal is viewed as psychic energy as well as an energizing or activating function of the autonomic nervous system, which is responsible for harnessing the body's resources for intense and vigorous activity.

Martens (1974) says, 'the engine of human machinery usually refers to both the activation of the brain and the innervations of different physiological systems'. Unlike the car engine, our human engine cannot be easily turned on or off—at least not while we are awake. When we are sleeping, there is electrical activity in our brain as well as in our muscles; thus, arousal is a natural and continuous state. However, when arousal level becomes too intense, one may experience unpleasant emotional reactions associated with the autonomic nervous system. This condition leads to a state called as stress or state anxiety or distress.

PHYSIOLOGICAL ASPECTS OF AROUSAL STATES

The physiological reactions of emotional arousal are the change in muscle tension, respiration, heart rate or blood pressure, galvanic skin response (GSR) and many other bodily functions. They have proved to be very sensitive to changes in emotional arousal. According to Krahenbuhl (1975),

> The functions for controlling emotional arousal are located in the brain, especially in the autonomic nervous system and primarily involve the cortex, reticular formation, the hypothalamus and the limbic system. These centres interact with the adrenal medulla and the somatic and autonomic nervous systems to determine overall arousal.

The most objective way of studying emotional arousal is through the investigation of the physiological changes that occur when the individual is upset or disturbed emotionally. Everyone is aware that certain changes take place within the body when we are emotionally aroused or disturbed. During an aroused emotional experience, the body reacts in a number of different ways:

1. Changes occur in the electrical resistance of the skin. It is commonly called GSR. It is measured through electrodes placed on the palms of the hands.
2. Blood pressure is elevated, and the volume of the blood in various organs of the body is altered.
3. Heart rate increases and, in exceptional cases, the individual may experience sharp pains around the heart.
4. Respiration becomes more rapid.
5. The pupils of the eyes dilate so that more lights fall on the retina.
6. Salivary secretion diminishes, and there is dryness of the mouth and throat.
7. Motility of the gastrointestinal tract slows or ceases altogether.
8. Muscles become tense and tremble.
9. The composition of the blood changes. The most notable change is an elevation of the blood sugar level.

In addition to these physiological changes, epinephrine is secreted into the blood by the adrenal medulla the non-endocrine part of the adrenal glands. Epinephrine heightens the blood sugar level, helps the blood to clot more quickly and increases the blood pressure. The other aspects of the physiology of emotions are as follow:

1. Different emotions have been associated with different patterns of physiological responses; for example, people with emotions such as anger, joy and disgust feel very differently to some degree in different biological reactions.
2. Different emotions have been associated with different patterns of activation in the cerebral cortex. Positive feelings are centred primarily in the left hemisphere of the brain, while negative ones are centred in the right hemisphere. Whereas positive feelings like happiness are associated with greater activation in the left hemisphere, while negative ones such as sadness or disgust are associated with greater activation in the right hemisphere.
3. It has been found on the basis of recordings of electrical activity in the brain (electroencephalogram) that happiness or amusement leads to greater activation in the left cortex, and disgust shows greater activation in the right cortex.
4. Depressed people show less left-frontal activation than non-depressed people.
5. Inhibited children who are shy and unwilling to approach new situations or objects show less left-frontal activation.
6. Cerebral hemisphere shows a degree of specialization with respect to emotion. So in the brain activity as well as in heart rate and other bodily processes, there is a relationship between our emotional experiences and physiological responses.

ROLE OF THE AUTONOMOUS NERVOUS SYSTEM

The autonomous nervous system is a part of the central nervous system, whose nerves run to the internal organs regulating body processes such as respiration, heart rate and digestion. The autonomous nervous system plays a major role in emotion.

The autonomous nervous system derives its name from the fact that it appears to operate as an independent system of control. It controls many of our body processes without requiring any conscious effort from us. We do learn to control some autonomic functions, such as urination and defecation, but these functions would be carried out even if we did not learn such control. The autonomous system controls such things as constriction of our blood vessels, the action of our sweat glands and the activity of our adrenal glands. In general, it controls involuntary actions.

The autonomic nervous system has two divisions—the sympathetic and the parasympathetic—which are often antagonistic in their action. Although many organs receive input from both systems, these systems are different from one another in structure and in the manner in which they operate.

Emotions are also affected by brain waves. The brain is the culmination of neural development. Our brain is highly developed and plays an important role in our lives, including our emotional life. The brain has the ability to contemplate and examine itself. Furthermore, the brain has the ability to change itself. There is evidence that physical changes occur in the brain as learning takes place. The brain is extremely versatile. Parts of it act like sensory organs. For example, some brain cells sense changes in the composition of the blood and cause other cells to make appropriate adjustments. Other brain cells act as if they are glands, and they produce hormonal substances.

As the spinal cord enters the bony skull, it enlarges into the brain stem, which contains all the ascending and descending nerve fibres that link the body with the higher brain structures as well as some important nerve cell centres or nuclei. The brain stem is the oldest part of the brain, which includes structures found in all vertebrates that regulate the complex reflexes, for example, respiration, heart rate, balance of body fluids, temperature and appetite—necessary for the maintenance of life. The activity controlled by the brain stem is much more complex than controlled by the spinal cord.

Emotions are controlled by the two components of the autonomic nervous system. The sympathetic nervous system arouses emotions, and parasympathetic nervous system calms emotions. The sympathetic (fight/flight) component speeds up heart rate as it signals to prepare for action, and the parasympathetic component slows down heart rate as it signals for relaxation. During the different events in life, we feel various types of emotions such as happiness, frustration, fear and sadness. Different emotions are felt as waves of energy, and the messages are sent through our nervous system to the heart, brain and body. Continuous surge of intense emotions, such as fear, frustration and anger, overburdens the autonomic nervous system with stress signals, and eventually, the autonomic nervous system becomes imbalanced by the chronic build-up of stress.

Amygdala, a region of the brain, is a centre for emotional arousal, and it acts as a coordination centre for responding to things in the environment. It is involved in causing physiological changes such as changes in heart rate, blood pressure and respiration during fear and anger. Amygdala is a paired structure, and it is located in each hemisphere of the brain. Earlier, it was believed that it is involved in negative emotions such as fear and anger, but now the latest studies have shown that it is also involved in positive emotions.

EMOTIONAL AROUSAL AND ITS EFFECT ON PERFORMANCE

Psychologists have been studying the effect of emotional arousal on performance for many years, that is, how arousal is related to performance, positively or negatively. There are individual differences in the emotional arousal of human beings. Some are too highly aroused, but some others may feel low or no arousal, and their responses to their stimuli are not the same ones. Why and how do arousals function to the advantage of one person and the detriment of another person? Researchers have come out with some findings, which have far-reaching effects for helping people psyching up and performing better.

To know why and how arousal affects performance can help us to regulate arousal, both in ourselves and in others for our benefit as well as for others' welfare. For example, if heightened arousal leads to increased muscle tension in a person, then relaxation exercises may help them to reduce state anxiety, which is accompanied by arousal, and it may improve performance. But on the other hand, thought control strategies may work better for another person who suffers from excessive cognitive state anxiety as they need to control thought. There are at least two views regarding how increased arousal influences performance, that is, (a) increased muscle tension and coordination problem, which affects performance adversely and (b) changes in attention or concentration levels, which also decrease the level of performance. The two views are briefly described below:

1. **Muscle tension and coordination problem:** Increased emotional arousal and somatic state anxiety will lead to increased muscle tension and can interfere with coordination activity, which may affect the performance negatively. Many people who face stress in life complain about muscle soreness, headaches and back pains. Many experience high levels of somatic anxiety, and there is an increase in their arousal, which causes muscle tension and can also interfere with the coordination of various activities. These phenomena will definitely affect the performance adversely.
2. **Changes in attention and concentration:** Increased emotional arousal and state anxiety also influence performance through changes in attention and concentration abilities (Nideffer, 1976; Williams & Elliot, 1999). The reasons may be as follows:
   a. Increased emotional arousal causes a damaging effect on a performer's attentional ability, which influences performance negatively.
   b. When arousal is too high, performers also likely to pay less attention to the environment.
   c. Emotional arousal and state anxiety cause changes in attention and concentration levels by affecting the attentional style (Nideffer, 1976).
   d. Increased emotional arousal will stimulate performers to shift to the intensity of attention style that may be less useful for any task.
   e. Increased emotional arousal and state anxiety also cause persons to attend to inappropriate stimuli.

All the above shows that the relationship between arousal and performance depends upon how increased anxiety affects attention or thought control.

SUGGESTIONS FOR PRACTICAL APPLICATION

The most effective way to help people achieve excellent performance in any task is to acquaint them how emotional arousal can lead to top-level performances. It is only possible if various psychological strategies (e.g., imagery and goal setting) can help them manage their emotional arousal. For implementing these techniques, the following important guidelines should be adopted:

1. To know the optimal arousal-related emotions needed for top performance
2. To find out the interaction of personal and situational factors, which affect the performance with excessive anxiety
3. To identify the symptoms of increased arousal and anxiety among participants
4. To recognize strategies and mental practices for individuals
5. To develop confidence among performers to help them to cope with increased emotional arousal

1. **Knowing optimal arousal-related emotions:** The various psychological strategies and skills can help the performers learn to regulate arousal. The main objective is to know the optimal emotional arousal for their best performance and then to learn how to set the arousal either by raising (psyching up) or lowering it (psyching out) their emotional arousal.
2. **Finding out the interaction between personal and situational factors:** The interaction of personal factors (such as self-esteem and trait anxiety) and situational factors (such as event importance and uncertainty) is a better predictor of arousal, state anxiety and performance. A positive attitude and a positive environment are an effective way to manage stress. It is quite clear from Box 6.1.

The above model clearly shows that the personal factors such as trait anxiety, self-esteem and self-esteem in combination with the situational factors such as importance and uncertainty of the events affect the performance, which is the main cause of emotional arousal. For example, in the field of sports, the higher the level of competition, the more will be the uncertainty of winning or the outcome of the competition along with the competitive trait

> **Box 6.1:** Interactional Model of Arousal
>
> | Personal Factors | P × S | Situational Factors |
> |---|---|---|
> | Trait anxiety ⟶ | Person-by | ⟵ importance |
> | Self-esteem ⟶ | Situation interaction | ⟵ uncertainty |
> | | **State anxiety arousal** | |
>
> *Source:* Weinberg and Gould (2007).

anxiety and self-concept of the athletes will definitely affect the performance, which in turn will lead to emotional arousal.

3. **Identifying symptoms of arousal and state anxiety:** There is a need to find out those people who are experiencing heightened stress and anxiety through their signs and symptoms. So it is essential to know the various symptoms of increased stress and anxiety. The symptoms of emotional arousal have been depicted in Box 6.2.

4. **Recognizing strategies for individuals:** There is a need to know the techniques and instructional practices for individuals. An individual with very low trait anxiety and high self-esteem performing in a non-threatening environment may need suggestions to increase arousal.

5. **Developing confidence in individuals:** Highly confident persons who believe in their abilities and capacities experience less state anxiety as well as arousal. Two important strategies are:
   a. Creating a positive environment
   b. Instilling a positive attitude towards life

> **Box 6.2:** Symptoms of Emotional Arousal
>
> a. Cold and clumsy hands
> b. A constant need to urinate
> c. Profuse sweating
> d. Negative self-talk
> e. Dazed look in eyes
> f. Increased muscle tension
>
> g. Inability to concentrate
> h. Butterflies in the stomach
>
> –Feel ill
> –Headache
> –Cottonmouth
> –Constantly sick
> –Sleeping difficulties
> –Consistently perform better in non-evaluating situations
> –Loss of attention
> –Pain in belly

Stress may be due to uncertainty and insecurity in the environment. It is possible only when people participate in a negative environment. For inculcating confidence among the individuals is to create a positive environment. For instance:

1. It is better to give objective feedback and encouragement when individuals face stressful events in their environment.
2. We should develop a positive and productive orientation towards unpleasant events, and we should learn from our failures. When individuals face failures, they often are overtly aroused and anxious. This leads to increased muscles tension which further deteriorates performance. Here, they need help, and for them, a positive environment may be created, and a positive attitude towards life may be developed.
3. It is useful for people to learn to view mistakes in a more productive way.
4. We should try to get success by staying cool and learn how to cope with stress in life.
5. If we master this strategy for reducing stress and anxiety, we can go for a more productive learning and performance enhancement.

The suggestions for practical applications are given in Box 6.3.

Box 6.3: Suggestions for Practical Application

1. Knowing optimal arousal-related emotions
2. Finding out the interaction between personal and situational factors
3. Identifying symptoms of arousal and state anxiety
4. Recognizing strategies for individuals
5. Developing confidence in individuals

EMOTIONAL AROUSAL REGULATION

It is very essential for individuals to learn how to regulate their emotional arousal. They should be able to increase it by psyching up when they are feeling boredom, fatigued and lethargic as well as to increase it when some stressors cause them anxiety and nervousness. The good news for them is to find their optimal levels of arousal, that is, to psych up without psyching out and to feel relax without losing intensity and focus. So there is a need to apply arousal regulation techniques so that we should help human beings in life situations to reach their optimal levels of arousal, especially when they are under tension.

The first step in this process of emotional arousal regulation is how to identify and learn more about anxiety and arousal states while performing some activities. We shall have to recognize how emotional states affect performance. It usually requires self-monitoring and self-evaluation as well as information about our arousal states. The following points suggest this:

1. We should try to imagine our best performance and visualize the actual situation as clearly as possible.
2. After it has been done, we should complete the items of our task in the checklist. The objective is to become aware of the relationship between psychological states and performance.
3. Then, we should repeat the process of giving our best performance.
4. Now, we should compare our performance in this exercise between two tasks.
5. In this process, the most important thing is to understand the relationship between how we feel covertly and perform overtly.

Before we can have self-control on our thoughts and feelings, we should be aware of our psychological states. Here, it is important to remember that how individuals cope with anxiety state, and how much anxiety they experience in life.

AROUSAL-INDUCING TECHNIQUES

There are some people who need to psyche themselves up because they might be feeling boredom, tired, lethargic and underactivated. It may be possible that they might have taken the task too lightly. There are certain signs from where we can judge that they are underactivated such as:

1. They are moving slowly and not getting set.
2. Their mind is wandering, and they can easily become distracted.

3. They are not concerned about how well they perform.
4. They do have a lack of motivation and enthusiasm.
5. They feel heaviness in the legs and arms.

Although these thoughts and feelings may appear at any time, they usually show that an individual is not physiologically and psychologically ready to perform. It may be that they could not get enough time for rest or might have worked too hard. For generating more energy and activating the organism, some suggestions have been given below:

1. **Increase breathing rate:** First of all, you should take deep breathing. Breath control and focus on breathing can produce energy and reduce stress and anxiety. Deep breathing tends to activate and speed up the nervous system.
2. **Act energized:** Then you should do light exercise to energize your body and mind before you start any work. At times, when a person feels fatigued, lethargic and slow, then at that time, they should act enthusiastically and work energetically that may help to recapture their energy level.
3. **Use positive statements:** Before you start any task, you should bring some positive feelings and thoughts in your mind. The mind can certainly affect the body; for example, saying or thinking good words about yourself can be energizing and activating. Positive self-talk, such as 'I am feeling alright' and 'I am okay', can also energize an individual.
4. **Use positive statements:** When you are tired and feel boredom after working very hard on some task for some time, and you feel that your performance is not well, then you should listen to music to overcome your fatigue. Light music can be a source of energy, and many people use cassettes with headphones before any task. You may take the help of your smart mobile phone also.
5. **Use energizing imagery:** Imagery is a good exercise. If possible, you may take the help of imagery, which is a useful psychological skill. Imagery is another way to generate positive feelings and thoughts. Imagery involves visualizing something that is energizing to an individual.

CONCLUSION

Emotional arousal is non-directive generalized bodily activation. General emotional excitement is a part of almost every situation in life. Arousal is a combination of both physical and mental activity in a person, varying on a scale of the continuum from a state of no feeling (apathy) to intense feeling (excitement). Sometimes, emotional arousal may be positively oriented when there are intense feelings of love, affection, enjoyment, happiness and success. On the other hand, the negative arousal may be in the moment of sadness, fear, anger, jealousy, worry and dejection. The low arousal is the coma state of the organism, whereas high arousal is the intensity state of the body and mind.

Arousal has typically been referred to as physiological activation in the autonomic nervous system. It has been considered in terms of physiological indexes such as heart rate, respiration and blood pressure, but it also represents a cognitive intensity of behaviour. Here, arousal is viewed as psychic energy as well as an energizing or activating function of the autonomic nervous system, which is responsible for harnessing the body's resources for intense and vigorous activity. However, when arousal level becomes too intense, one may experience unpleasant emotional reactions associated with the autonomic nervous system.

The physiological reactions of the emotional arousal are the change in muscle tension, respiration, heart rate blood pressure, GSR and many other bodily functions. They have proved to be very sensitive to changes in emotional arousal. The functions for controlling emotional arousal are located in the brain, especially in the autonomic nervous system, and primarily involve the cortex, reticular formation, the hypothalamus and the limbic system. The autonomous nervous system plays a major role in emotion. The physiological reactions that accompany emotions are regulated by the two parts of the autonomic nervous system, namely the activation of the sympathetic nervous system and the parasympathetic nervous system. Emotions are also affected by brain waves.

Psychologists have been studying the effect of emotional arousal on performance for many years, positively or negatively. There are at least two views regarding how increased arousal influences performance, that is, (a) increased muscle tension and coordination problem, which affect performance adversely and (b) changes in attention or concentration levels, which also decrease the level of performance. The most effective way to help people to achieve excellent performance in any task is to acquaint them how emotional arousal can lead to top-level performances. For implementing these techniques, some important guidelines should be adopted.

It is very essential for individuals to learn how to regulate their emotional arousal. They should be able to increase it by psyching up when they are feeling boredom, fatigued and lethargic as well as to increase it when some stressors cause them anxiety and nervousness. There are some techniques which can help in emotional arousal regulations, for example, (a) increase breathing rate, (b) act energized, (c) use positive statements and (d) use energizing imagery. Emotional arousal is the result of strains and stresses of modern life. So it can be said that stress and emotional arousal are related to each other. In the next chapter, we will describe the concept, causes, effect and some coping strategies to manage stress.

Stress Management Techniques

INTRODUCTION

Emotional arousal leads to many problems in life due to which strain and stress, anxiety, tension, maladjustment and frustration are caused. This century is now called an age of stress. So we will have to study the nature and concept of stress. What are the signs and symptoms of stress? How a man reacts to stressful life events? What may be the possible causes and sources of stress and consequences therof in this modern life? What types of coping strategies have been suggested by psychologists to manage stress? The answers to all these questions will be provided in the present chapter.

Everyone in this world faces stressors in some area of life. In this modern world, an individual is facing various kinds of problems in their social, psychological, economical, religious and political spheres. These problems have increased in the recent past due to various causes. An individual does not feel satisfied with what they have achieved, and they are always in search of what they do not possess. This constant search has led them to lead a life full of strains and stresses.

Modern life is full of strains and stresses. In everyday life of human being, there are many situations, where we face challenges and problems. Some of them work as a motivating factor for us, but many others bring miseries and create problems. To face the challenges boldly or to avoid them has become a part of life. But it depends from individual to individual. Stress is caused when any challenge exceeds the coping abilities of an individual. Every person is facing stress in their own way. So it can be said that stress is a part of life, but too much stress can be deleterious to life.

STRESS: A PSYCHOPHYSIOLOGICAL PROCESS

Stress is inevitable in life. Stress is a physical, mental, emotional and behavioural response to a wide variety of stimuli in the environment. The term 'stress' actually refers to pressures or stressors placed on some people by daily experiences that result in their physically and mentally arousing state when they are unable to face those pressures realistically. Stress is not only negative but, sometimes, positive also. Whether a stressor is negative or positive depends on your perception of the situation. Stress demands to initiate arousal of the mind and body. The emotional arousal, if prolonged, can make you tired, fatigued and may affect you adversely and put you in the state of distress, dysfunction and mental illness.

The term 'stress' indicates something undesirable and debilitating. Usually, stress is both a negative and a positive experience. The concept of stress has physiological, psychological and sociological consequences. The term 'stress' was made popular by an endocrinologist Dr Hans Selye as he was the first scientist who used this word, borrowed from Physics, to describe the results of some kind of traumatic impingement on the organism. In fact, he used the term for the event of traumatic experience of a person and the word 'strain' to show what happens to the individual. Later on, these terms began to be considered as anxiety, frustration, emotional arousal, mental conflict, ego threat, tension and so on, which show some psychological and physiological symptoms.

Selye (1959), a Canadian scientist, who is considered as the father of stress research, theorized the three stages of stress, which impinge on the organism. Accordingly, people's response to a stressor can be divided into the following three phases:

1. The first phase is the *alarm stage* which is the initial phase when the body is aroused. Emotional arousal is the first change that occurs when a person feels stressed. Alarm produces increased physiological arousal and people become excited, anxious or frightened. They may also have symptoms such as a loss of appetite, sleeplessness, headaches or harmonic imbalances. There may be increased heart

rate, breathing problem and blood pressure, sweating of the palms and dilation of the pupils.
2. The second stage is the *resistance phase* as the body tries to adapt to continued stress. It is followed by a longer period of resistance. In this stage, the initial phase of alarm response usually is replaced by resistance. During this stage, people are often irritable, impatience and anger prone. They go on experience continuous fatigue. This stage may persist for a few hours, or it may continue for many days or even years. If during this stage, if a person is unable to manage stress, they enter into the final stage of exhaustion.
3. The final stage is *exhaustion*; as with continuing stress, the body reaches the last phase of its capacities to handle stress. If your body cannot manage stress in a positive way, exhaustion is inevitable. As stress involves so much psychic energy, it tends to affect both physical and emotional health. People under extreme conditions of stress usually show disorganized and distorted behaviour. If their stress is not managed, they become too much exhausted and fatigued. The result is their maladjustment, withdrawal behaviour, and in some extreme cases, they may commit suicidal deaths.

Let us consider what stress is and what is a stressor? Selye (1956) says, 'Stress is a kind of non-specific response superimposed upon various specifics manifestations of an insulting agent impinging upon the organism.' Whenever forces in a situation affect someone physically and mentally, psychologists say the person is experiencing stress. Often several stressors such as money problems, work problems or marital problems act together to affect behaviour. Hence, a stressor is an environmental demand that acts on an organism physically or psychologically in injurious ways.

Selye (1956) says that 'stress is the process that involves the perception of a substantial imbalance between environmental demand and response capability under conditions where failure to meet demands is perceived as having important consequences and is responded to with increased levels of anxiety.' Many responses may be forthcoming from an individual under stress, and these responses from the same individual may not vary too much from time to time and from situation to situation, but there are marked inter-individual differences in stress reaction. There are four stages in this process, for example, (a) environmental demands on the individual, (b) individual's perception about those demands, (c) organism's actual response and (d) consequences.

We have noticed that stress does not seem to be long-lasting, whether they are unpleasant stress like fear or pleasant ones like joy. Yet on occasions, such stress may persist for long periods of time and may reach higher levels. In human beings, stress is always present to some degree. Indeed, humans are never without stress, and that some level of stress is actually desirable.

DIFFERENT VIEWS REGARDING STRESS

Different views regarding stress are briefly described below:

1. *Stress is reactive*. When stimuli in the external and internal environment are seen as a challenge to an organism's safety, comfort or preferred status, they provoke a variety of physiological, cognitive, emotional and behavioural responses. Such stimuli are referred to as stressors. Stressors can be chemical, climatic, physical, bacterial, social or psychological. A stressor changes the way an organism responds, and it induces a response of stress.
2. *Stress is a kind of response, which may be non-adaptive* to an overt situation and may cause physical, mental or behavioural problems in a person. Stress is a state of strain, which affects one's feelings and thought process. When it happens excessively, it may affect one's capacity to cope with the environment adversely. People who are too much stressed may become angry, nervous and irritable, and they are easily provoked and are unable to relax.
3. *Stress is a state in which the natural equilibrium* of the body is disturbed. Stress is caused by any threat to the organism. Emotional arousal can also bring stress. Stress is more than reactivity to stressors. 'Stress results when an organism perceives that the demands upon it exceed its resources to manage the demands' (Lazarus & Folkman, 1984). Appraisal, therefore, comes before the identification of stress and coping process with it. Thus, a

particular situation may be highly threatening to one person and not to some other person. It is the individual's perception that is important, that is, thoughts about their initial emotional responses to stressful stimuli.
4. *Stress is considered in terms of an overload of the demands*, which are made upon us, and we are not capable of meeting them adequately. Sometimes, stress may also occur when there is less demand for us or when we are under load in a job. Of course, stress may occur from sensory deprivation, social isolation or stimulus impoverishment.
5. According to Spielberger (1972), 'stress is limited to the magnitude of objectives danger that is associated with the stimulus properties of a given situation.' The term 'stress' is used usually to denote environmental circumstances that are characterized by some degree of physical or psychological danger.
6. Whenever you experience stress, whether it is the physical when you are fixed in a traffic jam or emotions of being broken up with a close friend or break up of love affair with a girlfriend, the organism consciously or unconsciously initiates some physiological responses which are called the flight or fight reaction. The body's nervous system and hormones naturally prepare up to fight or flee the approaching threat.
7. *Stress is an unavoidable part of life.* So it is imperative to learn to live with it. Some stress is good for us, while other stress, such as failure in an examination, may be harmful. It is an experience to know the joys and frustrations of stress. It depends upon how you interpret it in a strictly negative way or in a positive way.
8. Appley and Traumbull (1967) state that psychological stress is elicited by conditions that approach the 'upper thresholds of tolerability' and produces states of anxiety, tension and upset, emotional disturbances, distress, ego threat and arousal. The emotional responses are sadness, anger, irritable, frustration, excited, anxious and bored or depressed.

To sum up, it can be said that a stressor changes the way an organism responds, it induces a response of stress. Stressors usually produce anxiety, tension and emotional arousal.

POSITIVE AND NEGATIVE STRESS

There are various consequences of stress, which may be pleasant and unpleasant. So stress can be classified as eustress or distressed. There are two types of stress—positive and negative. Usually, we consider stress in negative terms, which brings distress and frustration in life. Sometimes, we also face some situations when there is positive stress, which is called *eustress*. When we get happy news, we feel stress which is positive in nature. For example, employees get the news on their mobile about their promotion, which they were not expecting, they will be in a state of ecstasy and hilarious mood and unable to control themselves out of joy and unexpected news. We can say they are in a state of positive stress, which is eustress. Suppose they are having their lunch at this time, they will feel lack of appetite and immediately will like to go to the washroom as they may be feeling digestive disorder.

Hence, stress can be either positive or negative. Selye (1974) differentiated among eustress or positive stress and distress or negative stress, suggesting that not all stressors should be perceived as negatives. Some new situations, for example, unexpected promotion in life may create positive stress, or unexpected victory in a match against a strong team may also create positive stress, which is called eustress. Sometimes, any bad news on your mobile may create negative stress, which is called distress. Similarly, the unexpected defeat against a weak team, not selected for the contest in spite of the excellent performance previously, too much pressure to win a match, to exhibit the peak performance within a short time may be the negative stress, which is called distress. On the other hand, new and pleasant experiences of the persons may have positive stress.

Stress is required in every person for the activation of physical and mental responses. But it should not be too high or too low. It should be at the required level or optimum level. So stress can be classified as (a) eustress and (b) distress, which are discussed below:

1. **Eustress:** Eustress means the presence of an optimal level of stress in an individual, which may contribute positively to the enhancement of their performance. In this situation, employees who are

enjoying their work in their jobs may be having optimum stress. In certain works, such as marketing, journalism and television announcement, where some level of stress contributes positively to good performance. When stress arises on getting some happy news when it is not expected, we experience a state of stress, which is called eustress.

2. **Distress:** Distress shows the presence of high level of stress, which affects one's job performance in an individual in a disturbing way adversely as well as creates many types of physical, psychological and behavioural problems. This state of stress brings grief, sorrow and sadness. When we receive unexpected sad news about the demise of someone nearer to us, we may feel it a state of distress.

McGRATH MODEL OF STRESS

Besides Selye, McGrath (1970) has also proposed a simple model of stress as depicted in Box 7.1. It is a process or a sequence of events that will lead to a particular end. It consists of four interrelated stages, namely (a) environmental demands, (b) perception of demand, (c) stress response and (d) behaviour consequences.

Box 7.1: The Four-stage Stress Process

Stage I   Environmental demand (physical and psychological)
Stage II Perception of the environmental demand
Stage III Stress response (physical and psychological)
 • Arousal and state anxiety (cognitive and somatic)
 • Muscle tension and attention changes
Stage IV Behavioural consequences

Source: Gould and Krane (1992).

According to McGrath (1970), four events must be considered in studying stress as a social psychological process:

1. The physical or social environment that places some demands on the individual are called environmental demands.

2. The individual's perception of the environmental demands, the way they respond to them and how they perceive those environmental demands.
3. A stress response is given when the individual acts physically and psychologically in the shape of arousal state, cognitive and somatic anxiety and muscle tension.
4. The behavioural consequences resulting from the responses in performance or outcomes.

Here we briefly describe each stage below:

1. **Stage I—environmental demand:** In the first stage of the stress process, some type of demand is placed on an individual. The demand might be physical or psychological, like parents putting up too much demand on their children to stand first in the class when they do not have the required ability. This stage consists of an environmental situation placed upon the persons when they are unable to perform it.
2. **Stage II—the perception of demand:** The second stage of the stress process is the individual's perception of the environmental (physical or psychological) demand. For example, one student may enjoy sitting in the first row in the class for attracting the attention of the teacher, whereas another student may feel shy and afraid of the teacher and likes to sit in the last row. So they perceive an imbalance between the demands placed on them and their ability to meet those demands.
3. **Stage III—stress response:** The third stage of this process is the individual's stress response to a perception of the situation. It may consist of increased emotional arousal and physiological changes in the case of state anxiety. If the perception between demands and response capability of someone becomes imbalanced, they may feel threatened, increased worries are aroused, and moreover, heightened physiological activation will result.
4. **Stage IV—behavioural consequences:** The fourth stage of the stress process is the actual behavioural consequences of the individual. If people perceive an imbalance between their capability and external demands, naturally their performance will deteriorate.

Sometimes, it so happens that the final stage of the stress process takes an individual back into the first stage. If a student becomes overtly threatened and performs poorly in front of the class, the other children may laugh, and this negative social situation becomes an embarrassment for the child and then an additional demand on the child (Stage I) is put.

This model delineated between stress as an environmental influence mediated by one's perceptions and anxiety as the cognitive manifestation of stress. There are four advantages to this model (see Box 7.2).

> **Box 7.2:** Some Important Points of McGrath Model of Stress
>
> 1. Stress is the outcome of events, which leads to a specific kind of behaviour.
> 2. Stress is viewed in a circular condition.
> 3. Stress may be considered as both negative and positive.
> 4. The stress is the result of both a person's perception of the situation (P) and the situational demands put on them (S).

REACTIONS TO STRESS

Different people have different ways of reacting to strains and stresses. Some people show an increase in physiological and emotional arousal, while some others exhibit significant physical symptoms, and many others may exhibit anxiety. Some other persons may develop some deviant behaviours or serious behavioural disturbance. High level of stress, however, clearly results in too much emotional arousal. So stress is the result of many dimensions of our lifestyle and environment. There are physiological, cognitive and behavioural responses to stress, which can be discussed as below:

1. **Physiological reactions:** In the physiological type of responses, the effect may be an increase in heart rate, elevation of blood pressure, muscular tensions, slowing down of digestive system and release of adrenalin and noradrenalin hormones. There will be a headache and a backache.

2. **Behavioural reactions:** The behavioural reactions become more acute, for example, decrease in performance level, avoidance of stressful situations and passivity/inertia. There are changes in performance, poor concentration, forgetting and becoming unsociable.
3. **Cognitive reactions:** The effect of the cognitive responses are distortions of thinking, decrease in intellectual functioning, unproductive, ruminative, anxiety generating patterns of thought and indecisiveness. There is a feeling of helplessness and hopelessness and low level of tolerance. There is a low level of adaptability to new situations due to mental blockage.

Stress produces behaviour that deviates momentarily from the normal behaviour that reflects the presence of some symptoms, which include muscular tremors, stuttering, performance shifts, increased reaction time, erratic performance rates, malco-ordination and fatigue. Different individuals react differently to the sources of stress that are due to the environment.

Many people give different types of reactions to stress, for example:

1. They feel frustrated or anxious, happy or excited and bored or depressed.
2. The cognitive and perceptual aspect of their world varies from situation to situation.
3. Such persons may experience a mental burden.
4. They may be too much sensitive to criticism.
5. They may face difficulty in concentration.
6. They may respond to stress cognitively and emotionally.
7. They may face some problem in the social group.

Psychological stress creates mental pressure, emotional disturbances, distress, ego threat and arousal. The emotional responses are sadness, anger, irritable, frustration, excited, anxious and bored or depressed. The reaction to environmental demands includes: (a) emotional responses, that is, sadness, anger, irritability and frustrative response and (b) behavioural reaction, that is, changes in performance, poor concentration and forgetting.

SOURCES AND CAUSES OF STRESS

Sources of stress or the situations that cause stress are known as stressors. There is a long list of potential stressors, which may include many sources, for example, use of drugs, not doing physical exercise, marital discords, failures in examinations, job-seeking problem, having children problems at home, ageing, disease, excessive eating, insufficient sleep, unsuccessful in winning a lottery, unable to buy a house and so on. Many of these stressors represent changes that can occur in personal life.

There are many causes of stress. Some are external factors that come from our environment, while others are internal. Some are physiological, and some are based on individual personality. The following are major causes of stress:

1. **External factors:** External factors are caused by the interaction between persons and social environment. The obvious external stressors are crowding in the urban area, besides noise and air pollution in the environment, the threat of nuclear war at the international level and the high rate of climatic change. Physiological causes of stress include erratic food and diet, wrong posture, including ergonomics, heat or cold, and light and so on. Moreover, social problems that produce stress are discrimination among people on the basis of caste, creed and religion, economic conditions and bureaucracy. Traffic jams, waiting for a bus or train, appearing for competition for jobs and insecurity on the job are all examples of social stressors.
2. **Personality and stress:** Much of the stress we experience is caused by our personality characteristics as well as different thought patterns and perceptions. The way we think, perceive and feel can increase or decrease to stressors. How we perceive the different events and experience them is often determined by our personality traits. There are individual differences so far as personality characteristics are concerned. So we react differently to various situations in life. Those who are more sensitive to life events, they are more stress-prone, while others are not as they can act to reduce negative thought processes and stress

responses. Developing a positive attitude towards others will help us to manage stress.
3. **Type A and Type B personality:** The personality type of individuals affects their reactions to stress and becomes a cause of stress. People with Type B personality traits tend to be relaxed, and contemplative, while those with Type A personality are likely to be rushed, aggressive, highly motivated and involved in doing several things at one time. Type A people tend to be more sensitive, sometimes in an aggressive manner that disregard and antagonize other people. It has been found that people with this personality (Type A) are more prone to stress as well as heart attacks.

Another personality style is called anxious reactive. People who are anxious reactive, tend to think the worst in any situation and go into depression. Their reaction to a stressor is to worry, which creates more anxiety leading to a chronic state of stress. Some people are more prone to stress from the combined effects of home, college and social commitments.

Besides, there are many physiological, biological and situational (life events) causes of stress, which need to be discussed here:

1. **Biological sources of stress:** Stress may be observed and measured through its physiological responses, and certain biological characteristics may predispose individuals to high anxiety states. Among the parameters frequently employed for such assessment are heart rate, blood flow, sweat production and muscle tonus. Selye (1982) conceived stress as the unsettling of the body's delicate homeostasis resulting from any demand. Stressors can be chemical, climatic, physical and bacterial.

   Selye gave the concept of general adaptation syndrome, which includes non-adaptive changes, for example, (a) adrenocortical changes, (b) modification of muscles tone, (c) heart rate, hyperactivity and (d) blood content and gastrointestinal function, (d) physiological malfunctioning, that is, headache, backache, high blood pressure, insomnia and so on and (e) cognitive level, that is, thinking level, feelings of helplessness and hopelessness. Due to these, the organism consciously or unconsciously initiates some physiological responses, which are called the flight or fight reaction. The body's nervous system and hormones naturally prepare up to fight or flee the approaching threat.

The physiological symptoms of stress may be enumerated as (a) headache/migraine, (b) insomnia, (c) lack of appetite, (d) digestive disorders, (e) coronary heart disorders, (d) sexual disorders and (e) temperamental changes.
2. **Situational causes:** Stress has become a part and parcel of everyday living. Stress is an unavoidable consequence of modern life. With the invent of technological advancement in this age, there is a rise in industries, overcrowding in the urban areas due to overpopulation and many other kinds of problems in day-to-day life are some of the reasons, which can be counted as reasons for the increase in stress.

There are many stressful life events, which may cause strains and stresses in an individual, for example, the demise of the life partner, a separation which leads to divorce, marital discord, death of close family member or friend, injury in an accident or serious illness, retirement in the service or loss in business, theft of some valuable article, sexual problems, son or daughter leaving home and even sometimes marriage if it is broken, later on, trouble with the in-laws family and so on. There may be many other events such as disease, trauma, heat, cold, thirst and fatigue, which can all be the causes of stress. Similarly, there may be many other events which cause stress, for example, marital discords, failures in examinations, job-seeking problem, having children problems at home unsuccessful in winning a lottery and unable to buy a house.

CONSEQUENCES OF STRESS

Stress has various consequences physically, psychologically and socially. It has many effects on physical, mental and social health of a person. Let us discuss its various ramifications on the life of a human being:

1. **Physical health:** Stress affects physical health adversely. It leads to an increase in the frequency of minor or major physical diseases. Individuals who are under stress are more likely to have severe headaches, backaches, stomach aches and chest pains and so on. These are minor physical illnesses. But stress can also cause major illnesses. People under stress are more likely to have many risk factors such as slow pulse rate fast or slow heartbeat or difficulty in breathing. Blood pressure also rises with the onset of stress, systolic going beyond 140 and systolic beyond 90, which is quite dangerous. All these factors cause physical disorders such as heart diseases and diabetes. Stress is a major contributor to ulcers, arthritis, drug and alcohol abuse. Stress decreases longevity. It shortens one' life. Stress not only leads to major illnesses but also contributes directly to life-threatening disease.
2. **Psychological well-being:** Stress has a marked impact on mental health and psychological well-being:
   a. Stress leads to anxiety. Individuals have fear and worry about how they will deal with threatening situations.
   b. Stress causes frustration. When people are not getting what they desire, they feel frustrated. They may become irritable, nervous and lose their temper over trivial matters. They may develop a negative attitude towards others as they start finding fault with everything.
   c. People go into depression. When they are frustrated, they often become sad and fearful. They may become pessimistic and lose their self-confidence and self-prestige as they feel depressed.
   d. Many people may develop suicidal tendencies. For many reasons, many people may be unable to cope with stressful events and all other negative aspects of their life. So they decide to die and commit suicides.
   e. Other psychological effects of stress are tension, anxiety, irritability, boredom and procrastination. There are changes in an individual's attitudes and disposition due to stress.
3. **Performance:** Stress may also have a negative effect on an individual's performance. If the stress persists for a long time, performance

begins to decrease. If the stress continues, their physical and emotional energy gets exhausted. They may have trouble in sustaining concentration. Due to stress, there are changes in an individual's attitudes and disposition.

STRESS AT WORKPLACE

Stress is likely to occur in everybody's life, whether they are working in an office or as a labourer in some farmhouse. In these days, stress is increasing in all types of jobs, especially in the corporate world. In business, there are always ups and downs due to the fluctuating conditions of the market.

Stress is a part of one's professional life, but too much stress brings miseries in the life of an employee. Job stress can be defined as the physical, emotional and behavioural responses that occur when employees perceive an imbalance between the demands put on them and their capabilities and capacities or resources to meet those demands. In simple words, it can be said that it is the physical and psychological reactions that may be given adversely. Stress arises when there is conflict between requirements of job demands and how an employee perceives them and reacts to them.

In fact, job stress arises from the working conditions/environment of an organization. Job stress has become an important issue for maintaining the mental and emotional health of an employee (Box 7.3).

Box 7.3: Effects of Job Stress

1. Stress puts physiological and psychological effects adversely on employees.
2. Stress is a major cause of employee burnout and alienation.
3. Stress is contagious. Stress on one employee may affect the health of other employees.
4. By managing stress, an organization can be helped in minimizing stress on employees more effectively.

The job stress is due to the negative environmental factors and is caused due to work overload, role conflict and poor working conditions. It may be caused by some other factors, for example:

1. Work environment (physical hazards, pollution, noise, extreme heat, cold and humid condition),
2. Change in working hours
3. Time pressure
4. Work and responsibility
5. Overload and monotony
6. Demotion, change in shift pattern or transfer
7. Qualitative changes in job
8. Job complexity
9. Ambiguity about future
10. Inequality or under-utilization of abilities
11. Marital disharmony and disturbing life events
12. Stressful life events like loss of loved ones on the job
13. Loss of self-esteem
14. A threat to status, goals, health and security
15. A threat to the organism, through disease, trauma, fatigue and so on
16. Emotional arousal

Other causes are (a) inappropriate attitude towards failure, (b) belief that one is incompetent, (c) the attempt to accomplish too much in too little time, (d) sensitivity to the feelings of others and (e) undue promotion of the junior.

Job stress results from the interaction of the employee and the conditions at the workplace. It is employees' response to an organizational work environment that threatens them physiologically, mentally and emotionally. The employees' stress level increase with an increase of imbalance between job demands and their capacities to meet those demands. Job stress results in low and adverse organizational performance.

Job stress is increasingly becoming a significant cause of economic loss in the organization due to employees' low performance and productivity. Job stress may produce both overt physical and mental distortion. An individual with job stress is likely to have job dissatisfaction, increased frequency of habit of drinking and smoking, which may create negative psychological symptoms with reduced aspiration level and self-esteem.

SOURCES OF JOB STRESS

The various stressors can be grouped into four categories: individual, group, organizational and extra-organizational, which have been described below:

1. **Individual stressors:** There are many stressors at the individual level, which may be categorized in the context of their personal life. These are (a) life events and career changes and (b) role characteristics. They are given below:
   a. **Stressful life events and changes in career:** Stress is produced by several changes in life and career. Stressful life events have been reported among young people between 20 and 30 years of age. It has also been found that stress is more prevalent amongst city people than village people. Stress has also been more even among educated people. Due to lifestyle changes, there may be changes in professions, which may be in the form of promotion and demotion, transfer and separation. These life events may cause stress in life.
   b. **Role characteristic:** Stress may be due to either of role conflict or role ambiguity. Role conflict is caused due to the conflicting of two or more roles on the account of job tasks, resources, rules, policies and other people. When people become members of any club, voluntary organization, work organization and so on, they are expected to play different roles and also to fulfil certain duties and obligations. But in most of the cases, the different roles may have conflicting demands due to different roles and statuses when people experience stress because they are unable to perform their jobs well. Another source of job stress is the role of ambiguity or have confusion about their roles in which people are not clear about their duties and expectation to perform. It may be due to inadequate knowledge or misinformation for the job.

2. **Group stressors:** Group stressors affect human behaviour. Therefore, some factors may cause stress, which is related to group processes. The main group stressors are as follows:
   a. **No cohesiveness in the group:** Group cohesiveness is very much needed for the satisfaction of the needs of individuals in group situations. When these are not being fulfilled, they lead to stress. The lack of group cohesiveness becomes a source of stress as they get negative responses from group members.
   b. **No social support:** When members of the group do not get social and moral support from other members of the group, they are under stress. When they do not get social support, it is stressing for them.
   c. **Conflict:** Any conflict among the members about the interpersonal and social relationship in the group may become a cause for stress for them, as it may be the conflict among the group members. For example, in an office, two officials who are working together as a team, may differ on some points and while discussing that point may start quarrelling with each and break up in a friendly relationship with each other, and they would not be able to work together efficiently. It may cause stress and affect not only their relationship but also affect their family members.
3. **Organizational stressors:** Stressors may also exist in an organizational context. The major organizational stressors are as follow:
   a. **Organizational policies:** Unfavourable and ambiguous policies of an organization may affect the group functioning, and members of that group may experience stress. Thus, ambiguous job description, frequent re-allocation of duties, rotating work shifts on a daily basis, unclear procedures, rigid rules, inequality of pay and salary as well as wages and bonus and so on work as stressors.
   b. **Organizational structure:** The structure of the organization provides formal and informal relationship among members of an organization. The organization which does not provide an opportunity to the members for group participation have fewer chances for the members in decision-making, lack of opportunity for growth and promotion, and moreover, if there

is a conflict among the staff members etc. these all work as stressors because relationship among individuals and group does not work effectively.
  c. **Organizational processes:** Faulty organizational processes, such as miscommunication among members as well as members and boss, poor and inadequate or negative feedback of work performance as well as conflicting roles, may affect the unfair organizational system, which may be one of the causes of organizational stress.
  d. **Physical condition:** Physical facilities provided to the members of an organization affect work performance. Due to poor physical conditions such as lack of space and accommodation, crowding and lack of privacy, lack of provision of toilets and washroom, excessive noise, excessive heat or cold, air pollution, safety hazards and poor lighting produce stress on employees.
4. **Extra organizational stressors:** Sometimes, events happening outside the organization also work as stressors. These are called extra-organizational stressors. Thus, social class conflicts, community conditions and so on work as stressors. Not surprisingly, there are a number of major stress factors which are parallel to those found in other occupations. For example, 'time pressure' and working conditioning are two such factors.
  a. **Work environment:** If the work culture in the organization is not conducive one, for example, when the workload is too light and under stimulating or it is too heavy and burdensome may prove to be one of the sources of occupational stress. Fears of retirement, no promotion, organizational changes or transfer can create pressure and anxiety. Stress at work expressed as illness and absenteeism cost both the worker and employer time and money in increased medical costs and payments. Moreover, work-related pressure can cause headaches, migraines and ulcers or cardiovascular disease (heart attack).

  In order to relieve stress or to cope effectively one becomes alcoholic or drug abuse. Moreover, responsibility, deadlines and no chance to relax on the job can ultimately lead to decreased work efficiency.

b. **Time pressure:** Some people's sense of urgency and competitiveness drives them to go faster and faster. Type A personality individuals tolerate too much stress in the environment for too long; they have heart attacks because they have reached the stage of emotional exhaustion and burnout.
c. **Life cycle events:** They can entail stress, because:
   i. Marriage is exciting but also stressful.
   ii. Parenting is rewarding, but subsequent responsibilities can cause stress.
   iii. An adolescent's problems in adjusting to adulthood can be stressful for parents.
   iv. Divorce is a stressful experience.
   v. Death of a friend and loved one can be stressful.
   vi. Life crisis includes psychic trauma, breakdown of social network and occupational stress.

Stress is accompanied by many of life's important events, even enjoyable ones. Because stress is often unavoidable, proper management of stress is important.

EFFECTS OF JOB STRESS

During the high level of stress, as well as low level of stress, the performance on any job is affected badly, and it is very low, but at the optimum level of stress (in the case of eustress), the performance is maximum. It is a kind of inverted U-hypothesis, that is, high- and low-level stress will produce low performance, whereas the optimum level of stress will help in increasing the performance. The ramifications of job stress may be physical, mental, social and personal. These are being discussed below:

1. **Physical problems:** Stress causes physical problems including an adverse effect on the autonomic excitability of nerves, increased heart rate, low pulse rate and a decrease or increases in body temperature. High level of stress produces high blood pressure and high cholesterol and may result in heart disease and diabetes. Now, research is going on to know if cancer is also caused by stress. It has

been found that such serious ailments, however, are not caused exclusively by stress alone, but physical problems of the individuals may also play their roles. These psycho-somatic ailments have a drastic effect on the individuals, their families and organizations.

If an employee has job stress due to overwork or work ambiguity, they can discuss their problems with their officers and get the work divided equally with other officials in the organization. If they have the problem of job ambiguity, they can get the work clarified from the competent authority. They should know what their functions are and what they are expected to perform. If they are having stress due to job conflict, they can understand the whole scenario and try to have a balanced relationship with their professional career and family life.

2. **Psychological problems:** High level of stress may create psychological problems such as anger, anxiety, depression, nervousness, irritability, tension and the individual's ability to cope with stress. The effects of psychological problems of individuals may be changes in mood and other emotional states, lowered self-esteem, resentment, inability to concentrate and decision-making ability and job satisfaction. They may have an adverse effect on productivity in the organization.

The psychological effects of stress are very much disastrous. It may not only affect their mental functioning, but it may change their attitude, their lifestyle and other daily activities. They may develop a negative attitude, animosity with their friends and develop withdrawal behaviour, which is not conducive for their personality development. It may be possible that they may have anti-social behaviour.

3. **Personal problems:** People have personal problems because of the high level of stress. Such problems may be in the form of habits of alcoholism, drug addiction, increased smoking, sleeplessness under/overeating and so on. In extreme cases, when the individual is not able to cope with stress, they may develop suicidal tendencies. At the workplace, people may show behaviour such as obstinacy, absenteeism and turnover. In all these cases, the organization is going to suffer. They may become, suspicious, fearful and aggressive and may develop a paranoid personality.

The other effects of the occupational stress are given in Box 7.4.

Box 7.4: Effects of Occupational Stress

1. Lower productive efficiency.
2. Reduced employee motivation and physical ability to do a task well.
3. Low morale.
4. Increased anxiety and irritability.
5. Adverse effect on employee's family life.
6. To increase the likelihood of heart disease.
7. When stress is chronic, suicide becomes an alternative and strategy for adaptation is required.
8. The feeling of despair such as hopelessness and helplessness are developed.

COPING STRATEGIES

Stress cannot be eliminated, but it can be minimized with some coping strategies as suggested by psychologists so that an individual may be able to lead a normal life. Employees may balance their personal and professional life and coordinate their home life and workplace. Coping strategies are aimed at reducing stress, that is, feeling of discomfort. Some psychologists say that coping is individuals' attempt to respond to the reduced feeling of discomfort. Two common strategies of coping with stress are (a) direct action, whereby the person attempts to master the stressful transactions with the environment and (b) the person attempts to reduce the disturbances when unable to manage the environment.

It is reported that coping styles are responses to the ongoing stressors in daily life. They emerge as taking direct action against the perceived stressors, rationalizing or avoiding the stressors. Effective coping strategies are as follows:

1. Finding out the real issues and search for more information
2. Try to express both positive and negative feelings and have guts for toleration of frustration
3. Seeking help from others in a sportsman spirit

4. Solving problems gradually and effectively and working with others cooperatively
5. Active mastery of feelings whenever possible and acceptable
6. Have the capability for flexibility and willingness to change
7. Self-trust and belief in others and optimism about the outcome is very much important

Eight conceptual categories of coping have been identified, which have the major importance in providing guidelines. The author has himself conceived the following coping categories while working with the Indian athletes at Netaji Subhas National Institute of Sports, Patiala, while serving as a sports psychologist there. They are as follows:

1. Distraction
2. Situation redefinition
3. Direct action
4. Catharsis
5. Acceptance
6. Seeking social support
7. Relaxation and religion
8. Culture and religion

It is mentioned that coping strategies are directed at modifying the stressors, redefining the situation or reducing distress. Lazarus and Folkman (1984) described the idea of coping as referred to response or adaptive strategies, which an individual uses to confront stressors and reduce stress-generating on one's functioning. It was also mentioned that coping responses make an effort to prevent, avoid or control emotional distress. Three functional categories of coping responses have been delineated:

1. Responses to change of situation, which leads to a stressful experience
2. Responses to avoid strain by controlling the meaning of the situation, and
3. Responses to control strain after it occurs.

It has been pointed out that coping is usually an effort to manage stressors when a response is not readily available. People often analyse what is happening to them, judge an event as either threatening or challenging and then determine the magnitude and intensity of the threat or challenge.

The successful coping techniques help in the development of self-confidence, lower anxiety and create a sense of personal growth. Sometimes, coping is made deliberately while sometimes they may be at a reflexive level. It is important here that people living under conditions of psychological stress should be aware of coping strategies that are being applied, which can protect them from the negative effects of stress. Social support has a positive relation to coping strategies.

It has been reported that coping takes place whenever a person faces an event or a situation that requires some special effort to handle it. These are two functions of coping, one function is concerned with regulating emotional response, and the other is concerned with regulating goal-directed behaviour or problem-solving activities. Each one of us serves two types of functions—problem-solving and emotional regulating. The perceived availability of social support has a positive direct effect on problem-focused coping.

A problem-focused function is to solve the stress-creating problem, whereas an emotion-focused function is by means of intra-psychic activity such as rationalization or defence mechanism. Social support resources have a smoothing effect to reduce stressors. The lack of social resources creates a feeling of isolation in individuals, and they lack the capacity to cope with problems. But some moderate level of stress is required to activate the body and mind to perform well and to achieve the set goals in one's life.

Another coping strategy to reduce stress is the practice of breathing exercises. Psychological well-being of a person is related to their normal breathing. If one can control the breathing, mind can also be controlled. When you are feeling calm and quiet, your breathing also becomes normal, which produces a relaxing effect.

Yoga *asana* is another important exercise for a healthy body and stress-free state. A focus on deep breathing is an integral part of yoga, which brings relaxation. Kapalbhati and Anulom Vilom described by Swami Ramdev, a well-known yoga expert of India, are the breathing exercises which are helpful in bringing the relaxation of both body and mind. It has been found that Pranayama or breathing exercise is effective against stress, anxiety and sleeping disorders. They affect both physiological factors (by stimulating the parasympathetic nervous system) and psychological factors (by changing attention from thoughts). Meditation and yoga have been discussed in some other chapter.

According to Jain (2018), 'A breathing exercise called nadi shodhan pranayama (anulom vilom) is a popular yoga practice. It is called cardiac coherence breathing as it has been found that it has helped to decrease anxiety and chronic stress and stabilize the heartbeat.' Other breathing techniques such as Kapalbhati and Sudarshan Kriya (breathing exercises of yoga) have a positive effect on areas of the brain such as amygdale and hippocampus, responsible for emotions, survival instincts and memory.

Many people need both physiotherapy and psychotherapy to relieve the physical and mental ailments as well as the feeling of anxiety resulting from stress. Coping strategies should begin at a biological level. It has been proved that human bodies are affected by stress reactions, including changes in the hormone level, autonomic nervous system activity and the extent of neurotransmitters in the brain.

Many people are in the habit of using either defence-oriented or task-oriented coping techniques. Defence-oriented coping techniques not only reduce stress but also help the individuals to save themselves from bad consequences. They produce positive effects, can minimize distress and allow the people to face difficult situations and tolerate disturbances. But on the other hand, task-oriented coping strategies involve four steps:

1. To know the source of stress
2. To find out an appropriate device for stress reduction
3. To implement the programme
4. To get feedback after evaluating its success

There are certain biological and psychological coping strategies, for example:

1. Relaxation in a quiet environment, with closed eyes, in a comfortable position and repetitive mental device
2. Meditation and prayer with transcendental meditation or yogic exercises
3. Progressive relaxation or autogenic training technique
4. Biofeedback technique with GSR or EMG or electromyograph and so on

Besides the above, other suggestions can also be put forward, for example:

1. Adequate preparation for stressful events
2. Change general attitude towards doing something
3. Provide clear guidelines for coping action
4. Verbal self-instruction.

STRESS MANAGEMENT TECHNIQUES

Stress will remain as long as there is a life. It is always with us at home, at our place of work, in our environment and in our personal and professional lives. As stress is caused from so many different sources and conditions, it is impossible to control it completely, but we can reduce it. To manage the potentially detrimental effects of stress, we will have to change many aspects of our life and modify our lifestyle. For this, we will have to learn techniques and then apply them to reduce external aspect of stress and also to manage our own internal aspect of stress. We should consider some of these techniques, which can be divided into three main categories, namely physiological, behavioural and cognitive, which are discussed below:

1. **Physiological techniques:** Some common physiological reactions to stress include tense muscles, fast heartbeat, faster breathing, increased pulse rate, dry mouth, upset stomach, sweat, rise in

blood sugar level, intestinal disorders and so on. But several coping strategies can be effective and have proved useful. One of the most effective procedures is through progressive relaxation technique as devised by Jacobson, a well-known psychiatrist of the USA. This technique is meant to reduce the tension in our own muscles. To use this technique, we should start by alternately tensing and relaxing our muscles to find out the difference between relaxed and tense muscles. Next, we might take out our arms and then let them relax by our sides. Then, relax the shoulders by slowly taking them up and down. Now, we should relax the neck, step by step, and extend this process until our whole body is completely relaxed from head to foot. Deep breathing is also important. These relaxation exercises are effective in reducing emotional as well as physical tension.

A relaxation technique is an important type of emotion-focused coping strategy. When we cannot change the stressful situation with the task-oriented strategy, we can cope with it more effectively if (a) we are in a calm and quiet environment, (b) we close our eyes gently, (c) we lie down into a comfortable position and (d) we keep on repeating a simple sound to block out negative thoughts. In this way, relaxation exercise can decrease muscle tension, optimize heart rate, blood pressure and rate of breathing. With proper diet, proper exercise and sufficient sleep, we can keep our body in a better form for coping with stress.

Another important technique for coping with stress is vigorous physical exercise. Morning walk with slow running or jogging has proved very useful in some of the cases and has certainly done wonders for many. Of course, physical exercise does not solve the serious problems, which we face at work, but it certainly increases the capacity to cope with the stress and definitely makes one feel better.

2. **Behavioural technique:** There are many other techniques which can be applied to reduce the stress in our lives. If stress is due to overload of work, one method is time budgeting, that is, learning how to make a timetable of work and better organize time. Focusing on a well-planned schedule can help us to do our work

more efficiently and to eliminate behaviour that interferes with our main goals. The main principles of time-management techniques are shown in Box 7.4.

> **Box 7.4: Schedule of Behavioural Technique**
>
> 1. On each day in the morning, you should prepare a list of tasks which you want to accomplish.
> 2. You should make a priority list of the work which you want to do.
> 3. You may plan to do the important tasks first and keep in balance the non-priority tasks for the later part of the day.
> 4. You may try to monitor your schedule to make the best use of those hours when you want to work the best.
> 5. You should be flexible about changes which you make in your daily schedule so that you can handle unexpected events.
> 6. You should also plan for some leisure time activity and hobbies during your day.
> 7. You should try to balance your work and playtime.

In this way, you can get the best out of your day.

3. **Cognitive techniques:** The cognitive techniques are related to thought control processing. The process of replacing negative thoughts of stressors with more positive ones is called cognitive restructuring. To use this technique successfully, you should begin by self-talk—what you want to say to yourself during periods of stress. You may begin to change these thoughts by thinking more positive thoughts. For example, you may try to find out something enjoyable or pleasurable things about the situation or visualize creative ways to reduce or eliminate the source of stress. Family members and friends with their social support can often help you to monitor stressors and perceive stressful events as less threatening and under control. They can help reduce the negative feelings that often accompany stressful events or situations. Friends can provide an outlet for throwing out your stress and can help you to build self-confidence or self-esteem.

Besides the above physiological, behavioural and cognitive techniques of stress management, there are a few more techniques, which can be used for tackling with the stressful life events, for example, delegation, handling criticism, the role of nourishment and many more, which can be easily applied in our life. These are briefly discussed below:

1. **Delegation:** It is just giving power and responsibility of the work to anybody on whom they have full confidence. If officers feel that they are overworked and unable to discharge their duties efficiently and if they are under stress, they can think of giving their power of duty and responsibilities to next junior officers and give them full freedom to take a decision on some matters. The principal of a college or head of any institution can impart their official powers and duties to vice-principal of the college or any other senior-most officer of the institution in whom they have full confidence.
2. **Criticism:** Usually, we are under stress when we face some criticism from others. The criticism from others is unbearable. Criticism may be positive or negative. The positive criticism should be taken in a sportsman spirit and consider it as feedback from others to improve upon the things. But on the other hand, if the criticism is negative and destructive in nature, you should not lose your temper and tolerate it. It is a kind of leg-pulling. Do not give any importance to such types of remarks from others if you are fully convinced that you are right, and others are wrong.
3. **The role of nourishment:** In our life, proper food and diet play an important role in maintaining our physical and mental health. They also improve our immunity, help keep ourselves fit as well as save us from illnesses. Stress affects both our physical and mental well-being. Stress is the outcome of the bad state of physical and mental health. If we eat taking good nutrition daily, there will be no reason that we may not be able to face stressful life events.

CONCLUSION

Stress is a physical, mental, emotional and behavioural response to a wide variety of stimuli in the environment. The concept of stress has physiological, psychological and sociological consequences. The term 'stress' was made popular by an endocrinologist Dr Selye who was the first scientist to use this word, borrowed from Physics, to describe the results of some kind of traumatic impingement on the organism. He theorized the three stages of stress, namely (a) alarm stage, (b) resistance stage and (c) exhaustion stage. Selye (1956) says that 'stress is the process that involves the perception of a substantial imbalance between environmental demand and response capability under conditions where failure to meet demands is perceived as having important consequences and is responded to with increased levels of anxiety.' There are different views regarding stress.

There are positive and negative stresses, which can be classified as eustress or distressed.

Eustress means the presence of a required level of stress in individuals, which may contribute positively to their performance. Distress shows the presence of high level of stress in an individual in a disturbing way, which affects job performance adversely and creates many types of physical, psychological and behavioural problems.

Besides Selye, McGrath (1970) has also proposed a simple model of stress, which consists of four interrelated stages, namely (a) environmental demands, (b) perception of demand, (c) stress response and (d) behaviour consequences.

There are many causes of stress. Some are external factors that come from our environment, while others are internal. Some are physiological, and some are based on individual personality. Besides, there are many physiological, biological and situational (life events) causes of stress. Stress has various consequences physically, psychologically and socially. It has many effects on the physical, mental and social health of a person.

Stress is a part of one's professional life, but too much stress brings miseries in the life of an employee. Job stress can be defined as the physical and behavioural responses that occur when an employee perceives an imbalance between the demands put on them and their capabilities and capacities or resources to meet those demands. The job stress is due to the negative environmental factors and is caused due to work overload, role conflict and poor working conditions. Some of the causes are (a) inappropriate attitude towards failure, (b) belief that one is incompetent, (c) the attempt to accomplish too much in too little time, (d) sensitivity to the feelings of others, (e) undue promotion of the junior.

Stress cannot be eliminated, but it can be minimized with some coping strategies, as suggested by psychologists. Two common strategies of coping with stress are (a) direct action, whereby the person attempts to master the stressful transactions with the environment and (b) the person attempts to reduce the disturbances when unable to manage the environment. It is mentioned that coping strategies are directed at modifying the stressors, redefining the situation or reducing distress. The successful coping techniques help in the development of self-confidence, lower anxiety and create a sense of personal growth. A problem-focused function is to solve the stress-creating problem, whereas an emotion-focused function is by means of intra-psychic activity such as rationalization or defence mechanism.

Some of these techniques which can be divided into three main categories are physiological, behavioural and cognitive. There are a few more techniques which can be used for tackling with the stressful life events, for example, delegation, handling criticism, the role of nourishment and many more, which can be easily applied in our life. Not everybody experiences stress in the same way, and not everybody responds to stress in the same way. However, most people want to reduce their stress. There are many coping strategies which help the people to adjust themselves to stress more easily. In the next chapter, some more techniques and strategies for managing stress and reducing anxiety will be discussed with psycho-regulative techniques.

Psycho-regulative Techniques

INTRODUCTION

The present age is full of various strains, stresses, anxiety, tension, emotional arousal, conflict and other psychological blocks. There are too much pressure and stress on individuals. Everyone in this world faces stressors in some area of life. An individual is making every effort to make themselves adjusted in this stressful environment. They apply some psychological skills to cope with the vicissitudes in their life; otherwise, they will lead a miserable life. So they have to adopt some mechanism to make their life healthy, happy and worth living. Psychologists have devised some psycho-regulative techniques, which help the people to lead a tension-free and stress-free living. Jacobson has given us a progressive relaxation technique through which we can overcome our stress and anxiety. Similarly, Schultz has a suggested self-regulated technique to remove the signs of strains and stress of life. His technique is called autogenic training. Similarly, there are many other relaxations exercises which have proved to be very useful, besides bio-feedback training which is an innovative technique in the field of clinical psychology.

NEED FOR PSYCHO-REGULATIVE TECHNIQUES

In these days of fast life, everybody is suffering from some level of stress, anxiety, depression or emotional upheaval. So they cannot lead a smooth life due to multifarious problems, which remain unresolved. The key issue is how to overcome the daily hustles in this fast life. The inability to effectively cope with the pressures in this competitive life leads to some psychosomatic problems. So the individual has to learn some psychological skills or techniques through which they may make an adjustment with the environment.

Psychologists have found out some procedures and techniques to optimize their emotional arousal, regulate their activation level, to manage their stresses and strains and to control their anxiety level so that they may give their best performance during this competitive life. These devices are called psycho-regulative techniques.

The rationale behind these techniques is that too much stress and anxiety can affect performance through muscle tension. For example, when your muscles become too tense, your movements appear inappropriate, awkward, jerky, rigid and uncoordinated. Moreover, high levels of anxiety can also produce negative thoughts. Have you ever had the experience of becoming anxious, distracted and thinking negative thoughts before or during an important performance?

With arousal control, psychologists should consider a variety of techniques. One management strategy is not likely to succeed for all. For instance, perceptions about physiological fluctuations (somatic) may require a reduction in autonomic activation and muscle tensions, worry about a forthcoming competition and personal performance (cognitive) require interventions that may change one's assumptions, attitudes and thinking. Hence, these stress-management techniques should be specific to the task; because desirable levels of arousal for optimal performance vary according to the task and the personal attributes of the performer. Many different interventional programmes to enhance performance by managing anxiety or stress have been examined by researchers in an effort to assess their effectiveness.

Here, we will discuss some relaxation procedures commonly used in life situations.

PROGRESSIVE RELAXATION TECHNIQUE

Jacobson's progressive relaxation technique has become very important and popular in these days, which has attracted the attention of psychologists for their research work as well as for applying in the modern relaxation procedures. This technique is being used in most of the modern clinics for reducing tension. This technique was devised by an American physician Edmund Jacobson in 1938, which was meant for the reduction of residual muscular tension in people whose tensions were negatively influencing their normal functioning in their lives in some way or the other. Jacobson named the technique progressive relaxation because the tensing and relaxing progress from one major muscle group to the next until all muscle groups are completely relaxed. The term progressive refers both to the increased level of relaxation and tension. This technique has been improved much over the years, but its objective was to help people learn to feel the tension in their muscles and then be able to overcome this tension. His original array of muscle groups is often modified so that less time is needed to learn the procedure.

Using electromyography equipment, Jacobson observed that high levels of anxiety and stress are incompatible with deep skeletal muscle relaxation. Muscular tension is a consequence of the body's preparation to deal with a stressful situation. So he developed a technique to show subjects the difference between tense and relaxed muscles and to help them get rid of residual tension. This technique involves tensing and relaxing specific muscles. The tension-relaxation cycles develop one's awareness of the difference between tension and lack of tension. After learning this skill, a person can detect tension in a specific muscle or area of the body, like the neck, and then relax that muscle.

Procedure

The following steps are suggested in this technique:

1. First of all, the subject is instructed to sit comfortably and remove or loosen tight-fitting clothing. The subject is asked to close their eyes gently and direct their attention to breathing since deep rhythmical breathing is relaxing and has a neutralizing effect on the autonomic nervous system stress response.
2. Then, the subject is directed to tense the body's large muscle groups, beginning with the hands. Major muscles groups are tensed and

relaxed in response to instructions such as 'Clench the hand, hold it, hold it, feel the tension, feel the tightness and now relax.' Permit the muscular tightness to escape and let the hand relax.
3. Now, muscles of the neck, face, shoulder, abdomen, legs and feet are tensed and then relaxed. During each tension and relaxation, the subject is encouraged to observe the difference between the two conditions.
4. After a number of practice sessions, the tension part of the procedure is abandoned, and the subject is asked to directly relax a particular muscle group. With practice, the subject is able to relax all major muscle groups simultaneously in just a few seconds.

Essentially, this technique involves placing the individual in a comfortable position and then helping him to gain an awareness of the exact degree of muscular tension in their whole body, in various parts of the body and particularly in the head and neck region (Cratty, 1973a). In this technique, the individual is, first of all, asked to tighten all their muscles as hard as they can and then following a period of relaxation, they are again told to tighten their muscles half that hard, then again one quarter as hard as they can and so forth until the individual can contract their muscles the amount they wish. The procedure also includes asking the individual to contract to varying degrees, muscles in specific parts of the body.

The first few sessions of progressive relaxation will probably take up to 20–30 minutes. With practice, less time is required. After three or four practice sessions, you might be able to relax within 5–10 minutes. When you can achieve relaxation regularly within 10 minutes, you can omit the muscle tension component. The main objective of progressive relaxation is to learn to completely relax in a short time, which can be extremely valuable in many activities.

Jacobson thinks that there is a direct connection between the muscular systems to the emotional state. Hence, this technique can be usefully applied to people who can use it on themselves because it has been assumed that peripheral muscular tension adjustment affects internalized emotional and physiological states. It is believed, however, that these methods do offer some help, particularly to those individuals whose emotional states are reflected by excessive muscular tension.

AUTOGENIC TRAINING

The autogenic technique is a modification of the previous technique called the 'progressive relaxation' technique. It is one of the techniques, which was originally developed and devised by a German psychiatrist, Johannes Schultz in 1950. This technique consists of a series of exercises designed to produce physical sensations, specifically of warmth and heaviness. It was extensively used in Europe but less in America. It was later revised by Schultz and Luthe (1969). Later on, this technique was adopted by many psychiatrists, psychotherapists and sports psychologists.

Basically, it is a method of self-genic, and it is a mental technique because attention is paid on the sensations a person is trying to produce. As in the relaxation exercise, it is important to allow the feelings to happen without any interference. Accordingly, the autogenic training programme is based on six hierarchical stages, which should be taught in the following order:

1. Heaviness in the body parts
2. Warmth in the body parts
3. Regulation of heart activity
4. Regulating breathing
5. Feelings of warmth in abdominal
6. Feelings of cooling the forehead

Starting with the statements such as 'my right arm is heavy,' 'my left arm is also heavy' and 'my right arm is warm and relaxed' are all examples of commonly used verbal cues given to the patient in this programme. But it takes a long time to respond properly because the person has to learn this exercise thoroughly. It usually takes several weeks or months of regular practice, 15–30 minutes per day to become proficient, experience heaviness and warmth in the body parts and produce the sensation of relaxation, quietness and warmth with a change in the heartbeat and respiratory rate in the whole body and coolness in the forehead.

Muthiah (1980) says,

> In Europe, coaches developed under the supervision of sports psychologists special technique called 'Autogenic Training' to adjust activation levels in a specific way. This was developed primarily for psychotic patients and has been found to be useful for athletes to adjust their tension levels just before the competition. It can be used for individuals suffering from either too high or too less tension.

Individuals adopt the following procedure either to increase or to decrease the tension level. First, they are placed comfortably in a lying position. They are then suggested to concentrate on their breath and its depth while breathing deeply. Then, they are asked to tighten and release their different muscle groups alternatively. This alternative relaxing and tightening is performed three or more times. After this initial practice, they are asked to concentrate on their various body parts and to try to relax them as much as possible.

They are then asked to make their arms too heavy to be lifted, which is repeated with legs, abdomen and chest. This suggestion to relax may be repeated until they gain complete relaxation. Moreover, they are asked to ignore their surroundings and to concentrate on their different body parts. The psychologist may lift their hand to see whether they are relaxed or not by dropping it on the floor and by observing whether they lower it slowly or it falls suddenly by its weight.

After this initial relaxation training, they are suggested that their limbs are becoming warmer and warmer. This suggestion is repeated several times involving the different parts of the body until they experience a real feeling of warmth. It may also be suggested that a warm wave is passing from the head to the foot and from foot to the head. The statements such as 'my left arm is heavy,' 'my right arm is feeling heavy,' 'my left arm is warm and relaxed,' 'my right arm is also feeling warm and relaxed,' 'my heartbeat is regular and calm' and 'my forehead is cool' are all examples of commonly used verbal signals in the autogenic training.

At this point, they are suggested to often sleep lonely. If the purpose is to activate them to a level appropriate for the competition, then they are again asked to tighten their muscles and to think that they are in the competition. This is repeated until the psychologist feels that they have gained the desired level of activation. It is a common belief that the person returns after first relaxing to an appropriate level suitable for optimal performance.

According to Cratty (1973),

> This method emphasizes concentration on the muscular and autonomic function as well as on the mental state. The individual is asked to relax in various ways and also to imagine his limbs or his abdominal area growing warmer; he is helped to regulate his heart rate and respiration rate, and he is asked to visualize various body parts 'becoming heavier'. This method also includes other instructions for self-regulation of mental state, including requesting the individual to imagine himself in various states of feeling, to visualize other person or concentrate on abstract objects and to experience colors.

Autogenic training is a concentration technique based on three main principles:

1. **Signal response relationship:** This is by concentration to produce a signal such as a mental picture or a sentence or even a single word, which gives rise to an associated response by the body.
2. **Relationship between muscular and psychological tension:** When people become psychologically tense, they also tense their muscles. It is impossible to be psychologically tense and muscularly relaxed. Therefore, people can control their psychological tension to a large extent by controlling their muscular tension.
3. **Principle of generalization:** If relaxation can be achieved in one part of the body, the relaxation will gradually spread to other parts and thus become generalized.

Stages of Autogenic Technique

The autogenic technique is divided into three stages, and each stage should be fully learned before moving on to the next stage.

1. **First stage:** A person should begin by concentrating on the feeling of quietness and on breathing slowly and quietly. It should be done for 10–15 minutes each day for about one week. This concentration on quietness will gradually produce an associated response from the body.
2. **Second stage:** After concentrating on a feeling of quietness for three–four minutes, the person should now concentrate on a feeling of heaviness. First, they should begin by concentrating on the right arm feeling very heavy and relaxed. This stage of the training will last one–two weeks. They should not be surprised if the arm actually begins to feel heavy to the extent that it may feel difficult to lift it. At the end of the session, they have only to concentrate on the arm feeling normal again and perhaps tense the muscles. When this stage of the training is complete, the feeling of heaviness should be extended to include the left arm, right leg and left leg. The total session will now last 15–20 minutes. By the end of about one month, they will be able to concentrate quite on the feeling of relaxation and heaviness in all four limbs.
3. **Third stage:** After first concentrating for about five minutes on quietness and heaviness, the person should also begin concentrating on a feeling of warmth. They should proceed in the same way similar to the second stage. Now, the arms and legs may become a few degrees warmer. Here again, if they concentrate on everything is normal, it will be so at the end of the session. This stage will take about one month to achieve competency. Each session should last about 20 minutes. It should be noted here that its effect will not happen overnight, and so it must be done regularly. But in the early stages of training, it is best to practice every day and to do so in a quiet and relaxed atmosphere may be in a bedroom either sitting or lying down with the eyes closed.

When all the three stages of autogenic training are completed at each session, the basic technique has been learned. Most people will take two or three months to reach this stage. The next step is to make the technique become automatic by continuing with a daily session of about 20 minutes for a period of two months. Once this has been achieved, it becomes unnecessary to go through all three stages each time. Concentration on only the first stage (e.g., quietness) will be sufficient to set all the stages in motion. It is not necessary to have quiet surroundings to practice, and hence, it becomes possible to use the technique in competitive situations.

Psychological Preparation

The autogenic technique should be used in combination with physical activity, which is a part of the pre-event warm-up programme for psychological preparation in life. This can be done in the following ways:

1. The person should have fairly hard physical arm-up exercises for about 20–30 minutes.
2. They should then remove the sweat with a towel and change the kit if needed. Then, they should use the method of autogenic relaxation training for about 20 minutes.
3. At the end of this session, they should spend about five minutes on a mental rehearsal of the event, especially if the event requires a high level of skill. Massage can be used during this session and then relaxation.
4. Then they should do a light physical warm-up exercise of 10–15 minutes, especially mainly for those events requiring strength, power or endurance.
5. Finally, they should do about five minutes of mental concentration on the coming event. They should not only concentrate mainly on the positive aspects of doing well in the event but also on any other technique that may be required.

Autogenic training can also be used to help bring the peak performance for very important events. Although for peak performance, physical conditioning of the person is considered very essential, psychological preparation has also become very important in these days, and autogenic training is an important part of the psychological preparation. To ensure peak performance when required, one should use autogenic training (Box 8.1).

> **Box 8.1:** Application of Autogenic Training
>
> 1. This technique should be used every day three or four weeks before the event.
> 2. Before the skill training starts, one should have a 15 minutes session daily.
> 3. After the training session, another autogenic session of about 10 minutes should be used.
> 4. During the second session, one should concentrate on the positive aspect of the possibility of improving on the previous personal performance in the coming event.
> 5. If the event is in the evening, the second session of autogenic training can be done just before going to bed.
> 6. For all other occasions, one should continue to use autogenic training at least once a week to ensure the retention of the ability to go through the routine automatically.

Effect of Autogenic Technique

The autogenic technique has two main training effects. First, it can bring the muscular and psychological relaxation of the person. Second, it will bring the tension level of the person to the optimum level prior to the event. Besides these uses, autogenic training can also be used to provide psychological rest to help build up nervous energy, for example, before an important event, people could use it. It can also be used several hours before the event so that they do not become tensed up too soon. Finally, it is believed that improvements in performance may be possible by using this technique.

There are a few limitations of the autogenic technique. First, learning of this technique takes a long time. It usually takes several months of regular practice, 15–30 minutes per day to become proficient in order to experience heaviness and warmth in the different body parts. Second, it also takes a long time to produce the sensation of relaxation, calm and quietness, warmth with changes in heartbeat and respiratory rate in the abdomen as well as coolness in the forehead. Third, many people have not reported positive results regarding this relaxation technique and hence could not become very much popular in America.

The author of this book, while serving as a sports psychologist at Netaji Subhas National Institute of Sports, Patiala, during 2000–2002, worked as a team psychologist with Indian athletics team as well as Indian women hockey team. He had the applied autogenic technique on the players as a part of mental training in order to reduce their competitive anxiety and found useful results. The mental exercises consisted of 5 minutes of Shavasana as a relaxation exercise, 10 minutes autogenic training for making the muscles tense and relaxed, 5 minutes for visualization as a mental rehearsal and 2 minutes for self-talk for developing self-confidence.

BIOFEEDBACK: A TECHNIQUE OF STRESS MANAGEMENT

Biofeedback training is a method of teaching participants to regulate organic responses to a variety of stimuli, stressors as well as those that result from stress reactions. It enables persons to learn to control different levels of muscular tension, arousal or other unpleasant effects of stress. Biofeedback is a technique of making involuntary bodily processes perceptible to the senses in order to manipulate them by conscious mental control. It ordinarily involves an electronic monitoring machine that can detect and amplify internal responses. They provide visual or auditory feedback of physiological responses such as muscle activity, skin temperature or heart rate.

This feedback is typically associated with bodily functions such as heartbeat, muscle tension, brain wave activity, blood pressure and peripheral skin temperature. The electrical charges emitted by the function of any internal organ (e.g., heart, brain, stomach, etc.) are sources of feedback about the organ's function. Many of the chemical events occurring in the neurons of the brain generate electrical signals. In 1875, Robert Caton published the electric currents of the brain, which documented in the first recording of the electrical activity from outside the brain of an animal.

Biofeedback is based on cognitive behavioural treatment procedures applied in medical settings. Feedback from a measuring instrument that gives information about a biological function is called biofeedback.

The instrumental conditioning principle that behaviour is moulded by its consequences finds its echo in the feedback notion, and all kinds of rewards, punishment and knowledge of results have been labelled as feedback.

According to the operant conditioning principle, antecedents and consequences determine the behavioural aspect of a person on which applied behavioural analysis is based. As against this viewpoint, the cognitive behavioural perspective holds that human learning is cognitively mediated. Biofeedback is a window through which an individual can observe these internal bodily processes. Biofeedback instruments monitor one or more of these internal bodily functions and translate these activities into information, normally audio and visual, used in the learning procedure. The desired result of this learning existence is for the individual to gain a degree of mastery over a monitored body function. This frequency leads to clinical improvement in associated psychosomatic, psychological or neuro-muscular disorders.

In biofeedback training, the equipment measures, amplifies and translates or transposes personal physiological data into displayed and interpretable information through visual, auditory or sensation feedback modalities. Data may be displayed as beeps on a screen, buzzers or some other sound source or any other mechanism that is perceivable. With regard to stress management, the important thing to realize is that the stress stimuli themselves are not removed or decreased through biofeedback training, but the subject's response to them is controlled.

In the biofeedback technique, the subject assumes responsibility for modifying the intensity or frequency (pattern) of the visual or auditory display. The subject understands that the frequency or intensity of feedback data corresponds to an increase or decrease in the organ's activity. Awareness of bodily functions is developed, and attempts are made by the subject to somehow regulate or change the displayed information. The subject uses cognitive techniques (thoughts, ideas, imagery, etc.) until they find one that effectively changes displayed function.

BREATHE CONTROL (BY BREATHING EXERCISES)

Breath control is another physically oriented relaxation technique. Breathing, in fact, is one of the easiest and the most effective method to manage anxiety and muscle tension. Deep breathing is often considered good for achieving relaxation. When you are in a relaxing position, your breathing is likely to be smooth, deep and rhythmical. But when you are under tension, your breathing is likely to be short and irregular. For this reason, in some rehabilitation clinics, deep breathing exercises are taught as rhythmic breathing is important to maximize the effectiveness of stretching and lifting movements. By inhaling, they are instructed to take oxygen from the outer environment, while exhaling, they are asked to throw out their fatigue, tension and boredom from their body.

It has been found that breathing in and holding your breath increases muscle tension, whereas breathing out decreases muscle tension and brings relaxation. Some athletes have learnt to exhale audibly each time they perform. Unfortunately, as pressure builds in a competition, the natural tendency is to hold one's breath, which increases muscle tension and interferes with the coordinated movement necessary for maximum performance. Hence, deep breathing is very essential in our ordinary life. If you take a deep, slow and a complete breath usually, it will bring a relaxation response. When you are in stress and under tension, deep breathing exercise is very important.

The advantages of these breathing exercises are that they will help you to maintain your calmness and manage your anxiety during stressful times. By concentrating on your breathing, you are not likely to focus on irrelevant cues or distractions. Deep breathing also helps to relax all muscles; it allows you to feel strong, centred and ready for action. Finally, deep breathing provides a short mental break from the pressure of work and can renew your energy.

RELAXATION RESPONSE: A KIND OF MEDITATION (MENTAL RELAXATION)

Relaxation exercises are some of the techniques for controlling anxiety and stress. Some relaxation procedures focus more directly on relaxing the mind and body. The reason is that relaxing the mind will, in turn, relax the body. Herbert Benson, a physician at Harvard Medical School, popularized a relaxation technique that he called the *relaxation response* (Benson & Proctor, 1984). Benson's method applies the basic elements of meditation, but it does not include any spiritual or religious aspect. Benson (1975) describes a naturally occurring relaxation response considered as opposed to the fight or flight reaction in human beings. This state, involving the decreased activity of the sympathetic nervous system, results in reduced oxygen metabolism, respiration rate, heart rate, blood pressure, and muscular tension.

Benson advocates teaching to the people to achieve a restful state by sitting quietly in a comfortable position with eyes closed and muscles relaxed in a calm and quiet situation as deeply as possible. In order to encourage the natural relaxation response, the person is instructed to direct their attention to the breathing rate and to repeat a word (such as 'Om') during exhalation for about 10–15 minutes. They are asked to maintain a passive attitude and permit relaxation to occur.

Many people have used meditation knowing that it improves their ability to relax, concentrate and become energized. However, it has been found that the effectiveness of the relaxation response results in enhancing performance. The state of mind produced by meditation is the outcome of keen awareness, effortlessness, relaxation and focused attention. The relaxation response requires four elements as shown in Box 8.2.

Box 8.2: Mental Relaxation

1. There is a need to have a calm and quiet place where the distractions and external noises are minimum.
2. You should sit in a comfortable chair or lie down on a bed and be in a comfortable position.
3. You should select a word such as 'om' and repeat the word while breathing out. Every time you exhale, repeat the word. You should concentrate on one word.
4. If something comes to mind, you should avoid it and focus on your word and try to continue to refocus your attention on your word.
5. Think in your mind that while inhaling, you are taking oxygen in your body, and while exhaling, you are throwing out tour fatigue, anxiety and tension from your mind.

Relaxation response takes time to learn. You should practice it for about 15–20 minutes a day. You will find out how much difficult it is to control your mind as it wanders again and again. You should try to focus on one thought or object or any one point on your forehead. The relaxation response teaches you to quiet the mind, which will help you to concentrate and reduce muscle tension.

RELAXATION TRAINING

Relaxation training is one of the most popular approaches used by some people to manage stress (Harris & Williams, 1993). This procedure is referred to as a mental state or physiological response (Lavey & Taylor, 1985), and relaxation training is part of many currently used stress-management techniques. Relaxation training refers to maintaining heart breathing and metabolic rates as well as a decrease in blood pressure.

Psychologist Jones (1993) has provided four phases of the relaxation training:

1. **Phase I:** The first phase involves about 10–20 minutes of recorded instructions through the tape-recorder or your mobile in which the person generally learns the exercises of the relaxation response. It consists of (a) concentrating on breathing, (b) on breathing, use a mental device of repeating the word 'om' or some other single word on each exhalation, (c) listening to music for relaxation, (d) counting down from 10 to 1 on each exhalation and (e) counting up from 1 to 7 on each inhalation. After two sessions of this form of relaxation exercise, the person practises using the recorded message at least once in a day for the next two weeks. In this way, they will be able to achieve a deep state of relaxation.
2. **Phase II:** During this phase, the period of relaxation is reduced to approximately five–seven minutes. Here, the person continues to listen to the recorded instructions on their mobile or smartphone, but after sometimes, the music is stopped and the mental device

of 'om' is changed to 'relax'. In addition, the counting procedure is also changed downward from five to one and then up from one to three. The person does this exercise daily for two weeks. During the second week, they also practise five-minute relaxation without the help of the recorded instructions. By the end of the second week, they become proficient at reaching the optimum level of relaxation procedure.
3. **Phase III:** During this phase, the person tries to concentrate on each inhalation and silently says 'relax' to themselves on each exhalation. While they do this, the relaxation technique is reduced to approximately 10–20 seconds, requiring four or five breaths. They are now using a relaxation technique. They should now feel that they are relaxing.
4. **Phase IV:** The fourth phase is the practice session. The person practices the relaxation technique as much as possible during this phase. They get their quick relaxation response, which is simply to focus on some point on the forehead and to relax as much as possible. They may use this technique in some other situations also. Now, they should bring the feeling that they are fully relaxed.

Relaxation may be considered a human response that is located on a continuum at either end by sleep or over-arousal. Some relaxation techniques employ active participation where subjects concentrate on their breathing and thus restrict awareness of physical and mental stimuli. Other approaches require subjects to be acutely aware of all stimuli entering their consciousness.

ROLE OF MEDITATION, YOGA

Meditation and yoga are Indian techniques for overcoming stress and anxiety in our ordinary life. They are also useful for the improvement of the self, which can change the attitude and widen the nature of the learners at different stages of life. To study the ways to strengthen the development of self through meditation and yoga, let us discuss with reference to the terms as follows:

Meditation

Meditation is that heightened stage of the human being where all murky blackness which shadowed reality is washed away and where all clouds that hide the sunshine are blown off, and reality in its true pristine glory shines forth.

Meditation does not mean 'samadhi' only. For some thinkers, to meditate means to think and to contemplate. Actually, meditation is an individual's innate nature. According to Shoonyo Ji Maharaj, 'Meditation is transcendence into a sublime state of no-body, no-mind, no-intellect, no-heart, no-ego, and no-form --a blissful state where there is full consciousness, full knowledge, full freedom, and full liberation.' The steps involved in the development of self through meditation are mentioned as follows:

- Withdraw attention from the outer being, external influences and senses.
- Contemplate and focus the attention on the inner self as a point of light/energy radiating positive waves.
- Afterwards, concentrate the attention on higher power/supreme being and feel the energy waves flowing into the inner self.
- Finally, realize as the practice becomes matured.

Meditation generates the power to respond more effectively to the people and the circumstances. It increases the ability to concentrate, which ultimately enhances the creativity to be effective in problem-solving. It is good to refine the intelligence of spirit because it is related to three distinct way of knowing, that is, sensory, intellectual and contemplative. Sri Sri Ravi Shankar asserts that meditation improves and balances the physical, mental, emotional and spiritual spheres of a man.

Yoga

Yoga is a systematic and regulated way of life. The word *yoga* literally means *union*. The union means it brings one to the ultimate reality where individual manifestations of life are clearly felt, and we are able to know the ultimate nature of the existence. It plays an important role in physical mastery as well as in all the domains of life.

The practice of yoga can be performed by individuals of all religions. The very useful benefit of yoga is that it increases the intake of oxygen during the exercises and helps to understand the real worth of the self and to attain the spiritual life. Baba Ramdev's, an Indian yoga expert, yogic exercises are very popular, especially Kapalbhati and Anulom Vilom. How yoga may contribute to the development of self is mentioned as follows:

1. **Encourages patience:** The yogic exercises help in bringing down the heart rate and increasing overall endurance, thereby giving the direction for the right way to live while one practises a challenging posture as it paves the way to learn patience.
2. **Social skills:** Yoga does not affect personal functioning alone; rather, it enhances the ability to socialize also. One learns to broaden the thinking of giving selfless love to others beyond satisfying one's own needs.
3. **Health**: Yoga is also useful in physical and mental health, as advocates the right way of eating that ultimately contributes to good health. Due to the positive effects, many people have started to use yoga as part of their daily living. Many individuals with serious diseases have claimed to have less pain after practising breathing exercises and yogic exercises.
4. **The all-round development of personality:** The practice of yoga not only helps in improving the body's physical aspects but also helps with the spiritual and mental aspects. It means that it helps in the development of the all-round personality of an individual.
5. **Relief from stress and a sense of well-being:** The practice of yoga helps in encouraging relaxation and in bringing down the cortisone levels in the body, causing relief from stress. Yogic exercises are very useful in reducing stress and anxiety, and they are very helpful in inculcating psychological well-being and human wellness.
6. **Improved concentration:** When we learn to perform *asana* and *pranayama*, our breathing becomes long and deep. It leads to improve concentration, greater reaction time and enhances memory skills.

7. **Inner peace**: By following regular practice and a proper diet, yoga helps to realize the inner self that ultimately is a great source of peace.
8. **Transformed of character**: Yoga helps to develop good character and attain public excellence as a result of the disciplined lifestyle.

CONCLUSION

Psychologists have found out some procedures and psycho-regulative techniques to optimize people's emotional arousal, regulate their activation level, manage their stresses and strains and control their anxiety level so that they may give their best performance during this life. In fact, excessive stress/anxiety can produce too much muscle tension, which in turn can affect the performance Physiological fluctuations (somatic) may require a reduction in autonomic activation and muscle tensions and worry about personal performance (cognitive), which requires interventions that may change one's assumptions, attitudes and thinking.

Jacobson's progressive relaxation technique has become very popular these days, which have attracted the attention of psychologists for applying relaxation procedures. This technique was devised by an American physician Edmund Jacobson in 1938, which was meant for the reduction of residual muscular tension in people whose tensions were negatively influencing their normal functioning in their lives in some way or the other. So he developed a technique to show subjects the difference between tense and relaxed muscles and to help them get rid of residual tension. This technique involves tensing and relaxing specific muscles.

The autogenic technique is a modification of the 'progressive relaxation' technique, which was originally developed and devised by a German psychiatrist, Johannes Schultz in 1950. This technique consists of a series of exercises designed to produce physical sensations, specifically of warmth and heaviness. Basically, it is a mental technique because attention is paid on the sensations a person is trying to produce. Accordingly, the autogenic training programme is based on six hierarchical stages, which should be taught in the order as (a) heaviness in the body parts, (b) warmth in the body parts, (c) regulation of heart activity, (d) regulating breathing, (e) feelings of warmth in abdominal and (f) feelings of cooling the forehead.

Biofeedback is a technique specifically designed to teach people to control physiological or autonomic response. It ordinarily involves an electronic monitoring machine that can detect and amplify internal responses. These electronic instruments provide visual or auditory feedback of physiological responses such as muscle activity, skin temperature or heart rate.

Breath control is another physically oriented relaxation technique. Herbert Benson, a physician at Harvard Medical School, popularized a relaxation technique that he called the relaxation response in 1984. His method applied the basic elements of meditation, but it does not include any spiritual or religious aspect. Benson advocated teaching to the people achieve a restful state by sitting quietly in a comfortable position with eyes closed and muscles relaxed in a calm and quiet situation as deeply as possible.

Meditation and yoga are Indian techniques for overcoming stress and anxiety in our ordinary life. Meditation is a heightened stage of human being. Meditation is transcendence into a sublime state of no body, no mind, no intellect, no heart and no ego. Yoga is a systematic and regulated way of life. *Yoga means union*, which brings one to the ultimate reality where individual manifestations of life are clearly felt, and we are able to know the ultimate nature of the existence.

These techniques are quite helping in developing our attention and increasing the concentration ability. So we will study the concept and characteristics of attention, types of attention focus as well as attention affecting attention. We will also discuss some guidelines for improving attention skill and concentration ability.

Attention Skill and Concentration Ability

INTRODUCTION

After studying some important psycho-regulative techniques, which not only help in managing stress and reduce anxiety, but these techniques are also useful in increasing the attention and concentration ability of a person. So it can be said that attention skill is another vital psychological skill for human wellness and successful performance. Superior performance is done when persons are in the optimal psychic energy characterized by attention and concentration being directed totally at performing the skill. Focusing on attention is required for people when they get ready to perform for some action and when they evaluate actual performances. Even in sports competition, a brief loss of concentration can mar the total performance and affect the outcome. So we will have to study how to effectively cope with the pressures of competitive situations and to maintain concentration despite momentary setbacks, errors and mistakes. Thus, two terms, that is, attention and concentration are used interchangeably.

Attention should not be considered as power, capacity or faculty of our mind, which can be switched off or on at will or form that can be given to this or that situation. But we should understand it in terms of an act, a process or a function. It should be considered as a process involving the act of looking at or concentrating on a topic, object or event for the attainment of desired results.

CONCEPT OF ATTENTION

Attention is the process that comes to our consciousness and leads to awareness as soon as information becomes available to our senses.

At every time, our sensations are bombarded with various stimuli from the environment. When we are aware of these sensations which we are experiencing at every time in our life, we perceive them and give interpretation to them. Perception is the process of giving meaning to our sensations and also knowing objects, persons and events. Perception occurs only when we attend to our senses. The process of decision-making requires attention to what we perceive. Thus, attention is a cognitive process whereby a person directs and maintains awareness of stimuli coming from the different senses. Attention is influenced by the person's level of alertness and capacity to process the incoming information on the basis of sensations.

If we do not attend to the stimuli in our environment, we do not perceive them, and hence, we do not experience them. What we experience is limited entirely where we direct our attention. Attention mechanism exerts ultimate control over our ability to perceive sensations and manage psychic energy by regulating the sequence of events that constitutes our awareness. If you can attend to all the relevant stimuli for the task, you are performing well. Moreover, you are more likely to perform optimally and experience the flow state of mind.

Csikszentmihalyi (1975) states that the flow occurs only when attention is focused totally on the relevant factors for executing the task. One is experiencing flow which can occur in two ways: (a) when the task demands full attention and (b) when people control the attentional process so well that they can direct their psychic energy totally into the task. The flow occurs by participating in tasks that attract one's attention.

Now, the question arises how to shift attention as needed and how to intensify one's attention and concentration, which are important psychological skills essentially for performing optimally.

CHARACTERISTICS OF ATTENTION

The following are the characteristics of attention:

1. **Selectivity:** Attention is a selective activity of the mind. It represents a narrow field of awareness. It helps in our consciousness of our environment.

2. **Instability:** Attention is unstable and short-lived. It may be called shifting or mobile, that is, it fluctuates from one object to another very rapidly.
3. **Purposiveness:** It is with some purpose that we concentrate our attention on an object. The more meaningful is the purpose, the more intense the attention.
4. **Presence of effort:** Both physical and mental energy is used as a result of attending to some task. It needs more effort on the part of an organism.
5. **The aspect of mental activity:** Attention implies all the three aspects of mental activity, that is, cognitive, affective and conative.
6. **Newness:** Attention is always attracted to new things. Concentration provided by the process of attention helps us in a clear understanding of the perceived object.
7. **Motor adjustment:** Attention leads to motor adjustments, automatically in our bodily postures.

TYPES OF ATTENTION FOCUS

The latest research reveals that there are many types of attention focus, which are useful in many activities. The most applied research on the role of attentional style was conducted by Nideffer (1976) who considers attentional focus along two dimensions, which are as follows:

1. Width of attention (broad versus narrow)
2. Direction of attention (internal versus external)

1. The width dimension refers to how many stimuli the person should attend. There are two types, that is, broad and narrow in width. A broad attentional focus allows a person to perceive many occurrences simultaneously. This is particularly important where persons have to be aware of many events and sensitive to a rapidly changing environment. On the other hand, a narrow attentional focus occurs when you respond to only one or two events.
2. The direction of attention dimension refers to whether attention is focused inwardly on the one's thoughts and feelings or outwardly

on the events happening in the environment. An internal attentional focus is directed inward on our thoughts and feelings, whereas an external attentional focus directs attention outward on an object such as on another person.

By combining width and direction of attentional cues, four different categories emerge, appropriate to various situations. These can be depicted in Figure 9.1.

Figure 9.1 *Nideffer's Two-dimensional Model*

	Broad		
Internal	(2) Used to analyse and plan	(1) Used to assess a situation	External
	Analyse	**Assess**	
	(3) Used to mentally rehearse an upcoming performance or control an emotional state.	(4) Used to focus on one or two external cues	
	Rehearse	**Perform**	
	Narrow		

Select a few skills and analyse them according to this model. Break each skill down specifically enough to clearly assign it a place, as in the following figure:

EXTERNAL

BROAD	(1) Assess	(3) Perform	NARROW
	(2) Analyse	(4) Rehearse	

INTERNAL

On the basis of the above figure, we can deduce four different types of attentional styles, for example:

1. **Broad external style (assessing):** People with this attentional style are able to attend well to rapidly changing situations, taking a lot of information. However, broad-external ones are subject to much information which results when we are unable to decide how to respond to rapidly changing events that are readily perceived.
2. **Broad internal style (analysing):** These are thinking process when people plan everything in their heads and they are quick to make tactical adjustments to the situations and skilful at analysing the activities of their opponents and making anticipatory responses.
3. **Narrow external style (performing):** This style presents problems when the environment changes and decisions need to be made about how to respond to the change. This is the stage of performance.
4. **Narrow internal style (rehearsing):** It is the stage for rehearsing as this style is conclusive for diagnostic purpose when one tries to diagnose performance, but such diagnostic tendencies carry the risk of becoming highly critical self-analysis.

Considering the above-mentioned attentional styles, people must deal with constantly changing external and internal environments. It also requires them to shift and control the width and direction of their attention.

FACTORS INFLUENCING ATTENTION

There are some factors which influence one's ability to shift attention effectively, which are given below:

1. **Attention style:** Many people have developed dominant attentional styles because they experience success with a particular style and become comfortable using it.
2. **Timing the shift:** People not only have to learn how to change the width and direction of their attention, but they also have to learn when to change it. Many errors of attention occur because they shift too slowly or too rapidly from one focus to another.

Through careful observation and discussion with those people who are making these types of errors, we can help them.
3. **Stress:** The width and direction of attention is substantially affected by stress as well as changes in the psychic energy level of the persons. The width of their attention narrows as psychic energy increases, first, eliminating irrelevant stimuli and later under high negative psychic energy or stress, eliminating task-relevant stimuli.

   Not only the high negative psychic energy in the form of stress results in narrowing ones' attention too much, but the stress also causes them to focus their attention internally. They are caught up with their negative thoughts and the analysis of the events, thus not focusing fully on the task at hand. High trait anxious persons focus more internally on self-evaluation and negative thoughts, while low trait anxious ones focus more on task-relevant cues. Thus, stress makes it impossible to shift attention effectively.
4. **Pain:** Another factor decreasing ones' ability to shift attention is when some stimulus is overwhelmingly strong and difficult to push aside. This may be some type of life crisis, creating a great deal of stress, grief or excitement. When these types of events prevail in the minds of people, they will have difficulty shifting attention effectively to the appropriate stimuli.

One powerful stimulus that affects people frequently is pain. Without strong attentional skills, the pain of continuing in an endurance event or the pain of an injury will preoccupy the person. But people with low pain thresholds are especially susceptible to this problem. The skill of redirecting attention away from the pain has been shown to be a highly effective way to manage pain.

Pain is a useful signal to the body that something is wrong. People with low pain thresholds can learn to become less pain-sensitive in endurance events when they can redirect their attention elsewhere.

ATTENTION SKILLS

Now, the question arises how to help the people who suffer from attentional problems. Knowing what to pay attention to, how to shift attention as needed and how to intensify one's attention or concentration are skills essential for performing optimally. People can be taught these attentional skills. Now, we should know how to teach attentional skills to people.

1. **Role of attention in perceiving and decision-making:** Attention plays an important role in the perception of events as well as in making decisions for some problems on life. Once you have perceived the objects or events, then you must make a decision about whether or not you will continue to work on it or only remain aware of them. The process of this decision-making requires attention to what you perceive as it is evident from the following figure:

   Sensation < _____ < Perception _____ < Decision-making

   _____ **Attention** _____

2. **Information processing model:** Attention is a vital aspect of any performance. (Nideffer, 1976; Boutcher & Trenske, 1990). Research has established the existence of two related forms of information processing: (a) control processing requires effort and (b) automatic processing is effortless, quick and efficient.

   Information processing model provides a framework for examining the characteristics of perception, memory, decision-making and attention. Attention is considered as the ability to switch focus from one source of information to another as well as the amount of information that can be attended to any one time. There are three interacting processes in this model: (a) selective attention, (b) capacity and (c) alertness.

   a. **Attention selectivity:** Selective attention refers to the process by which certain information from the internal or external environment enters the information processing system. In any situation, the organism is constantly being bombarded with various stimuli from both internal and external environments. Therefore, the selection of stimuli is necessary. The organism focuses attention on certain aspects that directly affect behaviour.

      An essential attention skill is the ability to select the correct stimuli or cues to which persons should attend from irrelevant and competing stimuli. It is learnt through countless repetition that the decisions are made by the right brain. In the game of cricket; the batsman will have to concentrate on the position of the incoming ball, speed and space of the ball and also to look to the different fielders as well as to their own co-player who has to run after hitting the ball to get a score.

According to Weinberg and Gould (2007),

> Selectivity of attention can be voluntary or involuntary depending on whether the selection is due to the organism or to the actual stimuli itself. Selection can take place in a large variety of behavioural situation, i.e.; an individual may choose to focus 'inwardly' or certain strategies and past experiences or outwardly on a wide range of environmental cues.

Selective attention has obvious advantages; in that, it allows us to maximize information gained from the object of our focus while reducing sensory interference from other irrelevant sources.

b. **Capacity:** The degree to which people respond to their environment depends upon their mental capacity, which is the ability to process the incoming information from their senses. As the environment becomes increasingly complex, capacity may be approached resulting in deterioration in performance. Thus, people need to narrow their attention focus, shift attention correctly in the rapidly changing environment and sustain the attention for the duration required.

c. **Alertness:** Being alert or paying attention requires mental effort and thus is often measured by psychic energy indicators. When the mind becomes tired, it is difficult to combine the psychic energy demanding work involved in executing attention—selecting, attending, shifting and concentration skills.

In the competitive environment, if attention is not directed to the specifics of the task, then the orienting response would keep the person constantly distracted by noise, movements on the sidelines and so on. Besides these external factors influencing what persons attend to through the orienting response, three internal factors greatly influence attention, for example, (a) interest, (b) mindset and (c) ability to screen out irrelevant stimuli.

1. **Interests:** Attention follows interests. A teacher can capture the attention of their students by utilizing this principle. When giving instructions to the students, the teacher should always explain why as well as how to do something. They should explain why they are teaching them a certain skill so that they may know where it fits into the total plan of action and how it will benefit them. They should explain why to increase interest in order to improve attention.

   Students in the classroom are likely to face problems regarding their attention. It is essential for the teacher to make practices, which may appeal to their interests to make them have fun, and then their attention can be focused on the plan. A teacher can also enhance attention in practice by letting students select what skills they would like to practice. This gives them a feeling of responsibility and control. It will increase motivation, and the increased motivation directs attention to the source of motivation, that is, practice.

2. **Mindset:** The second internal factor influencing attention is the mindset of the person. Through experience, people can develop a mindset to be alert to certain cues in the environment or within themselves. The technique of *thought-stopping* is based on developing a mindset. It is in fact programming people's minds to detect negative thoughts and quickly stop them.

   Mindsets can be positive or negative. People can learn to attend to appropriate stimuli in the environment and positive internal thoughts, or they can develop mindsets that focus on distractions and their own negative thoughts. Helping them develop constructive and positive mindsets is a very important task.

   When people have excellent knowledge of the correct cues to attend to and what potential distracters to avoid attending, they are able to anticipate events and therefore respond more quickly. Such anticipatory skills as reading the movements of the opponent are essential in highly skilled performance.

3. **Ability to screen out irrelevant stimuli:** Individuals differ in their abilities to screen out various stimuli in their environment.

Those who can screen are less anxious, lower in empathy and more selective in what they respond to as compared to others. They have difficulty in selecting the appropriate stimuli in their environments and shifting their attention from one stimulus to another. They are easily distracted and upset by events. Thus, people who are non-screeners need more help in identifying what stimuli to select and the priority that each stimulus should receive when attention is shifted.

Other factors determining what people attend to is their own will power—the power to direct their attention to what they want—which needs to be developed. Moreover, the orienting response can exert influence on the direction of a person's attention. So we have to examine what persons should direct their attention.

GUIDELINES FOR IMPROVING ATTENTION SELECTIVITY

The following suggestions may be considered for improving the selectivity of attention:

1. The attentional demands for each specific skill should be analysed by the person. They should identify whether the attention should be internal or external and how much broad or narrow it should be.
2. When attention is focused externally, a teacher should teach their students what cues should be attended to and in which order, they should keep the cues as few as possible.
3. When attention is focused internally, a person should attend to positive and constructive thoughts and leave negative thoughts unattended.
4. When actually performing the skill, a person should attend to the present and immediate forthcoming action, not to the past or future.
5. A person should focus on task factors such as form and execution rather than on the score or the pending outcome. They cannot concentrate on two different things at the same time.

6. A teacher should help students develop mindsets about which cues to attend to and which cues not to attend. Then, they can teach them the appropriate responses to these cues.
7. A teacher should teach their students the cues that help them to anticipate certain responses and then analyse when it is appropriate to make anticipatory responses.
8. When learning skills, a teacher should direct students' attention to the feeling and sensation in their muscles as they execute them. Attending these kinaesthetic cues increases the rate at which students may learn skills, and imagery is an excellent means of teaching kinaesthetic awareness.
9. When practising, a person should do attentional-demanding instructional activity early in the practice period when the psychic energy level is high.
10. A teacher should minimize distractions during the learning–teaching process when students are first learning skills, but then later introduce contest-simulated distractions so that they can practice their attentional skills.
11. When the environment contains a great deal of uncertainty, especially when the students may perceive as a threat to their self-worth, the situation stresses them and increases the tendency to be distracted. Therefore, it is helpful to decrease uncertainty.
12. People who are uncertain about their goals and their own self-worth are especially vulnerable to distractions. They should develop stable positive perceptions of themselves.
13. Although uncertainty about persons' self-worth is undesirable, the uncertainty that introduces variety and novelty in practices can keep interest and therefore attention high.

Courtesy: Martens (1987).

Many psychologists have recommended some guidelines which may help to improve the flexibility of attention. Some of the recommendations have been given in Box 9.1.

After selecting the correct stimuli to attend and having the skill to shift attention to these stimuli, they must be able to attend with great intensity, which involves concentration and mental alertness.

> **Box 9.1:** Guidelines for improving flexibility of attention

Some recommendations for helping persons shift attention more effectively are given below:

1. People should be educated about the factors that influence their ability to shift attention.
2. People differ in their attentional styles, and these styles can be measured to identify weaknesses in those attentional skills specifically needed. They should practise attentional exercises in case of weaknesses.
3. Managing stress is essential in helping people shift their attention effectively. The ability to redirect attention is very helpful in managing stress.
4. Attention may be redirected from pain and other powerful stimuli to the right cues when performing the skill.
5. Psychic fatigue impairs the ability to shift attention effectively. Thus, the mind must be conditioned to sustain the attention demanded.
6. People can learn how to shift attention by observing and talking with other persons who have excellent skills.

ATTENTION SKILL TRAINING

The training for leaning attention skills is very important. The following guidelines are essential for the student, which should be followed:

1. Educate the people about the attention process and attention demands.
2. Assess the people's current attention skill using the attention skill test.
3. Compare the people's strengths and weaknesses to the attention demands.
4. Plan a training programme to help each person develop attention selection, shifting and concentration skills. A teacher needs to think of ways to help students select the right cues to attend to shift attention at the right time and concentrate appropriately.
5. A teacher should be ready to have students practise those skills, which they need to develop.
6. Imagery is a vital tool for attention skill development because imagery requires some attentional skill to begin with. So through

imagery, students are practising their ability to direct and sustain their attention on the objects or activities of their mind's choice.
7. Attention skills should also be practised in practice sessions.

Role of imagery: Imagery is especially useful for re-creating the competitive situation in order to identify the cues to attend to and to practise shifting the direction and width of attention as the situation changes. In imagery, the rate at which the situational changes can be slowed down and speeded up as the mind wills it. Imagery also provides opportunities to attend fully to the environmental stimuli without worrying about making the appropriate response.

It is also vital to remember that attentional skills cannot be developed in isolation from other psychological skills. Imagery and stress management skills are especially necessary to improve attentional skills. And as attentional skills improve, they permit the further development of stress management and imagery skills.

IMPLEMENTING AN ATTENTION TRAINING PROGRAMME

Educate, acquire the skill and practice: The learning of skills begins with a teacher educating their students of the attentional demands of the various skills and various activities as follows:

1. To teach people how the attentional mechanism works
2. To identify the specific attentional demands of each skill to be performed
3. To understand which factors cause attentional problems
4. To know that selection, shifting and concentration skills can be developed to overcome these problems

These should be possible if people know that:

1. A person's attention involves three basic skills of selecting the right stimuli to focus on, which involves both the direction and width of attention.

2. The person must be able to shift attention as the environment changes.
3. The person must be able to sustain attention or concentrate as the task, requires, and then the person can begin to analyse many skills for their attentional demands.

CONCENTRATION ABILITY

Concentration is defined as the narrowing of attention, fixation of attention to certain stimuli and sustaining attention on some selected stimuli. It is also called a span of attention. It is the ability to maintain and sustain attention on selected stimuli for a certain period of time. Concentration means focusing, not forcing one's attention on a task. It is like parking the car (mind) at the parking place (some fixed object).

Intense concentration requires a great deal of psychic energy because when we concentrate for any length of time, we feel mentally fatigued and alert. When seeking to improve concentration skills, we try to face the task with fierce mental effort. Concentration is the learned skill of not being distracted by irrelevant stimuli. Concentration means being totally in the present state of mind.

Concentration ability is not starting hard at something. It is not trying to concentrate directly. Concentration is considered as an effortless trial, and it is the attraction of the mind for the object upon which we pay attention. People should park their mind squarely on the task and nothing else. Concentration requires parking the mind. But the question is where the mind should be parked to concentrate. It should be parked in the present. The persons should park it squarely on the task and nothing else.

The ability to concentrate varies among people, some having a greater capacity to concentrate than others. Also, some of them are more susceptible to distraction because their attention-selection and attention-shifting skills are weak. It is important to improve these attentional skills. Concentration can be developed by exercising the mind with tasks that require concentration.

Since concentration requires so much mental effort or since people are unaware of the need to practise this skill, many of them never practise concentrating for the length of time their event takes place. Their concentration exercise is limited to some events. And so persons should also not go without practising this essential psychological skill. In concentration, you become so much absorbed in the tasks that you are not aware of anything else. It is achieving flow by enhancing it when concentration is developed.

Like other psychological skills, concentration ability is developed through dedication, devotion, determination and practice. In competition, brief losses of concentration can deteriorate total performance and even affect the outcome. Thus, it is critical to concentrate throughout the competition, despite potential distractions such as crowd noise, weather condition or irrelevant thoughts.

Concentration ability has two parts:

1. **Paying attention to the relevant cues in the environment:** Irrelevant cues need to be either eliminated or disregarded. The attentional ability is to focus and minimize all extraneous noise and movements which is important for the successful execution of a task.
2. **Sustaining attention focus:** Maintaining and sustaining attentional focus for the duration of the event is a part of concentration.

Hence, the proper attention focus is conducive to good performance. There are two types of attention strategies:

1. **Associative attention strategy:** It is related to monitoring bodily function and feeling such as heart rate, muscle tension and breathing rate.
2. **Dissociative attention strategy:** It is concerned with distraction. This strategy gives the physiological feedback to help deal with the boredom and fatigue of the people, which causes distraction. Fatigue certainly affects concentration. When the body is fatigued, it can be difficult to keep the flow for certain periods of time.

Courtesy: Williams (2006).

GUIDELINES FOR IMPROVING CONCENTRATION ABILITY

The following suggestions are being given for improving concentration ability:

1. As concentration is a more passive process, this skill is improved in part by preparing the mind to concentrate. It involves getting rid of stress—managing psychic energy and stress.
2. Another way to develop concentration is through the use of some routine works. They help reduce uncertainty and decrease the likelihood for distraction.
3. Concentration can be improved through the use of triggers—words or actions that remind people to concentrate. It is too demanding to expect them to maintain intense concentration for the duration of the time they are on the task.
4. Concentration is quickly developed through practice. People should spend time in practice sessions sustaining their attention in exactly the same way they must sustain attention when competing.
5. Staying mentally alert and managing psychic energy during practices and competition will help produce not only razor-sharp concentration but also better attentional selection and shifting skills as shown in Box 9.2.

Box 9.2: Steps for the Exercise of Concentration Training

Step 1: We should start with deep breathing and then focus on our breathing while continuing to breathe normally. For the next few minutes, we should again breathe more deeply and slowly.

Step 2: We should pay attention to what we hear in the surroundings identifying it and then mentally calling it, such as voices of a song or something else.

Step 3: We should become aware of our bodily sensations, like the feeling of something. We should enjoy the sensations, which are occurring in a different part of the body.

Step 4: We should attend only to our feelings or thoughts. Let each thought appear gently. We should try to identify the nature of our thoughts and feelings and also try to remain quiet and calm.

> **Step 5:** When this exercise is over, we should open our eyes gently and slowly. We should try to look to some object across the room directly in front of us. While looking ahead, we should see as much of the room and objects in the room as our span of attention will allow. Gradually, we will narrow our focus by narrowing the mind. In this way, our concentration is likely to be increased.

To practise the concentration, people should not experience psychic fatigue. These events require enormous psychic energy to perform optimally, and if they do not practise concentrating for these extended periods, they are not likely to maintain the attentional focus they need.

Concentration takes so much psychic energy, which the energy management skills are needed. Teachers should help their students to know when to make these changes. When concentration is not managed, people are likely to experience psychic fatigue, which causes all attentional mechanisms to collapse.

CONCLUSION

Attention and concentration are two other psychological skills which we have to learn if we are concerned with human wellness. Attention is the process that comes to our consciousness and leads to awareness as soon as information becomes available to our senses. Thus, attention is a cognitive process whereby a person directs and maintains awareness of stimuli coming from the different senses.

There are four types of attention styles, for example, (a) broad external style (assessing), (b) broad internal style (analysing), (c) narrow external style (performing) and (d) narrow internal style (rehearsing). The factors which affect attention are (a) attention style, (b) timing the shift, (c) stress and (d) pain. Besides these external factors influencing what persons attend, three internal factors which greatly influence attention are (a) interest, (b) mindset and (c) ability to screen out irrelevant stimuli.

Some guidelines for improving selectivity and flexibility of attention have been suggested. The training for learning attention skills is very important for school students. Imagery is especially useful for re-creating the competitive situation in order to identify the cues to attend and practise shifting the direction and width of attention as the situation changes. Suggestions have also been given for implementing the attention training programme.

Concentration is the ability to maintain and sustain attention on selected stimuli for a certain period of time. Intense concentration requires a great deal of psychic energy because when we concentrate for any length of time, we feel mentally fatigued and alert. Concentration is the learned skill of not being distracted by irrelevant stimuli. Concentration means being totally in the present state of mind. Since concentration requires so much mental effort or since people are unaware of the need to practise this skill, many of them never practise concentrating for the length of time their event takes place.

Attention and concentration skills are very much required in the life of an individual. They will help an individual to have self-confidence in their life, which is a very important component of their personality. They are interrelated. So it is very essential to study the concept of self-confidence and how to develop it. The next chapter deals with the nature, concept and development of self-confidence.

Self-confidence as a Skill Area

INTRODUCTION

The skill of attention and concentration ability depends on the skill of self-confidence. In fact, they are related to each other. In this chapter, we will study the nature, characteristics and techniques for improving self-confidence. Self-confidence is one of the important and useful psychological skills which have to be developed. It is a trait of one's personality. Self-confidence is vital to successful performance in life. It is a key to be successful in any activity for those persons who believe in themselves. Many people lack this skill to manage this essential psychological quality though they know its importance. Effective goal-setting skill influences self-confidence more directly.

Self-confidence plays an important role in mental functioning and also achieving success in life. Confidence is that factor which distinguishes between a highly successful person and less successful person. The most successful people consistently show a strong self-confidence and self-belief in themselves and their abilities and potentialities. Many psychologists contend that self-confidence is one of the most important psychological states for success in all activities.

DEFINING SELF-CONFIDENCE

Psychologists define confidence as 'a person's belief that they can successfully perform a desired act.' In essence, self-confidence is your belief that you can accomplish your work completely and also get success in the job. Self-confidence means to have a positive attitude and mental functioning. If you have belief in yourself and feel

Self-confidence as a Skill Area   205

confident in your abilities, then it means everything is alright and going to be achieved.

Vealey (1986), a famous psychologist who has done a lot of work in the area of self-Confidence says, 'Self-confidence is the belief about his or her ability to be successful in performing a desired skill.' He defines confidence as 'the belief or degree of certainty individuals possess about their ability to be successful in life.' Feltz (1988) defines self-confidence as 'the belief that one can successfully execute a specific activity rather than a global trait that accounts for optimism'. Whether confidence exists in both state (i.e., moment) and trait forms (i.e., stable and permanent) is unknown.

Vealey (1986, 2001) originally viewed self-confidence as both a trait and a state. Self-confidence is a social but also a cognitive domain of behaviour, which has both trait and state construct. In fact, state self-confidence is something you may feel today, and therefore, it may be stable or unstable. But on the other hand, trait self-confidence might be a part of your personality, and thus, it is always very stable. Whereas the state self-confidence is for a short-term, there the trait self-confidence is long-term personality construct.

Self-confidence is an expression of a person's self-belief, self-worth and self-sufficiency, which ultimately leads to self-efficacy. It is the confidence in one's ability that one can become competent. Many people think that self-confidence is believing in themselves that they can perform well. Full self-confidence is one's realistic expectation about oneself regarding accomplishing any work and achieving success in that work. Self-confidence is the result of one's unique experiences in achieving many successes in future activity. It is a vital part of one's personality.

Self-confidence is not concerned with people's future expectations, that is, what they expect to do in a future life but with what they realistically expectations, that is, what they are actually expecting in these days. It is related to their innermost thoughts about what they are capable of doing. It is not only pride in what they have done, but their considered judgment of what they will be able to do.

Confident people believe in themselves and their abilities and potentiality. Most important is that they believe in their capability and capacities to acquire the necessary skills and competencies to achieve their success in life. But on the other hand, some low-confident people doubt their abilities whether they would be able to perform a task well or not.

OPTIMUM SELF-CONFIDENCE

Overconfidence and low confidence both are considered bad in taste. What we require in our life is the optimum self-confidence, that is, at the required level of confidence. Optimum self-confidence means confidence which is required in a person to achieve something. It should not be too high confidence or low confidence in a person. Optimum self-confidence refers to a state when a person is in a flow state of mind and they have belief in themselves that they will achieve their goals and that they would work hard to achieve it. It is not necessary that they always perform well, but it is essential that they reach towards their potential. It may be possible that they commit some mistakes and take wrong decisions, and they might lose concentration occasionally. But if they have a strong belief in themselves, it will help them overcome the mistakes effectively and keep them striving towards success. Hence, it is essential that each person should have an optimal level of self-confidence in order to give a top-level peak performance.

Self-confidence has a strong positive relationship with performance. The relation between confidence and performance can be represented by an inverted U hypothesis. Performance of a person with a low level of confidence will be at a low level. Performance goes on improving as the level of confidence increases up to the desired level, whereas a further increase in confidence produces the corresponding decline in the performance. People strive for success in an event at the optimal level of confidence, but they can sometimes become either overconfident or under-confident. It is evident from the following figure.

Optimal self-confidence is a powerful personal characteristic for human beings, but it alone does not give assurance to the persons

Self-confidence as a Skill Area

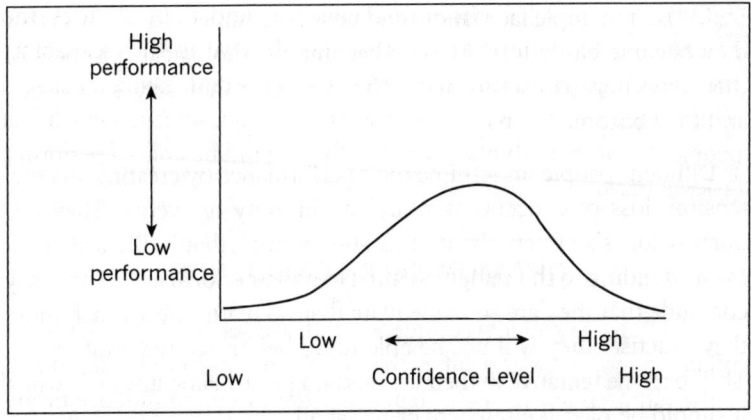

that they will perform well. They should also possess the physical and mental abilities to perform well. Self-confidence and mental competence always work together and helping each other. So strong self-confidence gives a person a powerful tool in tackling problems.

The self-confident persons should have the following qualities which are given in Box 10.1.

> **Box 10.1:** Qualities of Self-confidence
>
> 1. To think positive that any goal you truly set, you should be able to achieve.
> 2. Confidence is gained when it is earned.
> 3. Confidence is earned by working to become competent.
> 4. Confidence is obtained through enhancing your performance, which is achieved by setting realistic goals and striving to achieve your goals.
> 5. Self-confidence is there when one is more skilled and better prepared.
> 6. Think positively but within realistic terms. People should appraise themselves as favourably as possible but check against wishful thinking.

DIFFIDENCE OR LITTLE CONFIDENCE

Opposite to confidence, there is a term called 'diffidence'. Some people have too little confidence; they are diffident. Self-confident ones know mistakes because they know that losing is a part of any event in life.

But diffident people face failure and unsuccessfulness so much so that they become easily fearful. They become psychological prisoners of their own negative self-images. They perceive themselves as losers, and they become losers.

Diffident people undermine their performance by creating anxiety, tension, loss of concentration and uncertainty of events. They frequently focus so intensely on their shortcoming that it distracts them from attending to the things essential to good performance. They may conclude that they are so inadequate that no matter how much more they practise, they will not be able to do better, so they quit trying. They become tentative in their actions and place blame inwardly when it should be placed elsewhere or not at all.

Diffidence means false confidence or lack of confidence or no confidence. Some people may have the physical and mental abilities to be successful in a task, but sometimes due to lack of confidence, their performance is at a low level as they perform under stress and anxiety. So self-doubt, which is diffidence, affects performance adversely. It may lead to stresses and strains loss of concentration and develop indecisiveness.

OVERCONFIDENCE OR FALSE CONFIDENCE

Overconfident persons are actually those persons who have false confidence, that is, their confidence level is higher than their abilities. They develop feelings of superiority and think that the work is very easy, and they will be able to do it with due course of time. This occurs when individuals think that they will do it and to go to achieve it. This is overconfidence which is not required. But when it occurs, the results can be just disastrous as it means overestimating oneself. In fact, it is compensatory behaviour when some people show superiority complex in order to hide their inferiority due to lack of confidence.

False overconfidence is seen sometimes when people attempt to cover their self-doubts. Many teachers encourage their students to be confident when actually they are not comfortable showing self-doubt. Thus, they show overconfidence in order to hide actual feelings of self-doubt. People try to show an optimal level of confidence, but most of the time, they become either overconfident or under-confident.

People cannot be overconfident as their confidence is greater than their competencies warrant. Some of them honestly believe that they are better than they really are. They face disappointment. Some of them who act confident, yet they are actually diffident and worried about failing in life. They believe that this is the way they should act to show to others that they have confidence.

Self-confident people differ from overconfident ones as they distinguish reality from fantasy by accurately judging their abilities and efforts. Overconfident people misrepresent reality, confusing what is with what they wish would be or what ought to be. Self-confident people see hope in their personal efforts to achieve their goals, whereas overconfident ones cannot achieve.

People who do not possess self-confidence often show it because they know how important self-confidence is. False confidence is a psychological myth. The consequence of this is that they try to evade the real reason for their diffidence. They avoid those situations that threaten their self-confidence. They are falsely confident and find it difficult to admit their faults and make excuses, and they will not accept responsibilities for their errors.

SELF-WORTH: A PART OF SELF-CONFIDENCE

Self-worth is a fundamental psychological concept which has a great significance in life. Some teachers enhance students' self-worth. Self-worth leads to self-esteem and gives motivation. Early experiences in life are very important in shaping a person's self-confidence and self-worth. Those who experience early success become more self-confident, feel more worthy and are more motivated to pursue their goals. On the other hand, those who experience failure in life become more diffident and feel worthless. It means that success or failure leads to self-confidence, which increases or decreases self-worth.

Self-confidence can be developed among people who have a positive attitude towards others and better perceptions of their self-worth.

When a teacher encounters students who think poorly of themselves, they will have to help them develop a positive perception of their own worth in order to help them develop optimal self-confidence. A teacher can do three things to help students to develop and maintain wholesome perceptions of their self-worth:

1. Teach the techniques and tactics of skills effectively so that they develop the competencies needed to be successful.
2. Communicate your positive perceptions about your students' self-worth independently of their performance.
3. Help them recognize that the most important source of self-confidence is not performing but their own abilities to become competent.

The most important point in developing self-confidence is that people should possess the conviction that they will always be able to perform well, and they can correct their mistakes by working hard to become something the best in life. Their self-confidence lies in their ability to acquire both physical and psychological competencies.

SELF-CONFIDENCE AND SELF-EFFICACY

Self-confidence is a concept which is often associated with self-efficacy. Self-efficacy is a situationally specific form of self-confidence. It is people's conviction in their abilities to perform certain tasks successfully and also produce a certain desirable outcome. Self-efficacy combines state confidence with self-expectation. People should have a high degree of both self-confidence and self-efficacy. Bandura (1977) who has propounded the theory of self-efficacy defines it as 'beliefs in one's capabilities to organize and execute the courses of action required to produce given attainment.' As such, situation-specific self-confidence is a form of self-efficacy.

'Self-efficacy is the perceived ability to carry out a desired action' (Bandura, 1982). The higher a person's feelings of self-efficacy, the better that person tends to be on a wider range of tasks and higher the self-confidence. The feelings of success may create a more positive attitude which leads to more self-confidence. So self-efficacy is individuals' expectations concerning their ability to perform various tasks. If people say that they can do what they want to do to achieve the goal, their effort and performance will increase. It will add in their self-confidence because motivation will be strongly enhanced.

According to Bandura (1986), 'Self-efficacy cognitions represent the convictions or beliefs that, one can successfully execute a course of action to produce certain behaviour.' So self-efficacy is a kind of situation-specific self-confidence. For example, an individual may feel very confident of their ability to perform some specific tasks, but they may be completely fearful at the thought of public speaking. Bandura (1982) suggests that 'when faced with stressful stimuli, low efficacious individuals tend to give up, attribute internally and experience greater anxiety or depression.'

If we want to develop self-efficacy in an individual, then they must believe that they are in control of the situation, and they will act and perform intentionally. If people believe that they have the ability to produce specific results, they will be motivated to do things happen. In this way, the importance of self-efficacy increases, as people with high self-efficacy are motivated, who will work hard to achieve success because they believe in their successful achievement.

Self-efficacy theory, as advocated by Bandura, provides a sound theoretical orientation to study the relationship between self-confidence and performance. Self-efficacy is a good predictor of performance if one has the requisite ability and sufficient capacity to accomplish the task. Bandura (1977) says that 'Self-efficacy is a set of beliefs and expectations about how capable a person feels in performing the necessary behaviour to achieve a desirable outcome.' High self-efficacy results when the person is likely to be engaged in some activity with more vigour and vitality. Individuals who believe that they are capable of performing the required tasks to meet situational demands will be likely to engage in those activities in a better way.

Self-efficacy is the perception of one's ability to perform a task successfully, and it is related to self-confidence. These two terms are used interchangeably. Psychologist Bandura (1977, 1986, 1997) brought both the concepts of confidence and self-efficacy together.

He redefined 'self-efficacy to encompass those beliefs regarding individuals' capabilities to produce performances that will lead to anticipated outcomes.' In this regard, the term 'self-regulatory efficacy' is now used, which focuses more on one's abilities to overcome obstacles or challenges to successful performances. Hence, Bandura's theory of self-efficacy has formed the theoretical basis for most performance-oriented research in self-confidence (Weinberg & Gould, 2007).

Self-belief about one's ability to perform well in the examination occurs in almost every student. Sometimes, when anxiety state about examination (i.e., test anxiety) occurs too frequently and if it is not overcome at the right time, problems may arise in giving good results. Here, the psychologists suggest the application of self-efficacy model in which people have belief that they can give a successful performance.

There is a relationship between self-confidence and self-efficacy with performance. A number of studies have indicated that higher levels of self-efficacy are associated with superior performance (Morris & Koehn, 2004). Since successful achievements and effective performance are the predictors of self-efficacy, it is understandable that this will enhance self-confidence, and then, in return, these increased feelings of self-efficacy will have a positive effect on subsequent performance. Hence, we find a positive relationship between self-efficacy and performance.

Bandura (1977, 1982, 1986, 1997) proposes four main components which are effective in developing self-efficacy. Each of these components is very important in understanding how a person can develop self-efficacy and self-confidence. They are (a) mastery experiences, (b) verbal persuasion, (c) induced arousal states and (d) vicarious experiences (Bandura, 1997).

1. **Mastery experiences:** Successes in any activity in the past are mastery experiences. They are related to the challenge level in relation to one's abilities. Here, a person is more likely to assess their achievements in context to at a high level of challenge. Confidence is built up with achievements. The mastery experiences mean the previous successful performance. The person must experience success in order to develop self-efficacy. A student must experience

success in case they want to develop self-efficacy. The teacher must help them achieve success; otherwise, the student will believe that they will not be able to achieve success. For this reason, the past performance is the most useful source of self-efficacy.
2. **Verbal persuasion:** Verbal persuasion usually comes in the form of encouraging reinforcement from the teacher, parents or peers. It is a kind of verbal feedback. Positive and helpful verbal statements suggest that an individual is competent and can succeed in the most desirable way. On the other hand, negative comments and statements should always be avoided. A verbal persuasion can also take the form of self-persuasion. This is referred to as self-talk. Verbal persuasion is a positive approach, which usually comes in the form of reinforcement from the teachers.
3. **Emotional arousal states:** Emotional arousals are factors which are workable in self-efficacy. We must understand why we should be emotionally aroused and optimally activated in order to be attentive. Physiological symptoms are responsible to affect behaviour through the efficacy expectation. For example, muscle tenseness, a rapidly beating heart and shortness of breath can be interpreted as signs that one is incapable of physical activity. Alternatively, if these signs are viewed as the body's natural response to stress and they are alleviated with subsequent activity, efficacy is likely to be enhanced.
4. **Vicarious experiences:** Vicarious experience of a person is another component of self-efficacy. Research has revealed that some personal characteristics of the 'model' have an impact upon feelings of self-efficacy. In modelling, the learner first observes a task being performed, and then, they copy to perform the same task. Modelling can be shown on a film or video, which is a source of efficacy being observed or imagined of engaging in the task to be performed.

BENEFITS OF SELF-CONFIDENCE

Self-confidence is very useful in achieving success in life. It can help the persons to develop positive feelings and attitudes, focus concentration, set goals, put in increased effort and maintain momentum. Some of the benefits of self-confidence are as follows:

1. **Positive emotions:** Self-confidence develops positive feelings, emotions and attitudes. When people are self-confident, they are more likely to remain calm, quiet and relaxed under pressure. This state of mind allows him to be assertive, free and frank.
2. **Concentration:** Self-confidence helps to enhance concentration. When people self-confident, their mind is free to focus on the task. But on the other hand, when they lack confidence, they are worried about their performance, and they lose their concentration.
3. **Goals setting:** Self-confidence also affects your goals-setting programme. Confident people tend to set challenging and achievable goals and pursue them actively and confidently. Confidence helps them to reach towards their goals and realize the potential. People who are not confident tend to set low goals and never try to achieve them.
4. **Effort:** 'Self-confidence helps in increasing persistent efforts. But how many efforts someone should attempt and how long one will continue in pursuit of the goal depend largely on self-confidence' (Maddux & Lewis, 1995).
5. **Momentum:** 'Confidence affects psychological momentum, which is referred as shifts as critical determinants of winning and losing' (Miller & Weinberg, 1991) The positive momentum is an important asset for self-confidence, which is an important ingredient in this process. People view those situations as challenges which are called momentum.
6. **Relationship with Performance:** The relationship between confidence and performance is the positive one. According to Feltz (1984) and Vealey (2001), 'the factors which affect this relationship are organizational structure (high school vs. collegiate expectations), personality characteristics, demographic characteristics like gender and age, or affective one (arousal or anxiety) and cognitive (attributions for success or failure) which have been considered to be very important.' All these factors affect whether confidence is too low, too high or just right.

To sum up, according to Gould and Weinberg (1984), 'maintaining high confidence is accompanied by positive emotions (e.g.; elation, excitation, vigor), improved concentration, increased effort, lower susceptibility to mental distractions, reduced muscular tension, improved ability to remember and more rapid and accurate decision making.' Successful people possess and maintain consistently a high degree of self-confidence.

DEVELOPING SELF-CONFIDENCE

Self-confidence can be developed and improved through the following suggestions:

1. **Performance accomplishment:** Success in life gives you confidence and helps to do hard work to achieve more and more. So the successful accomplishments bring you to achieve performance and help you to set new achievable goals. Hence, self-confidence is very important for success.

   A person may feel confident about performing a certain task if they have the ability to do the job. For its development, training and practices can best enhance self-confidence. Performance accomplishments show the most powerful tool to develop confidence, and then, confidence will improve subsequent performance. Hence, we should have those conditions that encourage people to experience success and a sense of achievement in order to develop confidence.

2. **Work confidently:** A person can act confidently if they are likely to feel confident. Working confidently is a very important part and parcel of life. While giving a performance, people should try to show confidence. They can show their confidence by keeping their morale high even during a crisis. It is best to keep your head high to indicate that you are confident and will perform well.

3. **High thinking and simple living:** High thinking and leading a simple life will develop self-confidence. You will have the feeling that you can achieve your goals successfully. A positive thinking and a positive attitude are necessary for having a higher level of self-confidence. Correct technique, encouragement and motivation to perform the task more successfully should be the focus of self-confidence.

4. **Imagery:** Imagery is a psychological skill which always tries to help develop self-confidence. In imagery, you can visualize yourself

doing things in your mind which you have already experienced or have done it earlier. It is a kind of mental rehearsal when you think of the event likely to occur in future.
5. **Physical conditioning:** Physical conditioning is another key to feel confident. Physical training and good nutrition habits help you that you can stay out there as long as necessary to get the task done.
6. **Preparation:** Preparation for any job to be done will give you confidence that you have planned everything possible to achieve success. Planning and preparation are a general idea of what you want to achieve and how you will do it. Good preparation helps you not only in tapping your own abilities but also develop confidence.

As self-confidence is an important component of one's personality in one' life, there is a dire need for its improvement. It is not an innate but acquired trait, which can be learned. Although self-confidence is developed through life experiences, it can be learnt through training. For example, in schools, many students lack self-confidence and often complain that they are unable to remember their lesson in spite of hard work. They can be counselled by school counsellor or teacher by understanding their emotional problems and encourage them to develop the self-confidence. Similarly, in the field of sports also, until the athletes have the self-confidence, they cannot give their best performance and achieve their goals of winning. So the coaches have to increase their self-confidence by mental training. Even the skill of goal setting depends very much on self-confidence ability of an individual.

SELF-CONFIDENCE THROUGH SELF-TALK

Self-talk is a silent talk and a covert exercise in your mind. Self-confidence can be built with the help of self-talk. Self-talk is an affirmative statement that a person possesses the skills, abilities, positive attitudes and beliefs necessary for successful performance. These positive statements must be both believable and practicable. So the development of self-confidence is related to a person's willingness to work hard. An individual must build confidence with a record of success during the tasks to be performed before they feel confident of their capabilities during an actual event. There are a number of factors that could contribute to this situation.

The person could be suffering from some false beliefs about what causes success. For example, the person could believe that their success is due to luck or some external factor or hard work. Another factor could be that the nature of the task changes. An individual may feel very confident of their ability as a student during high school but lose their self-confidence when they go to college.

Sometimes, an individual may feel lack of self-confident in a situation, which will have a negative effect on how well an individual can perform. On this occasion, self-talk can be an effective tool in either increasing self-confidence or overcoming negative thoughts and feelings and replacing with positive thoughts. So self-talk is a useful cognitive technique for reinforcing self-confidence.

Self-talk is the inner dialogue which a person does internally and speaks out silently. It can be in the form of statements or words silently spoken or in the form of thoughts that come into one's mind, but these thoughts should be positive only. Self-talk is a psychological skill for improving self-confidence, which may lead to positive feelings about one's ability. People may speak out internally that 'I will do it, I can do it and I will have to do it.' There are three forms of self-talk which consists of (a) task-specific statements, (b) encouraging and rewarding statements and (c) mood words. These three categories are given as follows:

1. **Task-specific statements:** Self-talk should be in task-specific statements. This type of self-talk refers to positive words or statements that reinforce and build self-confidence.
2. **Encouraging and rewarding statements:** Self-talk should be in encouraging and rewarding statements. This type of self-talk refers to words or statements that provide encouragement for making more efforts and work harder.
3. **Mood words:** Self-talk should reflect the mood of a person. This type of self-talk refers to words that increase happy mood or optimum arousal.

If we want that self-talk should be effective, the following suggestions are put forth:

1. The statements should be brief and grammatically simple.
2. The statements should be logically sound.
3. The statements should be compatible with the correct timing of the task.

ADVANTAGES OF SELF-TALK

Self-talk should be effective for the enhancement of self-confidence. Some of the suggestions which are related to the enhancement of self-confidence through self-talk are being given below:

1. **Self-talk helps in developing self-confidence:** Self-talk is an effective tool which may stimulate thoughts and arouse feelings, which will create the belief that a person is fully competent and can perform a task efficiently and effectively.
2. **Self-talk helps in the acquisition of the self-confidence skill:** Self-talk can be an effective tool in helping the person to acquire a very important psychological skill of self-confidence. In this way, they will continue to work hard to achieve a worthwhile goal.
3. **Self-talk helps in changing mood:** Self-talk helps to change the negative mood to a positive one. Effective use of emotive words in self-talk may either create a desired mood or change the undesirable one. Words and statements in self-talk are powerful stimulators because of the meaning that they communicate.
4. **Self-talk induces controlling efforts:** Self-talk can be recommended to the person for the need to make more effort when it is needed for performance and also for enhancement of self-confidence. Self-talk words and statements can be effective in controlling efforts.
5. **Self-talk tries to focus attention or concentration:** Self-talk is necessary to stay focused or to concentrate on the task at hand. Both attention and concentration are important psychological skills for the enhancement of self-confidence as a skill.

CONCLUSION

Self-confidence plays an important role in mental functioning and also achieving success in life. Many psychologists contend that self-confidence is one of the most important psychological states for success in all activities. Self-confidence is defined as 'a person's belief that a person can successfully perform the desired act.' In essence, self-confidence is your belief that you can accomplish your work completely and also get success in the job. Self-confidence is an expression of a person's self-belief, self-worth and self-sufficiency, which ultimately leads to self-efficacy. It is confidence in one's ability that a person can become competent.

Optimum self-confidence means confidence which is required in a person to achieve something. It should not be too high confidence or low confidence in a person. Optimum self-confidence refers to a state when people are in a flow state of mind, and they have belief in themselves that they will achieve their goals, and that they would work hard to achieve it. People with optimum self-confidence set the most realistic goals based upon their own abilities, capacities and capabilities. Self-confidence has a strong positive relationship with performance. Optimum self-confidence is a powerful personal characteristic for human beings.

Opposite to confidence, there is a term called 'diffidence'. Diffidence means false confidence or lack of confidence or no confidence. The diffident persons undermine their performance by creating anxiety, tension, loss of concentration and uncertainty of events. Over-confident people are actually those persons, who have false confidence, that is, their confidence level is higher than their abilities. False overconfidence is seen sometimes when people attempt to cover their self-doubts. People try to show an optimal level of confidence, but most of the time, they become either overconfident or under-confident.

Self-worth is a fundamental psychological concept which has great significance in life. Self-worth is an important component of self-confidence, which is an expression of a person's self-worth.

Self-confidence can be developed among people who have a positive attitude towards others and better perceptions of their self-worth.

Self-confidence is a concept which is often associated with self-efficacy. Self-efficacy is a situationally specific form of self-confidence. It is the person's conviction in their abilities to perform certain tasks successfully and also to produce a certain desirable outcome. Some of the benefits of self-confidence are (a) positive emotions, (b) concentration, (c) goals, (d) effort, (e) momentum and (f) relationship with performance. For the development of self-confidence, the factors which work are (a) performance accomplishment, (b) work confidently, (c) high thinking and simple living, (d) imagery, (e) physical conditioning and (f) preparation.

Self-confidence can be built with the help of self-talk. Self-talk is an affirmative statement that a person uses for the successful performance of certain tasks. Self-talk is the inner dialogue which a person does internally and speaks out silently. Self-confidence will lead to the development of self as it is an important characteristic of the personality of a person. In the next chapter, we will discuss the understanding and development of self in detail.

Understanding and Development of the Self

INTRODUCTION

Self-confidence plays an important role in the development of self. In fact, self-confidence is a part of self-development. Suggestions, given for increasing self-confidence, help in developing a positive attitude, increasing concentration and accomplishment of goals. Self-development means the development of self-concept, self-image, self-sufficiency, self-worth and self-efficacy.

In a human's life, understanding the self has become very important in order to develop one's personality. PST helps an individual to understand and then to develop the self. Self is the hub of each person's social environment. We develop a social identity that includes how we perceive ourselves, including how we assess ourselves. For each person, this identity includes unique characteristics of life, for example, our name, age, gender and self-concept and many other aspects, which we share with others. Familiar categories include one's relationships such as man, woman, son and daughter; vocation such as student, musician, psychologist, salesman and athlete and political affiliation and attributes that at least some people like or dislike and ethnicity or religion.

These various classes are closely related to our inter-personal world, and they indicate ways in which we like or dislike other individuals. When a person's social environment changes, it puts a strain on their social identity that needs some kind of making an adjustment. Our self-identity, self-concept or self-image is acquired primarily through social interactions that begin with our immediate family members and friends and continue with the other people we meet throughout life. Our self-identity is a special framework that is affected by how we get information about the social environment around us along with knowledge about ourselves, such as our needs and motives, emotional states, self-assessment and abilities or intellectual functioning and so on.

CONCEPT OF SELF

The study of self is the cognitive and affective domain of one's behaviour or we can know about it through our experiences. The concept of self makes the distinction between the self as *I* and the self as *me*. Self as I is the subjective aspect, but the self as me is the subject that is known. The present contention of the self centres around the self as an important part in human motivation, emotion, cognition and social identity. It is possible to correlate cognitive and affective experience of self with other processes of human behaviour.

The self seeks to analyse essential characteristics that constitute a person's unique personality. There have been various measures to define these characteristics. The self can be considered in the context of consciousness, which is responsible for an individual's thoughts and actions or the consistent and persistent nature, habits and skills of a person.

The self is a complex but a core concept in many forms. Usually, two ideas of self are commonly considered, that is, (a) the self that is the ego,[1] superficial self of mind and body and an egoist creation and (ii) the self which is sometimes called the 'true self' or the 'ideal self'.

Every human being has a self as a person is able to see themselves as both subject and object in this world. Fortunately, it puts questions about who we are and also the nature of our own existence. Our religious practices make a distinction between the true self and the false self and perceive the true self positively and false self negatively.

The self is constantly changing due to the complexities of social culture. It has been found that the self is dependent on the culture of

---

[1] https://en.wikipedia.org/wiki/Self-concept

that society where the person is living. There are cultural differences between the Western countries and Eastern countries, especially the Indian culture, which may affect the self and self-concept. The self can be stated as a dynamic and changeable process due to past and present environments, including material, non-material social and spiritual aspects of the cultural patterns.

It is said that the self is shaped by our social, cultural as well as physical environments. An individual's social interactions form the social environment, which is a part of society, and each society has its own culture. If these individuals live in a certain culture, they have to conform to societal norms and standards and also follow a specific culture pattern of that society. That is why culture is important in the development of self and to explore how the self goes and changes. The self is complex and dynamic, and it will be changed according to social influences. The self in any culture takes place for its well-being.

Some experts have given the suggestion that the self acts as an agent in shaping and modifying the reactions of others, but the self is changed by how others react. If these interactive effects between self and other people operate, it is seen that they are even more important in a close relationship such as friendships and marriage. William James (1896) was of this view that while we have a central core self, we also have many different social selves that we express in different people in different social interactions. In this way, we have both specific and general self-concepts. The specific concepts for each individual are related to worker, wife, friend, daughter and so on.

So it can be said that each person's self-identity or self-concept is acquired through interactions with other people. The self operates as a mechanism that determines how we get information about the world around us and about ourselves. The self-effect here means that we get information about ourselves better than any other kind of information from other sources. As the self-concept is not static, so the self-concept changes in response to situational changes. The evaluation of oneself is known as self-esteem. Self-esteem or self-prestige can increase in response to positive experiences.

WHAT IS MEANT BY THE TERM 'SELF'?

Self is a 'co-source of manifest physical reality' (Zohar & Marshall, 2000).

Zohar and Marshall, taking a note of major contributors to the phenomenon of personality/self, proposed a detailed model of self that constitutes the three levels of self. The three levels of self have been symbolized in Figure 11.1 of lotus.

The three layers are expressed as follows:

1. **The outer layer of self:** It represents the personal ego.
2. **The middle layer of self:** It is the symbol of associative unconsciousness.
3. **The inner layer of self:** That is the central bud of the lotus, a central point, which indicates the transpersonal nature of the self.

Human beings generally identify themselves only as physical forms. Of course, they are also identified by terms such as nationality, race, gender and profession. This perception about the 'self' imbibes only the emotions of fear, anger and sadness in life. One's ego or identification

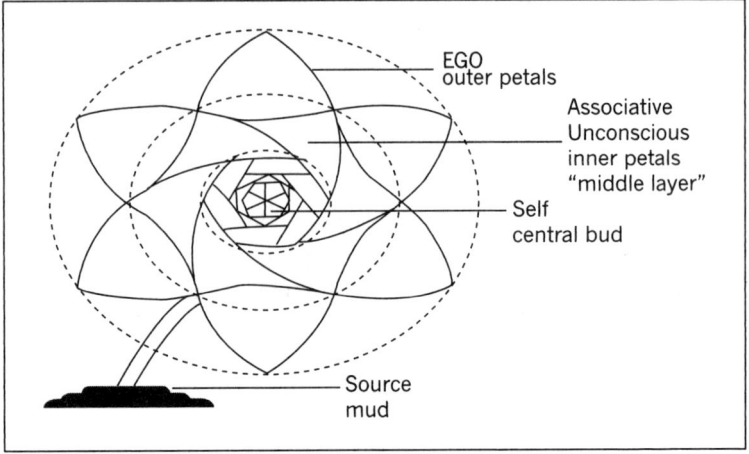

Figure 11.1 *The Basic Lotus of the Self*

Source: Agyajit and Prabhjot (2019).

of the self hides the true human nature, which is peaceful, loving and joyful. Thus, understanding of all the aspects of self may contribute to the qualities of a good life.

The construct of self has been researched by various in terms of self-actualization (Maslow's need hierarchy theory), self-efficacy (Bandura, 1977), self-esteem (James, 1896), self-concept (Carl Rogers & Maslow) and so on. Western psychologists, namely Cattell (1957), Freud (1923) and Jung (1933) and so on are well-known for their work on the concept of self from a different point of view.

J. G. Bennett (1964), who is well-known for his work, *A Spiritual Psychology*, elaborated the concept of self as the material self, the reactional self and the divided self in the following manner:

The material self: It is an instrument which should be used by something else behind it. It is the 'conscious mind'. The character of the material self is, first of all, indifferent, lacks sensitiveness and the tendency to externalized and separate. All these are recognized by looking at any sort of material object.

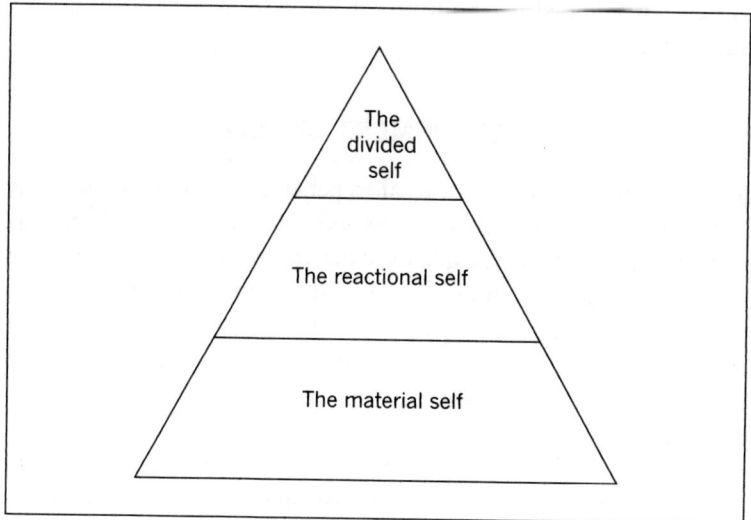

Figure 11.2 *The Symbol of* Me

Source: Author.

The material self is the proper and rightful lord of the material world that is where it has its rightful place. But as soon as it comes out of that world, then it is merely a thing, not to be treated with any more respect than other things.

The reactional self: There is a sensitive nature in an individual as there is material nature. In every situation that we find ourselves or before any complex influences that act upon us, there is always something that our sensitivity shrinks from and something our sensitivity turn towards. It is because of the sensitivity that we are drawn towards some ideas while shrinking away from others. In the sensitive self, it is the reaction, whereas, with the material self, it works by the movement.

The divided self: The point at the top (Figure 11.2) represents the 'true self' of a man. This suggests that we go upwards from the material self to the true self. In reality, we go inwards; there is no higher or lower in the way that the rungs of the ladder are higher or lower.

There is something in us, which is behind the body, behind the sensitiveness and deep down. It is a third way in which we can know ourselves that knowledge is the knowledge of the pattern of our desires and impulses.

DEVELOPMENT OF SELF

Self-development which is also called personal development includes activities that improve self-awareness and self-identity. It builds human relationships, enhances the quality of life, develops potential and talent and contributes to the realization of desires and aspirations. Personal or self-development takes place over the span of a person's entire life. The concept of self includes formal and informal activities for developing oneself and others, especially in roles such as teacher, doctor, nurse, guide, counsellor, manager and coach or mentor. Moreover, personal or self-development takes place in the society, so it refers to the programmes, techniques and assessment systems that support human development at the individual level in society (Aubrey, 2010).

Self-development also includes helping other people to develop. This may take place through different roles such as those of a teacher, doctor or guide or parent either through a personal competency or a professional service.

Self or personal development is a continuous process, starting from the day of birth and continues up to the death of a man. So it is a life-long process. It is a process through which people try to assess their habits, skills and qualities and also consider their aims and purposes in life and set goals in order to realize and maximize their potential. It helps us to identify the qualities we need for setting life goals which can enhance our workability prospects, increase our confidence and lead us to a higher quality life. We should plan to make positive and effective life priorities and decisions for our future to enable personal development.

Self or personal development includes the following qualities:

- Development of self-awareness
- Enhancement of self-knowledge
- Development of self-identity/self-esteem
- Empowerment of strengths or talents
- Improvement of economic or social status
- Inculcation of spiritual development
- To identify one's potential
- To build workability or human investment
- Chang of lifestyle or the quality of life
- Seeking for time management
- Improvement of both physical and mental health
- Fulfilment of desires and aspirations
- Execution of personal development plans
- Improvement of social abilities, and social relations
- Development of EI
- Improvement of skills and also learning new skills

In self-development, an individual often functions as the primary source of improvement. Personal development pattern may include goals that define the strategies or plans for achieving the goals, as well as a feedback system to provide information to change and progress. So self-development depends on self-awareness. So we will have to understand what self-awareness is.

Self-awareness

Self-awareness is the ability to introspect and the capacity to recognize oneself as an individual who is separated from the environment and other individuals. It is looking inside yourself in the thoughts, feelings and emotions for your benefit. It is related to self-concept. It is concerned with self-perception, self-analysis and self-evaluation. But it is different from consciousness. While consciousness is a term given to being aware of one's environment, self-awareness is the recognition of your intrapersonal relationships.

Self-awareness theory was developed by Duval and Wicklund (1972) in their landmark book *A Theory of Objective Self Awareness*. They state that when we focus our attention on ourselves, we evaluate and compare our present behaviour with our internal and covert behaviour as well as our own norms and values. Of course, it displays a state of subjective self-awareness. We try to become self-conscious as an objective evaluator of ourselves. So self-awareness should not be compared with self-consciousness.

Bandura's (1997) self-efficacy theory was devised on the basis of self-awareness. Self-efficacy is 'the belief in one's capabilities to organize and execute the courses of action required to manage prospective situations.' A person's belief in their inner ability is to get success and also to set the stage how they think, feel and behave. For example, someone with strong self-efficacy views tasks as challenges which must be faced boldly, and they should not be frustrated by failures. Usually, they are aware of their strengths and weaknesses and utilize their qualities to the best of their ability. But on the other hand, someone with a low level of self-efficacy does not face challenges and easily feels discouraged by failures. This concept is related to Bandura's social cognitive theory, 'which emphasizes the role of observational learning, social experience, and reciprocal determinism in the development of personality.'

Self-acceptance

According to Shepard (1979), 'self-acceptance is an individual's satisfaction or happiness with oneself' and is considered to be important for sound mental health. Self-acceptance involves self-development and self-understanding, which is a realistic and subjective awareness of one's strengths, weaknesses and limitations. It is the outcome of one's feeling about oneself that one is of 'unique worth'. Self-acceptance can be defined as:

1. Self-acceptance is the awareness of one's strengths and weaknesses.
2. Self-acceptance is the subjective appraisal of one's abilities, capabilities, and capacities.
3. Self-acceptance is the feeling of satisfaction with one's limitation.
4. Self-acceptance is the feeling of self-worth.

In positive psychology, self-acceptance is considered to be as the new concept in the personality construct. It can be achieved by overcoming our weaknesses and then accepting them to be existing within one's self. Ryff (1995) has included self-acceptance as one of the six factors in her model of psychological well-being.

People who are high on self-acceptance have some characteristics as listed in Box 11.1.

Box 11.1: People with High Self-acceptance

1. They will have a positive self-attitude.
2. They will acknowledge and accept all aspects of themselves.
3. They will not be self-critical or confused about their identity.
4. They will not wish that they are different from others.

Self-development among Children

Self-development means developing the life and social skills related to positive interpersonal relationships with friends, family members, peer groups, age-mates and community members. These skills and competencies enable children to have feelings and thinking about what they want to do and also about others who and what would like to do in their lives. Emotional and social development provides children with the capabilities and abilities that they need to have and also to function in order to live in society as well as in the world. There are many different stages in the life of a child about social and emotional development. The personal, social and emotional development consist of the following aspects:

1. **Attitudes and interests:** These are the first and foremost aspect in the development of a child. They are about how children become interested, excited and motivated about their environment. This is only possible if they have positive attitudes towards others in their lives.
2. **Self-confidence and self-esteem:** Self-confidence is very important for everybody, especially for children. It is about having a sense of their own self-worth and self-sufficiency for knowing the significant events in their own and other people's lives. Self-esteem also leads to self-prestige, which helps them to have a positive self-concept.
3. **Positive relationships:** It is essential that the children should develop a positive relationship with all others with whom they come in contact in their environment. It will help in working along with them as a companion as well as getting along with them. It is a quality of having social skill which is worth developing among school children.
4. **Commitment and self-control:** Children should develop the qualities of commitment, control and challenge (3 Cs). It is about how children develop an understanding of what is right and what is wrong and why together with learning about the sincerity of work and the will to do the work. Moreover, they should be self-disciplined. They should always think new tasks as challenging and will have the will power to complete them.
5. **Self-care:** Self-care is regarding keeping oneself physically and mentally fit and healthy. In this way, children will in a sense of self-respect and have concern for their own personal hygiene and care.
6. **Sense of we feeling:** Sense of we feeling means the sense of belongingness with the group to whom they belong. It is concerned

about how children understand and respect their own needs, views, values and beliefs in their culture and also those of other people in their community.

For the children' physical, social and emotional development and well-being as well as their overall health, it is essential that they should be well looked after, cared for and treated psychologically. It will lead to children gaining self-confidence, self-worth and inner strength through emotional attachments with these people.

The positive relationships with others will lead to the growth of self-esteem, self-confidence and self-sufficiency, which promote a sense of belongingness, which allows children to explore the world with a feeling of security and warmth. Children need to set a good example and also have opportunities for interaction with others so that they can develop a positive attitude towards themselves and others. Children who are given the freedom to feel free to express their feelings, such as joy, sadness, frustration and fear, can develop strategies to cope with new, challenging or stressful situations.

To sum it up, it may be stated that children should look smart or appear to be smart to others; it is only possible in a good and congenial environment where they may grow, develop, prosper and blossom, and where they are able to express themselves liberally, think freely and make decisions independently to solve their daily or day-to-day problems amicably. They should be given full freedom to work and learn to face difficulties in their lives.

Self-development among Adolescent

Indian society has its own rich culture and social heritage. It has established its own cultural norms, traditions, taboos and mores which the Indian people have to follow. Due to these, Indian adolescents have to face many problems as they have their own needs, desires and ambitions. They are in conflict whether they should adhere to their own traditional and conservative rituals and standards of society, or they should follow the new and radical way of life, which has been affected by the Western culture. Indian adolescents have the following types of problems and dilemmas of a newly established lifestyle. The following points are the determinants for the development of the self among Indian adolescents:

1. **Sex behaviour:** As the pre-marital relationships are not permissive in the Indian society, Indian adolescent boys and girls have many strains and stresses due to taboos of having sex relationships between them before their marriages. Hence, they become rebellious, non-corporative and anti-social, and sometimes, they commit immoral acts for which they develop guilt feelings in their lives and remain unadjusted socially in the future married life. Here, the school can play a very useful role in channelizing their surplus energy by organizing co-curricular activities, for example, physical activities such as sports and games, hiking and trekking exercises, outdoor activities and excursions.
2. **Unemployment:** Due to unemployment and underemployment in our country, most of the young people are not being placed well in their professional life after receiving graduate and post-graduate education. While studying in schools, colleges and universities, they think about their dark futures due to the prevailing scenario of the society. Hence, they feel frustrated, maladjusted and develop some type of mental disorder and create problems. They prove to be a headache for the parents and elders in the family. Even adolescents are not sure about their future career and unable to concentrate on their studies. The insecurity and uncertainty about their future life lead them in the trap of the wrong company, and they come into contact with gangsters and go astray. So there is a need for an arrangement of personal and emotional counselling by the competent and experienced psychologists.
3. **Drug addicts:** Due to many frustrations at homes and school and later on in their lives, they fall victim to drugs and become addicted to alcoholism and drug abuse. First, when they resort to these bad habits, they find pleasure and solace for overcoming their problem, but later on, they find that they have fallen prey to them; they repent and some of them go in depression. Here, the psychological help

and education are needed, which may be provided by parents, teachers and counsellors.

4. **Conflict with elders:** Due to generation gap, there is always a conflict between the parents and their adolescent children. Parents still believe that they are just children and try to dictate them, whereas adolescents think that they have grown up and want to be independent. Due to these diverse opinions and attitude of parents and adolescents, there is always a conflict between them, which create some problem of interpersonal relationships. For the development of the personality of adolescents, they have to be handled politely and compassionately by the parents and teachers and all those who come in contact with them.

5. **Parental deprivation:** Life in this modern age has become very complicated. As both husband and wife have to work for their livelihood and honourable living as well as for economic reasons, the parents do not have time for their adolescent children. Every child wants love, affection and attention from their parents. When they are unable to get the same at home, they will look forward outside the home from some other person. It is very dangerous for adolescent girls when they find their peer group to reciprocate with them and also to compensate with maternal love. They also try to discuss their new physiological changes, especially sex matters, with their friends, and sometimes, they are misguided and go astray to find the company of some member of the opposite sex and get pleasure from their physical relationships. The parents need to have knowledge about developmental psychology and adolescent psychology.

6. **The value system of the society:** The modern society is heading towards developing a new value system, and it expects from the new generation, especially adolescents, to adopt the new moral values. But adolescent boys and girls come into conflict with the new value system and try to disorganize the system as they blame society for the wrong deeds. In schools, moral and religious education should be taught to the students. In our secular country, it may not be possible to teach the tenets of one particular religion, but the students can be given education about the general ethical value systems.

Self-development among Adults

There are a number of steps for monitoring self-development among elderly persons. They are as follows:

1. **Developing a personal vision:** It is better if adults develop their own personal vision. Self-development cannot be taken for granted. Most of the people, however, may find it easier to motivate themselves to learn and improve if they have a goal in doing so. Developing a clear idea of what they want to be in their life has become a crucial issue. So adults should be clear what they want to do or what they want to be in your life.
2. **Planning for personal development:** Once they are clear about what they want to do, they can start planning how to do them. Developing a personal development programme is essential, but the planning process should be more realistic. If they are working hard to identify which areas should be considered for development and improvement, it will be helpful to know and assess.
3. **Starting the developmental process:** There are a number of different methods through which they can learn to develop. These methods suggest how different types of learning procedures may be more applicable in effectiveness for them.
4. **Keep a record of personal development:** It is very essential to keep a record of the personal and self-development. It is often a good idea to note down the events of their personal development. By writing down the main developments in them as and when they occur, they will be able to retrospect about their successes at a later time.
5. **Revising personal development plans:** It is good if they continue reviewing and go on revising their programmes for personal and self-development. Regular review of the personal development plans and self-development activities will ensure that they learn from their experiences about what they have done and revise the programme if they find that it has not proved useful. It will also ensure that their activities continue to go towards their goals and that the goals remain relevant to them.

Developmental Plan to Know Ourselves

It is a fact that in today's fast life in this busy world, most of our time is spent dealing with many of life's trivial matters and solving our problems that are obstructing our activities. The hard fact is that without a concrete plan of personal development, we will never be able to feel like growing ourselves. We should try to consider asking ourselves the following questions.

1. Do we feel that life is worth living?
2. Are we dissatisfied with ourselves and our life?
3. Have we read all the latest self-help books which can change our life?

If we answer yes to any one of these questions, we are not alone. Many people work very hard to develop. But when we do not know who we are or what we want to do in our life, we miss the opportunities for a meaningful life. If we want something to improve, we need to be clear about what we want. The following plan will guide us to create the right personal development programme for us if we implement it effectively.

1. **Know ourselves:** We should try to develop our personal development plan effectively and successfully. We should clarify who we are and what we want to do in life. In this way, we may feel confident and passionate about our life activities as we clearly identify what matters most to us. It is true that the more we know and express our assertive self, the more meaning, joy and happiness we will have in our life. We should follow the following points.
    - We should clarify our unique characteristics.
    - We should know our life challenges that hinder our ability to succeed.
    - We should identify how we give away our power and status.
    - We should discover what gives us a meaningful and purposeful life.
    - We should know the values that give us strength.

2. **Implement our personal development plan:** We should try to resolve the main issues and problems in our life. We should identify where we want a change in our life and then address those issues. We should try to follow the points given below:
   - **Manage our time:** We should budget our time schedule and make the most of the time of our life useful.
   - **Invest more money, prosperity and abundance:** We should try to make our life purposeful, wealthy and healthy as well as enhance our self-worth.
   - **Maintain healthier relationships:** We should maintain cordial and healthy relationships with others and explore our role in a relationship with the other important people in our life. We should try to find a more satisfying relationship with others.
   - **Develop your creativity:** We should develop our talent and potential and learn 10 easy creativity tools to solve our problems quickly.
   - **Make your life purposeful:** We should make our life meaningful and prosperous and uncover our essential aspects of life. We should try to explore our life purpose.
   - **Develop spirituality:** We should practise daily spiritual and religious prayers and connect with our own divinity.
   - **Identify your own needs:** We should know both our primary and secondary needs and try to fulfil them. It is better if we create our own self-development plan.

Through the process of personal development planning, we will be able to know ourselves and get clear idea about our needs, desires and aspirations. We will be empowered to take charge of our life and to focus on purpose, growth and achievement.

Development of Self through Meditation and Yoga

Meditation and yoga nurture the body, mind, senses and intellect. These attributes contribute to healthy development and also change the attitude towards life by enhancing one's self-esteem, self-confidence and self-respect. Our mind is controlled by meditation, rather than by mere spiritual knowledge. Through meditation, there is an accumulation of energy, which is not possible through knowledge only. The use of appropriate training in improving the self triggers the urge for qualitative thinking and service to humanity. As meditation and yoga help in understanding the meaning and purpose of life, it ultimately would lead to a peaceful life in the world of materialism (Jain, 2018).

POSSIBLE REASONS BEHIND THE TRANSFORMATION OF SELF

Human beings exhibit differences in behaviour due to various life events. The possible reasons that tend to bring changes in their inner selves as follows:

- **Environmental challenges:** Although children are born with certain innate emotional tendencies, as they grow, the basic needs of life impact on them internally to meet the environmental challenges.
- **Experiences:** During the span of life, one learns through *the direct experience*, that is, what one sees, hears or learns as well as *the vicarious experiences*, that is, what one learns from the experience of others.
- **Injuries and accidents:** Major injuries and accidents such as brain damage, head injury and drug addiction also bring physical and chemical changes, which contribute largely to the development of self.

ROLE OF YOGA

Yoga is a systematic and regulated way of life. The word *yoga* literally means *union* that brings one to the ultimate reality where individual expression of life is clearly felt, and in this way, we are able to know the ultimate nature of its existence. It plays an important role in physical and mental mastery as well as in all the domains of life.

The practice of yoga is performed by individuals of all religions. The very useful benefit of yoga is that it increases the intake of oxygen during the exercises and help to understand the real worth of the self and also to attain the spiritual life. How yoga may contribute to the development of self is mentioned as follows:

1. **Encourages patience:** The styles of yoga help in bringing down the heart rate and increasing overall endurance. Therefore, it gives the direction for the right way to live while one practises a challenging posture as it paves the way to learn patience.
2. **Social skills:** Yoga does not affect personal functioning alone; rather, it enhances the ability to socialize also. One learns to broaden the thinking of giving selfless love to others beyond satisfying one's own needs.
3. **Health:** Yoga is also useful in advocating the right way of eating that ultimately contributes to good health. Due to the positive effects, many doctors have started to use yoga as part of the patient recovery programme. Individuals with serious diseases have claimed to have less pain after practising breathing exercises and yoga postures.
4. **All-round development of personality:** The practice of yoga not only helps in improving the body's physical aspects but also helps in the mental, emotional and spiritual aspects.
5. **Relief from stress and a sense of well-being:** The practice of yoga helps in encouraging relaxation and in bringing down the cortisone levels in the body, causing relief from stress.
6. **Improved concentration**: When we learn to perform *asana* and *pranayama*, our breathing becomes long and deep. It leads to improve concentration, greater reaction time and enhances memory skills.
7. **Inner peace:** By following regular practice and a proper diet, yoga helps to realize the inner self that ultimately is a great source of peace.
8. **Transformed of character:** Yoga helps to develop good character and attain public excellence as a result of the disciplined lifestyle.

COMMON TECHNIQUES, STRATEGIES AND PRACTICES FOR DEVELOPMENT OF SELF

An important objective of education is to foster self-reliance and independence. It has been shown that self-development strategies can be used to improve performance, productivity, any task and to help in solving problem behaviour. The development of the self makes one aware about the knowledge of God, life values, character, interpersonal relationship, love and comparison, flexibility, brotherhood, equality of caste/creed, happiness, distress and so on. A number of techniques, strategies and practices that have been identified as beneficial for the development of self through meditation and yoga have been summarized in Box 11.2.

Box 11.2: Techniques for Self-development

1. It is to balance the life, to plan about the goals and to think desires and wants.
2. It is meant to see that your goals, needs and wants are fulfilled, and you may experience the emotional arousal with this fulfilment, look into the inner processes through the use visualization.
3. Its goal is to recognize your connectedness to others, nature, the world and the universe also try to integrate the personal and universal vision.
4. The needs, desires and wants should be fulfilled for which you should take responsibility.
5. Let you connect with more people with your life so that you may develop a sense of community.
6. An open mindset that tolerates uncertainty is beneficial to the growth of the self, whereas a rigid and closed mindset may hinder its development.

CONCLUSION

The study of self is the cognitive and affective domain of our behaviour or we can know about it through our experiences. The concept of self makes the distinction between the self as *I* and the self as *me*. The self seeks to analyse essential characteristics that constitute a person's unique personality. Every human being has a self as a person is able to see themselves as both subject and object in this world. The self is constantly changing due to the complexities of social culture. It is said that the self is shaped by our social, cultural as well as physical environments. So each person's self-identity or self-concept is acquired through interactions with other people.

Self-development includes activities that improve self-awareness and self-identity. It builds human relationships, enhances the quality of life, develops potential and talent and contributes to the realization of desires and aspirations. It is a process through which people try to assess their habits, skills and qualities, and also consider their aims and purposes in life and set goals in order to realize and maximize their potential

Self-development is related to self-awareness, which is the ability for introspection and the capacity to recognize oneself as an individual separate from the environment and other individuals. It is looking inside yourself in the thoughts, feelings and emotions for your benefit and self-concept. It is self-perception, self-analysis and self-evaluation. According to Shepard (1979), 'self-acceptance is an individual's satisfaction or happiness with oneself.' Self-acceptance involves self-development and self-understanding, which is a realistic and subjective awareness of one's strengths, weaknesses and limitations.

Self-development will help people to grow as good human beings. It includes guiding them to find out and accept their life purpose. Self-development means developing the life and social skills as related to positive interpersonal relationships with friends, family members, peer groups, age-mates and community members. The factors which affect the development of children are (a) attitudes and interest, (b) self-confidence and self-esteem, (c) positive relationships, (d) commitment and self-control, (e) self-care and (f) sense of we feeling.

The determinants of self-development among the adolescents are (a) sex behaviour, (b) unemployment in the country, (c) drug addicts, (d) conflict with elders, (e) parental deprivation and (f) value system of the society. The self-development among adults includes factors such as (a) developing a personal vision, (b) planning your personal development, (c) starting the developmental process, (d) keep a record of your personal development and (e) revising personal development plans.

For implementing the personal developmental plan, we should try to follow the points such as (a) manage our time, (b) invest more money, prosperity and abundance (c) maintain healthier relationships, (d) develop your creativity, (e) make your life purposeful, (f) develop spirituality and (g) identify your own needs.

Meditation and yoga play an important role in the development of self. Meditation and yoga nurture the body, mind, senses and intellect. These attributes contribute to healthy development and also change the attitude towards life by enhancing one's self-esteem, self-confidence and self-respect. Some common techniques and strategies for the development of self are (a) it is to balance the life, to plan about the goals and to think desires and wants, (b) it is meant to see that your goals, needs and wants are fulfilled, and you may experience the emotional arousal with this fulfilment, look into the inner processes through the use visualization, (c) its goal is to recognize your connectedness to others, nature, the world and the universe also try to integrate the personal and universal vision, (d) the needs, desires and wants should be fulfilled, (e) let you connect with more people with your life, so that you may develop a sense of community and (f). An open mindset that tolerates uncertainty is beneficial to the growth of the self. Whereas, a rigid and closed mindset may hinder its development.

Self-confidence and self-development which are interrelated are essential characteristics of the personality of a leader. A leader is a person who is a more assertive and popular person in their group. What are the qualities of good leadership? What should be the functions of a leader? What are the different styles of leadership? Who is the most effective leader? What do we mean by leadership behaviour? What type of relationship should be there among leaders and followers? Is there a need for leadership training? There are many other questions which need to be answered. In the next chapter, an attempt has been made to answer all these questions.

Leadership and Communication Skills

12

INTRODUCTION

After studying the understanding and development of self of an individual, we will discuss the concept and characteristics of a good leader as well as allied issues related to leadership styles and so on. In fact, in any type of grouping of individuals, there is always an individual, who is outstanding and who possesses exceptional physique, beauty and other qualities and who leads the group. Such types of people are socially better-adjusted individuals. They know how to get along with their fellows. So a leader is a person who has a unique position in their group in terms of role and status, that is, power and prestige or effective imitativeness.

LaPierre and Farnsworth mention that 'leadership is a behaviour that affects the behaviour of other people more than their behaviour affects that of the leader.' In fact, they lead the behaviour of other individuals. There is a dominance–submission pattern of behaviour. Dominant behaviour is a learnt behaviour among the leaders. In the group structure, they are the people who dominate, direct and influence other people.

CONCEPT OF LEADERSHIP

The leadership is such an affair in which two parties are involved. A leader acts as a model and gives commands to their followers. The co-operation of these two parties is essential for the proper functioning of leadership. They must always see that their followers take their advice, accept their opinions and perform those actions which they approve. They have a position of ascendancy. But they should always be prepared to adjust themselves to the wishes and desires of their followers.

Leadership refers to their status and role in the group—the particular skills and qualities they use and their popularity with other members. They take initiative in many activities, for example, a student leader, a cine leader and so on when other people try to copy their lifestyle also. Leaders have social skills to get along with other people. Leaders are different or superior to other members, for example, sports groups, gangs, military groups and so on. Their role behaviour is due to position and power and communicates with others effectively.

A leader is the individual highest in the status relationship of the group. They are the part of the group structure which may be more or less stable and more or less enduring. The reciprocal relationships with other members of the group and expectations denote their leadership role in the particular group. The abilities and skills which are prominent in the group seem to depend upon the values, goals and traditions of the group quite as much as on the personality of the leader.

According to Lindzey (1954), 'Leadership is a concept applied to the personality-environment relation to describe the situation when a personality is so placed in environment that his will, feeling and insight direct and control others in the pursuit of a common cause.' On the other hand, Cattell (1965) has defined a leader as 'a person who has a demonstrable influence upon his group.' There are two aspects in this concept of leadership:

1. Internal group relations
2. Performance effectiveness of the group

Shaw says, 'A leader is the group member who exerts more positive influence over others than they exert over him.' According to Daniel Katz and Robert L. Kahn, 'the term leadership has three main attributes':

1. An attribute of a position
2. A characteristic of a person
3. A category of behaviour

CHARACTERISTICS OF LEADERSHIP

According to Barrow (1977, p. 232), the following are some of the characteristics of leadership:

1. The leader is considered as the individual occupying a given office.
2. The leader is that individual upon whom the behaviour of group members is focused, that is, they occupy the position of central person.
3. The leader's personality is incorporated in the ego-ideal of the followers.
4. The leader is that group member who is so chosen by their colleagues.
5. The leader is the most powerful single individual in a social organization of which they are a member.
6. The leader is one person who is singled out as more effective than other members in initiating and controlling the activities of others.

LEADERSHIP BEHAVIOUR

Leaders are to be identified by the relative frequency with which they engage themselves in those acts which can be termed as leadership acts in a particular group. There are three aspects in this connection: (a) leader, (b) group and (c) situation.

The leader occupies a unique position in every group. They are responsible for all the activities in their group and help to create group structure, group atmosphere, group goals and group ideology. Leaders influence the group climate, which in turn has a significant effect on the behaviour of group members. The group morale cannot be sustained, enhanced or extended to all the members of the group without the positive efforts of the leader of the group.

The leader is expected to contribute to the success of the group, co-ordinate activities, promote their success and set an example. They are expected to exemplify the interests of other members to promote their interests as members. They are interested in the solidarity and cohesiveness of a group and possesses general good feeling (*esprit de corps*).

Any member can attempt to influence the behaviour or motives, attitudes, values and feelings of members of a group, which show the reflection at leadership. Any member can play leadership roles at some time or other. It is the role behaviour attached to the position of a leader and their attempts to influence others. A leader may communicate with other groups, which serve as a channel of information.

The leadership is a process which implies influences among group members. The leadership process always involves a leader–follower relationship in which the leader influences the group, and in turn, the group influences the leader. One must think of leadership as a process made up of such important elements as the traits of the individual leader, the group's structure, the method of acquiring leadership within the group, the nature of the task, the group goals and the past experience of the group. All these elements interact dynamically to form the leadership process.

A good leader has some qualities as shown in Box 12.1.

Box 12.1: Qualities of a Good Leader

1. High intellectual level
2. Self-assertiveness
3. Love for people
4. Ideal person
5. Knowledge of the subject
6. Knowledge of group psychology
7. Good orator

FUNCTIONS OF A LEADER

The functions of leaders depend on the type of the group of which they are a leader as well as the structure and the goals of that group. They also depend on the needs and attitude of the group which is being determined by whom they are selected. In fact, the behaviour of both leaders and groups depends upon the situation they face. Political, social or religious leaders have different functions to perform.

All functions of leaders fall into two broad groups: (a) inspiration and (b) execution.

1. *Under 'inspiration'*, we may include all the things that the leader does for motivating the members in the group, dramatizing its goals, rewarding and punishing members and getting them to work effectively with each other.
2. *Under 'execution'*, we may include what the leader does for the group: planning policymaking, selecting subordinates, dividing up the work, delegating authority and so on. The executive leader is concerned with the effectiveness of their organization. They neglect the feelings of their associates. They make people feel important and keep them happy, as well as others make them feel secure.

Besides the above, there are many other functions of good leadership, for example, delegation and trust.

1. **Delegation:** A good leader always has a positive attitude. They know that they have to perform so many works within a short period of time. They feel overloaded with many tasks to be done, and they may be under stress due to constraint of time. It is better for them to delegate some of their powers and duties to the next senior officer or next in command. Just like a vice-chancellor of a university can delegate their powers of taking some decision on some matter to the pro-vice-chancellor or dean of academic affairs, whosoever is senior in hierarchy. In the same way, a principal of a college may delegate some of the duties to the vice-principal or some senior professor to do their job on their behalf to be free from overwork.
2. **Trust:** Another important function of good leadership is that they should be trustworthy. Their followers and subordinate staff should have full confidence in them. If they lose the confidence of their followers, they would not be able to do full justification for their status, which they are commanding. They will not be able to get co-operation from them, and then they cannot be an effective leader. So a good leader should be an individual with trust, integrity, honesty, hardworking and an urge to work for others and serve the society.

'Leadership is both a function of the social situation and person, but it is also a function of interaction of both situation and person.' Leader is uniquely superior individual who leads in whatever situations they might find themselves. In various situations, different individuals take initiative in different tasks. So leadership is a way of behaviour exhibited by individuals in different ways and situations, such as behaviours such as effective initiative, individual prominence, sociability, consideration and the like.

Leadership refers to functions in actual groups in social life. Leaders initiate, direct and manipulate activities of the members, but leadership in a particular group is effective only within the range of tolerable behaviour determined by the leaders who reciprocate with other members and their group working.

LEADERSHIP STYLE

Leadership style, here, means the leadership roles and activities. It is related to power, which varies with the prestige of the leader who is attached to positions or status. The leadership style depends upon the perception, attitudes, values and ways of thinking. The particular manner and method of procedure that a leader adopts vary with the purposes of the group and its major norms. They also vary with the structure or organization of the group.

According to Lewin (1951), there are three types of leadership styles:

1. **Authoritarian leadership style:** This type of leader is like a dictator who exercises arbitrary power and has everything in their hands. They give orders without any explanation. They do the decision-making without consulting the group, assesses performance according to their own standards and controls the rewards and punishment. They are also called an autocratic leader who is to make all decisions themselves. They are to lay down all the policies, procedures and techniques.
2. **Democratic leadership:** This type of leader is the most popular one in the present scenario. They have positive and distinctive

attitudes and possess social skills to carry on with their followers. One of the functions of this type of leadership is to lay down the overall objectives for the benefits of their group and to help the group to understand its relation to the whole group. They are required to encourage and assist in group decision-making and planning. A democratic leader must develop skill in influencing and motivating others.

3. **laissez-faire leadership:** This type of leader is not really leadership but the absence of leadership. The leader has no existence as they do not exercise any positive influence. The members may agree that they have the status of a leader, but they play little or no part in initiating and coordinating activity. Such leadership is to allow complete freedom to the group with minimum leader participation.

There are two approaches to leadership styles, which are as follows:

1. **Trait approach of leadership:** Are great leaders born with special traits that give them a charisma? There is a special emotional appeal and attraction in this approach. It is true that leaders are characterized by certain traits, but traits alone cannot account for a person's becoming a leader. Leaders are generally more intelligent, more assertive and more talkative. Other traits are physique, self-confidence, extroversion and dominance. Leaders frequently participate at a high rate in group interaction, usually in communication or initiation of actions.

    The proponents of the trait theory of leadership argue that successful leaders have certain personality characteristics that make it likely that they will be leaders no matter what situation they are in. In fact, there are many particular set of traits which seem to characterize effective leadership, for example, assertiveness, independence, self-confidence, intelligence and so on.

2. **The situational approach of leadership:** When an individual is elevated to a position of leadership, the power of the group is invested in them. Such leaders tend to be the most verbally active members of their group. An effective leader must possess whatever resources are needed by the individual members of the group and

by the group as a unit in order to reach its goals. Fiedler (1967) states that it is of utmost importance to remember that 'becoming a leader depends on personality only to a limited degree'. Almost any individual can become a leader at any time if the situation and circumstances are appropriate.

There are two basic ways to become a leader:

1. One is appointed a leader by an authority above the group. Formally, structured groups tend to have appointed leaders.
2. One emerges as a leader from within a group. Informally structured groups usually have emergent leaders.

It is commonly assumed that a leader is also a popular group member, but this is not always true; much depends upon the situation. In many situations, more than one leader is needed. There are two general types of leaders: (a) task leaders and (b) social-emotional leaders, which are briefly described below:

1. The task leader is interested to get the work done as efficiently as possible. They emerge within the group to play the role of the task leader.
2. The social–emotional leaders help in creating and maintaining a good psychological climate within the group, responsive to the personal needs, problems and uniqueness of individual members. Hence, some fill the role of an emotional leader.

There are again two more approaches of leadership styles, for example, (a) behavioural approach and (b) interactional approach. They are briefly described below:

1. **Behavioural approach of leadership:** Another approach of leadership style which is quite common is behavioural approach. Attempts were made to find out the behaviours of effective leaders. It was found that anyone could become a leader by simply learning the behaviour of other effective leaders. It is said that leaders are made, not born. Leaders have a number of personality traits.

Leaders in life settings work through interpersonal relationships with others and also by providing direction, goals and structure to their groups. For example, when an individual takes over as a leader, they must try to establish open lines of communication, good interpersonal relations with their followers and clear goals and objectives.

2. **Interactional approach of leadership:** Trait and behavioural approaches emphasize personal factors. But now interactional model of leadership has emerged. The interactional approach has important implications for effective leadership.
   a. Many characteristics ensure successful leadership. In fact, great leaders have had in common personality traits appropriate to leadership roles, which are distinct from non-leadership roles.
   b. The behaviour of effective leadership styles fit into the specific situation. Some leaders function better in certain situations than in others.
   c. Leadership styles can be changed. In fact, leaders can modify their styles and behaviours to match the demands of a situation.

There are two types of leadership styles:

1. **Relationship-oriented leaders who develop interpersonal relationships:** They keep open lines of communication, maintain a positive social relations and ensure that everyone is involved and feeling good.
2. **Task-oriented leaders primarily work to get the task done and meet their objectives:** Their focus is performance and productivity, rather than on creating good interpersonal relations.

EFFECTIVENESS OF LEADERSHIP

Effective leadership depends on the outcome of a leader's personality and situational demands. It means that both the trait approach and state approach of leadership are required. The power of the group is invested in leadership. In fact, a leader will emerge from the group to become its head, guide its direction and often give it a unique identity to the group. A group needs changes, so do the demands on leadership. The effectiveness of leadership depends on the following factors:

1. The personality of the leader
2. The attitudes, demands and problems of the followers
3. The interpersonal relationship in the group that it encompasses
4. The situation as determined by such factors as physical settings, nature of the leadership task and so on
5. Some positive correlation between intelligence and effective leadership
6. People seem to prefer to be governed or led by people whom they understand

PERSONAL CHARACTERISTICS/TRAITS OF LEADERS

1. **Experience:** Experience of the leader is the main factor in leadership effectiveness.
2. **Intelligence:** Intelligence is the characteristics found to be most commonly associated with leadership.
3. **Dominance:** Dominance and assertiveness are important characteristics of leadership qualities.
4. **Adjustment:** The role of leaders is more demanding. Our perception of an individual's adjustment influences our willingness to accept them as a leader.
5. **Activity:** Leaders are dynamic and active. They are full of activities.
6. **Non-conformity:** Deviancy seems to imply psychopathology, which would be inconsistent with the notice that leaders are well-adjusted. It is essential to maintain cohesiveness of the group and to express non-conforming behaviour and to express solidarity of the group.
7. **Less neurotic:** They are emotionally more stable, so that they are able to use their ability to think independently
8. **Physical factors:** Factors, for example, height, weight, physical energy and health, appearance and so on are required.
9. **Other factors:** Other factors such as self-confidence, sociability and willpower are essential.

LEADERSHIP TRAINING

No attention has been paid to the leadership training due to the belief that 'leaders are born and not made. So there is no need for leadership training. But it has now been felt that in democracy, there is a need for leadership training. It has been more widely recognized that strong leadership of the right kind is indispensable in a democratic set-up of society. The need for leadership training in government, business, education, administration and all sorts of organizational activity is widely appreciated, and the success of leadership depends upon inherent features of their personality traits rather than the skills and attitudes that they possess and the kind of environment in which they function. Hence, there is a need for leadership training in these days.

In our society, the problem of leadership training arises in every type of organization, whether it may be industry, business, army, government, politics, labour, education and so on. Of course, much attention has been paid to the problems of selection of leadership personnel and the evaluation of their performance, but less emphasis has been laid to its training. There is recognition of the need for training for administrators. Hence, the problem of training for leadership involves: (a) knowledge and skills, (b) problem of human relationships and (c) formal and informal training.

Obstacles in Training

There are many factors which cause some obstacles in providing training to leadership. They can be enumerated as below:

1. Leaders themselves have failed to recognize that they are in need of training. Their mindset is not conducive to leadership training.
2. Leaders may not have the proper attitudes conducive to the training process.
3. The personality of leaders may prevent them from being easily trained.
4. Leaders may lack the necessary skills that are required in the new leadership role.

The primary purpose of leadership training is to help individuals to overcome this obstacle. The problem of leadership is a very complicated one. It involves the traits of personality, the nature of the situation and the goals of the group and also the training. Just as training is necessary to help people obtain various skills, so training the skills involved in leadership can also be improved. It helps the individual to become a better leader.

RELATIONSHIP BETWEEN LEADERS AND FOLLOWERS

Leader–follower relationships involve social interaction, face to face as well as indirect relations. They deal with each other by means of communication. The leader can perform the functions in that case only in which they can maintain a constant pattern of good relations with the followers. There should be a very close relationship between leaders and followers. The leader and the followers must have a credit balance of psychological satisfaction to both. Both of them must feel satisfied and establish such relationship that the maximum individual satisfaction result.

CONDITIONS FOR GOOD RELATIONSHIPS

Some conditions for good relationships are given below:

1. **Membership character:** They must have similar patterns of attitudes and reactive tendencies which are found in the other members of the group.
2. **The leader as a symbol of the group:** They must symbolize the ideals of the group.
3. **The leader as a father figure:** The followers should have a similar attachment to their leader as the children have towards their father.
4. **The leader as ideologist:** The leader should be the conserver of old culture, and they should have the formation of new ideas. They follow the group ideals themselves and motivate their followers to follow them.

5. **The leader must understand their followers:** The leader should know the attitudes, values, objectives as well as conflicts likely to occur in the group. This understanding helps them in providing proper guidance to their followers.
6. **The leader must have knowledge:** The leader must have knowledge as to when they should withdraw and admit their mistakes to their followers.
7. **A prestige of the leader:** It is related to the emotion of fear and love.
8. **An object of hero-worship and emotional fixation:** Their personality is a great attraction. they fulfil the needs, while others may seek security and protection from them.
9. **A figure of authority:** A leader is a figure of authority as they enjoy a good reputation and status.

The above points describe the conditions for a good relationship between leaders and their followers. It is not essential that only leader can influence and mould the behaviour of the followers. But sometimes, followers can also affect and modify the behaviour, attitude and opinions of the group leader. In a secular and democratic set-up of society, as we find in Indian democracy where media plays an important role, the followers of a political leader will shape their attitude towards some problem. When meetings are held, and the decision is taken by the majority vote, the leader will sometimes have to shift their stand on some issues. It has been observed in the academic field, especially in schools and colleges that sometimes the heads of the institution or principals have to withdraw the previous orders on the decision taken by the staff members.

COMMUNICATION AS A SOCIAL SKILL

Good communication between the leader and their followers is utmost essential for the effective functioning of a group. Interpersonal communication provides a means for understanding the behavioural aspects of leader–follower relationships. To be successful in influencing others or to be a good leader, they must possess communication skills, both verbal and non-verbal. Communication skill is one of the psychological skills which is needed for the leaders to become more effective.

Communication is a kind of interpersonal relationships between two parties. The process of communication involves (a) the decision to send a message, (b) encoding of the message, (c) sending the message, (d) the channel through which the message is sent, (e) decoding the message by the receiver and (f) an internal response to the message. Sending messages that are accurately decoded is a vital skill for leaders.

Several kinds of roles in communication processes can affect the leader–follower relationship. Leaders might choose to be authoritarian or democratic. Alternatively, they might adopt interdependent relationships with their followers or members of their group which they are leading. Similarly, depending upon factors such as their personality traits and the value they see in the leader–follower relationship, leaders might decide to be demanding, resistance, friendly, hostile or submissive. Sometimes, leader, as an expert, has authority over their followers, who are expected to be subservient to their beliefs.

Communication is just so important that knowing that leaders really notice how members in their group perform, recognizes the effort they are putting in and can provide positive or negative feedback, which may be constructive and honest will make all the difference in the process of communication. If a leader hardly communicates with the followers, then it is very difficult to motivate them. Leaders who communicate with their followers are more likely to know their strengths and weaknesses and thus are more able to create simulated situations during practice and to prepare them for upcoming situations. Talking and communicating do not necessarily require long meetings with followers. Regular talks between the leader and the followers can make all the difference and should be considered as the leader's priority, as they would be solving many problems of their followers.

The relationship between leaders and their followers is in constant change. There may be formal and informal communications with them. Formal communication consists of meetings with followers on some occasion. These meetings primarily aim to highlight performance-related issues. Here, feedback regarding their performance is also provided to them. Leaders should also know how to receive feedback and how to give it to their followers. Informal communication occurs all the time on and off the event. Moreover, there is a positive experience from having social activities for the whole group, which also helps in enhancing the cohesion of the group.

Communication for Leaders

Communication is usually an important component in all types of professions. We communicate verbally and non-verbally; we communicate by words and by actions. Communication may be through language or body language. It is hard to imagine a world without communication, without ever knowing what other people think and feel or without sharing our thoughts and feelings. Without communication, we cannot think of life would be hardly worth living. So by improving our communication skills, we improve our own lifestyle in a direct or indirect way.

Language is one of the greatest inventions of humankind, and it is an important tool in the process of communication. To be successful in influencing others or be influenced by others is the greatest asset of being a leader. It means that a leader must possess communication skills—both verbally and non-verbally. Communication skill is much like any other skill, and leaders should recognize the five steps as given below as they use them while interacting with their followers. Leaders will need to take the following steps to learn and improve their communication skill:

1. They should have felt the need to improve their communication skill
2. They should identify the behavioural aspects involved in improving their communication skills.
3. They may bring changes in the behavioural aspects of communication.

4. They may receive feedback concerning how well they are performing the behavioural aspects of communication.
5. They should integrate new or improved communication skills into their day-to-day communication patterns.

Successful communication is enormously difficult and depends on eliminating or controlling the noise. To communicate successfully, one must recognize that each person with whom one communicates has had different experiences. If one is to be understood by the other people and if one is to understand the other people, one must come to know people's frame of reference.

Sending Messages

In all professions, people send many messages. Leaders give instructions, encourage others, discipline them, organize events and evaluate others performances, all of which require sending messages. Leaders have been credited with being much better at sending messages than receiving them, but judge that about yourself after learning more about sending messages.

The most important decision a leader needs to take is when a message needs to be sent. Some leaders talk too much, discussing things that bore others or distract them from their work. But some leaders talk too little, assuming others to know what they think or want.

Feedback

Feedback is a special form of sending messages. Leaders, particularly, spend much of their time giving feedback to the followers through pep-talk or instructions. Feedback comes in various forms:

1. In the objective descriptive type, feedback describes as clearly and objectively as possible the behaviour observed. This type of feedback does not evaluate, but it seeks to help the other person look more clearly at their behaviour. The quality of this type of feedback is very important in facilitating followers' learning skills.

2. In the direct descriptive type of feedback, a person's behaviour is described and then describes how they reacted to it. This type of feedback is powerful because it gives the person receiving it a clear picture of their behaviour and what impact it had on them. Direct feedback of this type, however, must be given in a relationship of trust and concern with a desire to improve the relationship.

When giving feedback, leaders need to consider what their motivation is for doing so. It should be:

1. To reward and support the person receiving the feedback
2. To help someone improve his performance
3. To improve their relationship with that person

Unfortunately, at times, we give people feedback to punish, hurt or put them down that almost always hurts or destroys a relationship.

Just as it is important to give feedback effectively, it is essential to get feedback about one's own behaviour about one's performance as a leader. Leaders can receive such feedback by observing how others respond to their leadership style by requesting feedback directly from other individuals—perhaps from their followers—and also by getting written evaluations. When feedback is shared between leader and followers and how the leader responds to the feedback will determine if the followers will give correct feedback in future.

Here are a few suggestions for receiving feedback, which are given below:

1. **Listen and do not explain:** A leader should listen and try to understand the other person's point of view. He will only explain or justify his actions when he is criticized and his actions have been misunderstood.
2. **Ask for more feedback:** It will be good of leaders if they encourage to get more feedback by showing they are interested and open to the feedback.
3. **React honestly:** When people want to know what a leader's reaction is to their feedback, they should tell them their honest feelings.

4. **Express appreciation:** At the end, a leader should thank them and appreciate them for feedback.

Non-verbal Communication Skill

Non-verbal communication means expressing your viewpoints, feelings and thoughts through gestures, bodily movement and facial expression. Here, you speak through your body language. In non-verbal communication, the messages we send to others without uttering a word is a fascinating phenomenon. The field of non-verbal communication consists of (a) body language (kinesics), (b) spatial relation (proxemics) and (c) paralanguage or the way in which words are spoken.

Body language refers to how we communicate through our physical appearance, posture, gestures, touching behaviour and especially the changes in our facial and eye movements. We communicate with our postures. An awkward posture is a sign of feeling low, fatigued and inferiority, whereas an erect posture connotes feelings of confidence, openness and energy. The way people walk also communicates how they feel. When people are sad, they shuffle along, head down, hands in their pockets and moving along ever so slowly. A person who is lacking self-confidence will not have eye-to-eye contact with others. In the interview, they may not be facing the members of the board properly.

Happy achieving people show enthusiasm in their walk by a rapid, purposeful pace with free-swinging arms and upright posture. Even our breathing reveals something about how we feel. Rapid breathing is associated with excitement, fear, anxiety or extreme joy. Sometimes, leaders also have to take the help of non-verbal communication in order to convince others and give suggestions to followers. Some officers by their posture, walk and other gestures communicate arrogance, while others communicate self-confidence and still others meekness. This is non-verbal communication.

We especially communicate with gestures and various body movements. Touching others is another common form of body language used to express affection, to calm or to interrupt, depending on the context. A hug works well for expressing affection, holding the other person's hands in yours just in front of your chest is used to calm and reassure and a slight touch on the speaker's arm may be used to interrupt. The handshake is a common way we communicate by touch. Kissing is a sign of expression of love and affection for others.

Another means of communicating by kinesics is through the face, our most expressive body part. The eyes and mouth especially communicate a great deal, and we tend to study these when listening to others to determine the meaning of their messages.

Importance of Non-verbal Communication

We all recognize that non-verbal communication is very important in fully understanding a message when two or more people are communicating. Body language also reveals considerable information about our unconscious feelings and attitudes and our hidden selves. Our non-verbal messages are more powerful than verbal messages while communicating our feelings and emotions which often are more difficult to interpret accurately. Non-verbal communication is a more potent tool in conveying your message to others.

CONCLUSION

A leader is a person who has a unique position in their group in terms of role and status, that is, power and prestige or effective initiative. The leadership is such an affair in which two parties are involved. The leader acts as a model and gives commands to their followers. Leadership refers to their status and role in the group—the particular skills and qualities they use, their popularity with other members. A leader is the individual highest in the status relationship of the group.

In leadership behaviour, there are three aspects, that is, (a) leader, (b) group and (c) situation. The leader occupies a unique position in every group. Leaders influence the group climate, which in turn has a significant effect on the behaviour of group members. The leadership process always involves a leader–follower relationship in which the leader influences the group, and in turn, the group influences the leader.

There are many functions of good leadership, for example, (a) inspirational, (b) executive, (c) delegation and (d) trustworthiness. There are three types of leadership styles: (a) authoritarian leadership, (b) democratic leadership and (c) Laissez-faire leadership. There are two approaches of leadership styles: (a) trait approach and (b) situational approach. There are again two more approaches of leadership styles, for example, (a) behavioural approach and (b) interactional approach.

It has been more widely recognized that strong leadership of the right kind is indispensable in a democratic set-up of society. So there is a need for leadership training in these days. Hence, the problem of training for leadership involves: (a) knowledge and skills, (b) problem of human relationships, (c) formal and informal training. But there are many factors which cause some obstacles in providing training to the leadership.

There should be a cordial relationship between leaders and followers. The leader–follower relationship involves social interaction, face to face as well as indirect relations. They deal with each other by means of communication. The conditions for the relationship between leaders and followers are (a) membership character, (b) a leader as a symbol of the group, (c) a leader as a father figure, (d) a leader as an ideologist, (e) a leader must understand their followers, (f) a leader must have the knowledge, (g) prestige of the leader, (h) an object of hero-worship and emotional fixation and (ix) a figure of authority.

Good communication between leaders and their followers is utmost essential for the effective functioning of a group. Communication is a kind of interpersonal relationships between two parties. Several kinds of roles in communication processes can affect the leader–follower relationship. Communication is usually an important component in all types of professions. A language is an important tool in the process of communication.

Feedback is a special form of sending messages. Leaders particularly spend much of their time giving feedback to the followers through pep-talk or instructions. A few suggestions for receiving feedback are (a) listen and do not explain, (b) ask for more feedback, (c) react honestly and (d) express appreciation. The field of non-verbal communication consists of (a) body language (kinesics), (b) spatial relation (proxemics) and (c) paralanguage or the way in which words are spoken. We all recognize that non-verbal communication is very important in fully understanding a message when two or more people are communicating.

Leadership and communication are very important psychological skills for effective performance and to achieve success in life. Besides these, there are many other skills, which have already been described in the previous chapters. In the next chapter, an important psychological skill of decision-making and problem-solving will be discussed.

Decision-making and Problem-solving

13

INTRODUCTION

After studying many psychological skills which are quite useful for human wellness, there are a few more skills which need to be discussed. Decision-making and problem-solving are two other important cognitive skills, which are very important in the life of a human being, and both are related to human wellness. Decision-making process is very important in present-day business management. Essentially, the rational or sound decision has to be taken for the efficient functioning of management. Every officer or chief executive officer has to take many decisions consciously or otherwise making it as the basic function of a business manager. Decisions have important roles to play in the fulfilment both organizational goals and activities. Decision-making is a dynamic and an ongoing process and an important component of managing business activities.

Decisions have to be made at the lower level and higher level of business management to achieve business goals. Further, decision-making is one of the basic functions which is laden with values and belief system that every organization tries to implement to make sure of optimum growth and productivity in terms of services offered. Decisions are made in order to maintain the activities of all organizations. Decisions are also taken in our daily life to make our working comfortable and easy going.

PROCESS OF DECISION-MAKING

Decision-making process falls under the cognitive domain of human behaviour. It results in the choice of a correct line of action among several alternatives. Decision-making process consists of identifying and recognizing many alternatives but select only one choice based on the same values, beliefs and personal preferences of the person involved. Every decision-making process gives a final choice, which should have prompt action to follow.

Decision-making process also involves a problem-solving activity, which gives a solution considered to be correct, adequate and satisfactory. It is, therefore, a process which is based on more or less rational thinking and also depends on tacit or explicit knowledge and beliefs. Tacit knowledge is often used to fill the gaps in complex decision-making processes (Brockmann & Anthony, 2016). Usually, both of these types of knowledge, that is, tacit and explicit are used together in the decision-making process.

In the general term, it can be said that the decision-making process is the skill of selecting one appropriate line of action between two or more alternative choices. But in the wider context, the process of decision-making involves choosing between possible alternatives to a problem. So here, the process of problem-solving starts its functioning. Decisions can be made either through logical or illogical reasoning or the combination of the two.

Decision-making is a dynamic activity which is quite relevant and necessary for all types of organizations for their efficient and effective functioning. Since it is a continuous activity, it has gained much importance in these days in the area of business administration. Since many experts and intellectual administrators are involved in this process, it requires expertise and solid scientific background coupled with knowledge, skills and experience, besides the mental and emotional maturity. It can be stated that decision-making is the process as well as the action of making important decisions in day-to-day functioning in professional as well as personal or social life.

The decision-making process which is a part of human performance as well as cognitive aspect of behaviour consists of three domains of human behaviour:

1. **Psychological:** It means to examining the needs, demands, preferences and values of individuals who have to decide which way they want to go and which path they have to follow in their life.

2. **Cognitive:** Decision-making involves the thought-processing activity. So it is included in the higher mental functioning of human behaviour.
3. **Normative:** 'It is the analysis of individual decisions concerned with the logic of decision-making, or communicative rationality, and the invariant choice it leads to' (Kahneman & Tversky, 2000).

MEANING OF DECISION-MAKING

A decision may be considered as a line of action purposely selected from many alternatives to achieve organizational goals and also fulfil its objectives. Psychologically, decision-making is a process of arriving at the best possible choice for the solution of a problem within a minimum period of time. The decision means to find out some possible solution and to come to a conclusion. But the decision-making process involves only selecting one out of two or more alternative choices because if there is only one alternative, then there will be no need to make a decision.

According to *Oxford Advanced Learner's Dictionary*, the term decision-making means 'the process of deciding about something important, especially in a group of people or in an organization'.

Trewatha and Newport define the decision-making process as 'Decision-making involves the selection of a course of action from among two or more possible alternatives in order to arrive at a solution for a given problem'.

According to McFarland, 'A decision is an act of choice where in an executive forms a conclusion about what must be done in a given situation. A decision represents behaviour 'chosen from a number of possible alternatives.'

Henry Sisk and Cliffton Williams defined decision-making process as 'A decision is the selection of a course of action from two or more alternatives; the decision making process is a sequence of steps leading to selection.'

So it can be said that a good decision is the one that is made thoughtfully and reasonably, which includes all relevant factors, consistent with the individual's beliefs and values.

CHARACTERISTICS OF DECISION-MAKING

The following are the characteristics of the decision-making process:

1. It is a process of selecting one correct alternative out of many choices.
2. A decision is preceded by thinking, deliberation and reasoning.
3. Decision-making requires a lot of planning, organizing, initiating and executing a line of action which has been selected.
4. Rationality is another characteristic of the decision-making process, as the ability to learn, to remember and to relate with many other complex factors have made the rationality possible.
5. Decision-making involves control and commitment. The management is committed to make a correct decision because it leads to the achievement of the organizational goal, and also, every decision taken becomes part of the policies and programmes of the organization.
6. The objective of decision-making is to select the best alternative choice, which can be translated into concrete action.
7. In this process, actions for decisions are taken, so that any adverse consequences may be prevented from becoming problems.
8. Some steps are generally followed that may result in a decision model which can be used to determine the optimal level of the production plan (Monahan, 2000).
9. In case of conflict, the role-playing technique may be helpful for predicting decisions to be made (Armstrong, 2001).

SKILL OF DECISION-MAKING

Decision-making is a basic and important skill in the workplace if one wants to be an effective administrator. In case of the selection of employees in the company or choosing the clients in the market and type of the strategy to use for the marketing of the product, the ability to make a good decision is utmost essential.

There are different styles of decision-making. Every administrator prefers a different way to find out a decision. The four styles of decision-making are (a) directive, (b) analytical, (c) conceptual and (d) behavioural. These styles are being discussed as follows:

1. **Directive:** The manager of a company/organization should be a good director, as they have to give directions and suggestions to their company/organization employees to follow what to do and what not to do. It is only possible if they are quite well versed with the know-how of the organization rules and policies. They should also be a technical director.
2. **Analytical:** Another good style of decision-making skill is the analytical style of the manager. It means that all the decisions which they have to take should be based on rationality. All the decision should be made at the micro-level. The manager should think analytical on the pros and cons of each matter and think reasonably. In this way, all the decisions made will be accurate, which would help in the achievement of organizational goals.
3. **Conceptual:** This is another style of decision-making. In this style, the manager of the company/organization arrives at the decision at the conceptual level and not at the concrete level. If they have a higher level of abstract intelligence, their thinking ability will also be at an abstract level, which will help them make decisions at the conceptual level. It means that they will think of the problem at a global level and divide it into different parts and decide about each part of the problem separately.
4. **Behavioural:** This style of decision-making is based on some psychological principles. Before they are a good manager, they should also be a psychologist. If they may apply the principles of motivational mechanism, emotional arousal, learning process and so on, they may take quick decisions as well as correct decisions, which will help them to be an effective leader in their organization.

DECISION-MAKING ABILITY

Decision-making is a cognitive ability which is related to reasoning power of an individual. From the moment individuals wake up until they go to bed at night, they face many problems as life presents a continuous series of difficulties. They have to make decisions which clothes they should wear, what type of food they should eat, whether they should go to school or college or not, whether to attend meeting or miss it, these types of problems are there where decisions have to be made. Similarly, we may have many other big problems which we face in everyday life where much more important decisions have to be taken, for example, what type of school to join, which job to accept, what type of house to buy and in which locality, whether to continue or end a long-term relationships with somebody who is very close to you and so on. If you have the ability for rational thinking and decision-making, you would like to make each of these decisions in a cool, calm and rational way.

There are two factors which you would like to consider before you arrive at some concrete decision. These factors are:

1. The utility and value to you of the performance of the activity for which decision has been done.
2. The probability that such results would actually be productive.

After considering these two factors, you would like to make your decision on the basis of expected utility and the value of the performance of the activity. Moreover, the probability of the possible result is another consideration. Sometimes, you may make decisions informally on the basis of hunches, intuition or the opinion of others, which may prove wrong and incorrect. But on the other hand, even if you make decisions in a perfectly rational way, you may find later on that this was also not a good decision and you have to back out.

Decision-making ability is required when there is mental conflict, which is a common and frequently occurs in everyday life. Conflicts may be minor and resolved easily, but sometimes they may be of great importance and resolved only with considerable difficulty and under substantial stress. For example, a young lady going to a dance party has to choose between two attractive dresses, a student who has to take both mathematics and biology finds the courses offered at the same time or a young executive offered a promotion wants the higher salary but apprehensive of the additional responsibilities.

Among the various types of conflicts, decision-making ability has the most significant quality. A young man may have to decide out of the conflict when he may choose freely between two offered positions. A child may have to decide between reading an interesting book and going out to play football. A young woman who faces with decision-making between two equally qualified matches for her wedding occasion.

In many instances, we are simultaneously attracted to two mutually exclusive goals with a positive attractive value. As the two goals become alike in attractiveness, and the decision involved increases in importance, the length of vacillation period increases as does the stress produced by the conflict. But when both goals appear equally attractive, the vacillation period is likely to be a long one. The prospective medical student who has to choose between marriage and medical college makes their decision quickly if one goal is substantially more attractive to them than the other. Another student faced with choosing between two difficult courses may entertain the idea of dropping out of school.

PHASES IN DECISION-MAKING PROCESS

Every day, we are facing situations in life that require us to make a decision and to solve problems. Sometimes, making decisions is an easy task and can be done abruptly, but at some other times, making a decision becomes very difficult, and the individual may go into mental conflict. Easy decisions consist of things like what clothes one should wear, and usually, most people choose wearing clothes based on the weather of the day, or we can say that they wear seasonal clothing or where they might be going. If they are going to the workplace, they will wear formal and simple dressing, but if they are going to attend some party, they will wear a gorgeous dress, especially women. Other easy decisions consist of things such as what to eat, which movie to see and what television programmes to watch.

Decisions that seem to be the most difficult to take are those that require a higher level of thinking. Examples of difficult decisions consist of things such as which college to join, whether to take a medical group or non-medical group for studies. What professional career one should adopt in life. If offered equally two attractive jobs, which one to accept and which one to reject, because one's future depends upon the right decision at this juncture of life as one is unable to predict about their future. Moreover, a decision regarding marriage and selection of a spouse—whether or not to marry and start a family. These types of decisions are difficult because they are life-changing decisions, and they shape our future.

Making good decision is a skill which must be learned. It is not something innate, but it is a gradual process that is usually ascertained from life experiences. So it is acquired through various experiences, which we face in our stressful life. Because decisions can change so obviously from one situation to another, the experiences gained from making one important decision may be transferred to some other situation.

Decision making is a very important behavioural aspect of human life. Because man is born with some needs, both physiological and psychological. They are called as primary needs and secondary needs. When these needs are not fulfilled or partially satisfied, they create some problems and when they are not solved properly, they develop some mental conflicts. In order to resolve conflicts, we have to make correct decision in life, so that we may lead a tension free life. This whole process leads to the process of decision making which has now become a skill to be developed for human wellness.

For making a decision, there are many phases that can be taken into consideration, but when making good decisions there are only five phases that need to be followed.

1. **Identify the goal:** The first phase in making the right and correct decision is identifying the goal. One of the most effective decision-making strategies is that you should be very clear about your goal. You should ensure why this decision will make a good impact on your customers as well as your employees or subordinates. You should realize that you need to make a good and correct decision, which may benefit them. This simply means identifying the goal

as well as the purpose of your decision by asking yourself why and what exactly is the problem that has to be solved. Knowing what is most important to you will help you to make good decisions.

2. **Gather relevant information:** This is the second phase of decision-making. When making good decisions it is better to gather relevant information from various sources that are directly related to the problem. When getting information, first if all you should make a list of every possible alternative choice, even ones that may initially sound foolish or seem unrealistic. You should seek the opinions of friends that you have faith in them or consult the experts and professionals. In this way, you will be able to come up with various types of solutions while considering all your options for a final decision. You may use as many resources as possible in order to make the best decision.

3. **Consider the consequences:** This is an essential phase because it will allow you to assess the pros and cons of the different options that you have framed during the previous phase. It is also important because you want to feel confident with all your options and the possible outcome of whichever one you have chosen. This phase can be just as important as the first phase because it will ensure you how the final decision will impact you as well as your colleagues. During this phase, you may be asking yourself what is likely to be the outcome of your decision, and moreover, how it will affect your future.

4. **Make decision:** After identifying our goal and gathering all necessary information and weighing the consequences, it is time to make a decision after considering the alternative choices and actually executing our final plan. This phase may cause some people a lot of tension, but it is important because this is where we have to arrive at some point of decision. Sometimes, it may be possible that we may still be slightly indecisive about our final decision, but we will have to consider how this makes us feel. We should ask ourselves how this decision works best for us now, and also in the future. When we answer this question, we should feel good about the result.

5. **Evaluate decision:** The final phase of the decision-making process is evaluating the decision. Once we have made our final decision

and put it into action, it is necessary to assess the decision and the steps we have taken to ensure that it works. This final phase is just as important as phase one because it will help us to further develop our decision-making skill for future problems. This phase is also fundamental because it may require us to seek out new information and make some changes along the way.

This phase requires some patience, and it may also encourage perseverance as it may take some time to see the final result. We should remember that if the first decision is not working, we may have to go back to step two and choose another option.

HOW TO IMPROVE DECISION-MAKING PROCESS

The following are some of the suggestion through which one can improve the process of decision-making:

1. **Cost-benefit analysis:** You should analyse the cost benefit of each and every decision which you make in your lives. Before reaching the ultimate decision, it is essential to assess each and every aspect to ensure that you are making the best possible decision.
2. **Narrow your options:** There may be many alternatives out of which you have to select one. You should try to screen out and shortlist two or three choices. It will help to make the right choice.
3. **Evaluate the significance:** If you have many alternative choices, you should look into their pros and cons of each choice. Consider which is important and which is less important, and which is the most important.
4. **Do not sweat the small stuff:** You should not waste your time thinking on the less and insignificant problem. Concentrate on the right track.
5. **Do the research:** If you have the scientific temperament, look into the problem rationally. Try to do research on the problem and come to the logical conclusion.
6. **Get a well-informed opinion:** If you have made a decision, try to stick on and do not ponder too much and have no wavering mind.

PROBLEM-SOLVING

Every day we solve hundreds of small problems, and in the process, we learn routine actions for handling those that recur. The solutions become automatic and we no longer consider ourselves to be 'solving problems'. Only when an established routine fails to do, we begin to think again about familiar problems. Getting to school poses no problem unless your car or bike breaks down and the buses are on strike. Fixing a dinner is no challenge unless a power failure turns off all your appliances.

These problems are everyday puzzles, others such as repairing a stereo requires expertise, and still, other problem-solving activities are undertaken as the source of entertainment such as the mystery readers want to be a step ahead of the novel's skilled detective and solve the murder before the solution is revealed by the author. Jigsaw puzzles, jumbles and so on form hobbies for some people who find them interesting because of their problem-solving aspects of those activities. The bureaucrats have to solve the problems of their employees in their files after taking quick decisions.

Problem-solving is the ability to know the solution of the problem and also to understand what principles could be applied, which helps the individual in solving the problem. Sometimes, the problem requires abstract thinking, and at some other times, it requires a creative solution. There are two different types of problems, well-defined and bad-defined for which different methods are used. Well-defined problems have specific end goals and clear expected solutions, while bad-defined problems do not specific goals. 'Well-defined problems allow for more initial planning than bad-defined problems' (Schacter et al., 2009).

Problem-solving is a mental process and refers to the process of finding solutions to problems faced in life (Brandell, 1997). Solutions to these problems are usually situation specific. The process of problem-solving starts with the finding of the problem and shaping of the problem when the problem is discovered. The next step is to find out the possible solutions and to evaluate them. Finally, a solution is found and implemented and verified. 'Problems have an end goal to be reached and how you get them depends upon problem orientation and systematic analysis' (Robertson, 2001).

There are four basic steps in solving a problem:

1. **Defining the problem:** First of all, we will have to know the nature of the problem. Try to find out the operational definition of the problem at hand. What are the main objectives? What are the goals to be achieved? Until we are not conversant with these questions, it is not possible to find out the answer and solve the problem.
2. **Generating alternatives:** After knowing the nature of the problem, we should think of various alternatives choices which would match the solution of the problem. It will create some conflict in our mind and also confusion. But we should be courageous enough to face these situations.
3. **Evaluating and selecting alternatives:** This is the right step for finding out the solution to the problem. Out of the many alternatives, select the only one which you think the most appropriate and adequate enough to help you in solving your problem.
4. **Implementing solutions:** After you have found out one alternative which you think that it is helping you to solve your problem, then continue with the same alternative and do not change on the way. Try to implement it in solving the problem.

Stages in Problem-solving

Psychologists have viewed problem-solving as a process, which passes through various stages. The stages of problem-solving according to Graham and Wallas are as follows:

1. **Preparation:** The initial or preparation stage of problem-solving involves a great deal of information gathering, including an assessment that requires a clear definition of the problem. What is the problem? What are its starting and endpoints? What seems to be the obstacles? What kinds of information are needed to work toward a solution? If a problem seems familiar, reproductive

thinking might lead to the conclusion as a previously successful solution may be successful. Research has shown that one of the strengths of expert problem-solvers is that they can draw on their considerable experience to generate reproductive solutions.
2. **Incubation:** Incubation stage is present sometimes only. Incubation occurs when the problem has been put aside, that is, when the individual stops thinking about the problem and engages in some other activity. During this incubation period, the solution may appear suddenly, or a new approach may become apparent. This may occur because the incubation period allows the person to recover from the mental fatigue that has built up from working on the problem. But in many incubation instances, solutions to the problems do not appear.
3. **Production:** Production involves thinking of problem solutions. In this stage, potential solutions begin to be generated. Various strategies are employed to find out the correct solution such as trial and error, algorithm rules that guarantee a solution to a specific type of problem, the heuristics rule of thumb or quick-fix methods which mean end analysis, that is, breaking a problem into sub-goals that can be reached by smaller problems and working backwards for solving a problem by working backwards from the goal. Employing all or one strategy often leads to the solution to the problem.
4. **Evaluation:** In this stage, the solution is evaluated in terms of its ability to satisfy the demands of the problem. If it meets all the criteria, then the problem is solved. If not, then the person goes back to the production stage to generate additional solutions. In some cases, several solutions may be generated, all of which solve the problem. Yet some solutions may be better than others, that is, they are cost-efficient, involves less time, are more humane and so forth. These alternate solutions are compared at the evaluation stage.

Factors Influencing Problem-solving

The following are the factors that influence problem-solving:

1. **Motivation:** Motivation directs behaviour towards the goal. Motivation helps to solve the problem by giving direction to

thought. Just as in learning, motivation plays an essential role in problem-solving. A demotivated person will not work enough on the problem, leave aside, reaching the goal and solving the problem.
2. **Past experience:** Even though problem-solving behaviour involves a lot of creative thinking but, reproductive thinking is also involved. Whatever had been learnt in the past, in similar situations, is generalized in the present situation. This makes it easier to solve the problem. An individual's experience in a given field is worth considering in this process, as their concepts and generalizations will have a profound effect on solving some problem in that field.
3. **Creativity:** The more people think creatively in any problem situation, the more they will be able to take help from their past experiences and present strategies. They would be efficient enough to organize the whole information in such a novel manner that they may find not one but many solutions to the problem. But if people are rigid in ideas, they will be unable to perceive things from an angle conducive for the solution of the problem.
4. **Functional fixedness:** It means a strong tendency in an individual to think of applying objects only in those ways which they have been used earlier. Functional fixedness is our ability to solve many problems. If we do not use it, the process can be seriously affected. For example, functional fixedness probably leads us to think of this material as something to read instead of using it for some other purpose. Functional fixedness is an example of a mental set also.
5. **Mental set:** Another factor that often affects effective problem-solving is our mind set. Sometimes, after solving a series of similar problems, we fall into the use of certain procedures that might not be very efficient or might fail if a simple change in problem occurs. Difficulties arise when tendencies to stick to a familiar method cause us to overlook other more efficient approaches.

CONCLUSION

Decision-making and problem-solving are two other important psychological skills which are very important in the life of a human being and both are related to human wellness. Decision-making is a dynamic and an ongoing process and an important component of managing daily activities. The decision-making process consists of identifying and recognizing many alternatives but select only one choice based on the same values, beliefs and personal preferences of the person involved. The decision-making process also involves a problem-solving activity, which gives a solution considered to be correct, adequate, and satisfactory.

Decision-making is a dynamic activity which is quite relevant and necessary for all types of organizations for their efficient and effective functioning. A decision-making process which is a part of human performance as well as cognitive aspect of behaviour consists of three domains of human behaviour: (a) psychological, (b) cognitive and (c) normative.

Decision-making is a cognitive ability which is related to the reasoning power of an individual. Decision-making ability is required when there is a mental conflict which is common and frequently occurs in everyday life. Decision-making is an important function in all types of management, whether it is business, public services, education or sports administration. Decision-making is a part and parcel of today's administration, especially in business management, as it is related to planning, organizing, directing, executing and controlling functions of a director or manager in the company.

Some suggestions through which we can improve the process of decision-making are (a) cost-benefit analysis, (b) narrow your options, (c) evaluate the significance, (d) do not sweat the small stuff, (e) do the research and (f) get a well-informed opinion.

Problem-solving is the ability to know the solution to the problem and also to understand what principles could be applied, which helps the individual in solving the problem. Problem-solving is a mental process and refers to the process of finding solutions to problems faced in life. Problem-solving is a higher-order mental process and cognitive functioning, which requires a fundamental skill. So problem-solving is a psychological skill, which has to be learnt.

There are four basic steps in solving a problem (a) defining the problem, (b) generating alternatives, (c) evaluating and selecting alternatives and (d) implementing solutions. The stages of problem-solving are (a) preparation, (b) incubation, (c) production and (d) evaluation. The factors of problem-solving are (a) motivation, (b) past experience, (c) creativity, (d) functional fixedness and (e) mental set. The practical applications of these skills need to be analysed. So the implementations and applications of these skills have been discussed in detail in the next chapter.

Implementation and Application of Psychological Skills Training Programme

INTRODUCTION

Learning of psychological skills has become very important for everybody in their day-to-day work if they want to lead a healthy and prosperous life. As physical exercises and morning walk has become very essential to keep our self physically fit and also to maintain physical health, similarly, mental health has also attracted the attention of the psychologists who may teach some mental exercises to sustain their proper mental health and also to keep them mentally alert, emotionally matured and balanced as well as socially adjustment.

Life is adjustment and adjustment is life. Without adjustment and contentment, you cannot be happy, and if you are not happy, you cannot be mentally healthy. In that case, you may fall victim to some mental disorders and your personality integration would be disorganized. Hence, training of psychological skills has become one of the important functions for the psychologists. But only an experienced psychologist can teach these mental and other psychological skills to help the people learn them, so that they may become better human beings. Hence, there is a need to start a programme of PST. In this chapter, practical suggestions will be given for implementation of a successful programme of psychological skills, so that proper training should be imparted. The application of these skills in the different walks of life will also be discussed.

PST PROGRAMME

The first step to starting PST programme is to determine specific goals. The following should be the objectives:

1. To help the persons to be responsible in their lives
2. To enhance an individual's self-worth and self-prestige
3. To develop them more worthy by becoming more competent
4. To learn skills of the essential psychological qualities for being successful
5. To increase self-awareness which is important for developing these psychological skills
6. To develop these skills through systematic training

PST programme will add a powerful and exciting new dimension to one's endeavours. Here the consideration is whether to launch the full programme in a comprehensive way or begin more slowly, selecting certain skills and then building on them. Moreover, we should set our specific goals and use the principles of goal setting.

Basic Steps for Starting PST

According to Martens (1987), psychologists should help implement PST programme by outlining how they should. The following steps may be followed:

1. **Initial PST orientation:** Psychologist should begin the basic step of initiating a PST programme by introducing the entire programme to the trainees during the season of the training programme. These psychological qualities that help them to achieve their best performances are not inherited abilities but skills that can be learned through systematic practice. At the end of the session, he should evaluate their psychological skills with the help of a questionnaire.
2. **Evaluation of the psychological skill:** At the second session, the psychologist should have all the trainees bring with them their completed questionnaire. Explain how to score each questionnaire

and discuss how to interpret the results. The purpose is to help them become more aware of their present psychological skill level for a particular quality and also to see if they perceive any improvement after practising PST for a while; otherwise, it will affect their feelings of self-worth. They will record the results of their periodical self-evaluation and the record of their psychological training. It is important and essential in monitoring progress from learning psychological skills and recording their observations.

3. **To teach the basic skills:** Now, the psychologist is ready to introduce all trainees to a specific psychological skill requiring one–two-hour session. After completing the educative phase and answering any questions the members have, they should give a periodic session for acquiring each psychological skill. The number of sessions will depend a great deal on which skill is being taught and on the skill levels of the trainees.

   If the psychologist decides to teach all the skills that comprise PST programme, imagery should be taught first of all as it is the master psychological skill used to practise all other psychological skills. All the skills are interrelated and the development of anyone helps the development of others. Imagery and goal-setting skills must be taught in the initial stage. Imagery is a building block for further psychological skill development. On the other hand, goal setting, that is, the setting of performance goals, if achieved at the earliest, will be the booster factor and also a motivating to reach the peak level. In this way, they would be able to overcome anxiety and enhance concentration and self-confidence.

4. **Individual counselling:** The psychologist will meet each trainee to discuss their level of skill for each psychological quality. Discuss with them how to personalize the programme so that it can meet the objectives. This type of individual session is a terrific opportunity for the psychologist to get to know their trainees better. A psychologist can discover those things that are important for them, which become helpful to them in motivating them in future. This is one good opportunity to individualize both the physical and psychological training of the trainees. Psychologist has to work with the trainees to outline their PST practice schedule. Then, the actual

work needs to be recorded by the trainee along with any observations about the training. This individual session should close with the psychologist reinforcing how important he believes the PST programme is and encouraging the trainee to accept responsibility for developing these skills.
5. **Incorporating PST into practice and session plans:** In order to manage psychic energy and stress, improving concentration and setting effective goals programme must be worked out if they are to be functional skills. The psychologist needs to plan to practise with the time given to allow trainees to get into the flow and to work on integrating rather than always analysing. The psychologist wants to structure exercise and emphasize in their instructions the attentional demands of the task at hand. They want to find ways in practice for trainees to measure the achievement of their new performance goals.

   One of the most helpful things a psychologist can do during practice is to simulate conditions so that trainees can work on their psychological skills. Three levels of the simulation are:
   a. The practice of psychological skills by using imagery to simulate the environment
   b. To make practices simulate the day of competition as realistically as possible
   c. The trainees may have conditions for simulation in which they can practise their psychological skills for future more important events
6. **Monitoring progress:** As the PST programme progresses, the psychologist will want to consult periodically with each of their trainees to see how they are progressing in order to increase their commitment to the programme. Monitoring of their progress is very helpful in increasing commitment. The psychologist should also able to help trainees to try alternative techniques if they are having difficulty with certain skills.
7. **Evaluation of PST programme:** It is very helpful to have all trainees evaluate their psychological skills at the end of the session and determine what progress they have made. Based on the evaluation, it is a good time to plan additional psychological training that can be practised during the other session. Trainees should also evaluate

the PST programme with the help of the psychologist. They should also try to evaluate the psychological skills of each member of the group, that is, trainees individually. They should also evaluate the entire PST programme and consider how it can be improved.

Questions about Starting the Programme

The following are some questions about starting the programme:

1. **Should PST be used with all persons?** PST can be beneficial to any person. Many people have realized how important psychological factors are in their own performances. But there may be some younger ones who can certainly benefit from PST. Imagery and mental relaxation skills generally are easier to teach to young children, but it is essential to adjust the programme to their level of reasoning and language comprehension.
2. **Is PST just for the more skilled trainee?** PST can be beneficial to any and every trainee. The development of these psychological skills will release hidden physical skills.
3. **Should trainees be required to participate in PST?** All members of a group (trainees) should be required to attend the meetings that introduce the programme and explain the basics. After that, each one of them should be given the freedom to choose whether or not he utilizes the programme.
4. **When should psychologist initiate the PST programme?** It is best to do the basic training during the initial stage or as early as possible during pre-session training, especially when the trainees are free from their routine work. School students may be given training as soon as their final examination is over and before the new academic session starts. It will take a long time to learn psychological skills. Once the programme is initiated, then it must become a regular part of the training programme. It should be included in practice plans and the regular sessions.
5. **How much time will it take to implement the PST programme?** The psychologist should plan on spending one or two hours to introduce the programme and to teach each psychological skill. Once the basics have been introduced to the group, they need to

spend considerable time helping each one of them structure the programme to their specific needs. Then give about 15 minutes of time in each formal practice to work on one psychological skill. Later on, PST should become an integral part of the practice and other routines.
6. **What are some of the obstacles to implementing the programme?** Some obstacles occur when trainees are not committed to the programme or when psychologist decides not to do it or to make only a token effort to implement PST.
7. **Are there any other obstacles?** If the programme is not presented correctly, trainees may not take it seriously. If some of them joke about or ridicule others who are practising PST, the programme may be undermined.

Preparation of PST Programme

The psychological preparation involves preparing the integrator, setting realistic goals, mentally rehearsing the physical and mental skills as well as strategies to be used and preparing the mind for the psychological demands of the situation. It is meant to help our trainees prepare for any event.

General Psychological Preparation

Psychologists want their trainees in the best physical and psychological condition possible. They want to optimize their chances of experiencing flow and of reaching that optimal energy zone. They want their trainees to be high in positive psychic energy and to have little or no negative psychic energy. They should be prepared for the unexpected. The following activities are involved:

1. **Integration of psychological skills:** Psychologists, first of all, teach all psychological skills to trainees one by one, and when all the skills are mastered and perfected and when they know that trainees have learnt all the skills, they will try to integrate all the skills into one unit in their total game plan called PST. Two days before any event, they should shift from learning these skills to using these

skills. First of all, they should use their imagery skills to visualize the entire event perceiving themselves executing the skills and strategies to be used to the best of their abilities. Also, they should be encouraged to think of their psychological preparation for that event. It involves visualizing the attainment of the optimal energy zone, perceiving themselves manage any stress and strain, selecting and shifting their attention effectively and keeping focused on their performance goals three times per day for two days before that event. Next, psychologists may help the athletes integrate their psychological skills by simulating the event.

2. **Setting performance goals:** Psychologists should have the trainees record their goals before the event. These goals should be set by them in consultation with their psychologists.

3. **Engineering the environment:** Psychologists should be prepared to engineer the environment as much as possible to accommodate their trainees' preferences. To eliminate any hustles and bustles that may cause unnecessary distractions or stress at the higher levels of event, psychologists need to engineer the media too. The objective is to minimize disruption and to create a hassle-free environment that let the trainees focus on the positive side of the event.

4. **On-site preparation:** Psychologists should begin to consider any other environmental factors like weather that might influence the event. They may like to eliminate unexpected weather or other conditions. A trainee's health and other changes all may be good reasons for adjusting goals. Trainees need to begin moving toward their optimal energy zones. They begin psyching up to increasing positive psychic energy or psyching out using stress management techniques to find their optimal energy zones.

Learning Psychological Skills

Most people have learned these skills to a sufficient degree so that they function quite well in many day-to-day activities. But when confronted with the more highly demanding level situations, they may not possess these skills to the extent needed. This can be the most frustrating to them because they know that they do not have superior skills. They have displayed them time after time in practice or in less intensive events. They are unable to perform them in big events because the psychological skills needed to complement their other social skills are not equally extraordinary. But many persons who have developed psychological skills have done through many years of trial and error learning and training.

Some positive behavioural alternatives are of little use, for example, to say 'just relax' or 'concentrate' does not tell the trainees how to relax or concentrate. They need not be told, for example, 'stop getting uptight'. What they need is specific instruction on how to relax, so that they can perform better. The psychologist who lacks the ability to help them acquire the necessary stress management skills usually does one of three things.

1. *Uses empathy* to provide support for the trainee to overcome this problem
2. *Selects another trainee* who can perform better under the pressure, even though the other may have less talent
3. *Aggravate the problem* by placing more pressure on the trainee to begin performing up to their capability
4. *To include PST* into trainees' training programme

Essentials of PST

The following are some of the essential points of PST as suggested by Weinberg and Gould (2007):

1. PST programme should be planned, supervised and implemented by qualified psychologists as they have to plan the programme and then to execute it periodically and also to implement it regularly.
2. Psychological training is a continuous process that needs to be integrated with all other routine programmes in life.
3. It is always good if we initiate the PST programme during our free time or during that period when there is more time to learn something new.
4. It is not possible to teach new psychological skill overnight, and moreover, the trainees are not expected to learn it immediately.

5. The time taken for practising these psychological skills will vary from one individual to another depending upon what is being practised and how well it is learned.
6. As trainees become more proficient, they may be able to integrate the psychological training with any other type of training.
7. Once a skill has been effectively integrated into practice, it should be tried before being used during an actual situation.
8. It is better if we supervise the psychological training practice until the trainees are self-directed.
9. The psychologist can help to ensure compliance and also giving feedback to the trainees after the training is completed.
10. PST is a continuous process and it should continue for much more time.

Implementing PST Programme

PST is an educative system for mental training. Mental training includes the teaching of some positive variables such as positive mental attitude, mental toughness, aggressiveness, self-motivation, self-confidence, character-building, leadership, anxiety management, concentration, competitiveness and communication skills. For implementing PST programme, the following steps may be considered:

1. First of all, we will have to know which mental skills need to be learnt and they should be assessed. For this, interview and psychological tests can be conducted, which may provide useful information. The interview provides a good opportunity to know where and when they need help in their difficult time and then we should start building the trust and confidence among them.
2. After the interview and tests, psychologists should give feedback to each trainee to acquaint them with their specific psychological strengths and weaknesses. This evaluative feedback should include identifying the nature of psychological skills appropriate for each trainee meant for training.
3. Psychological skills to be learnt to depend upon (a) how much time of practice is available, (b) how much practice time can be

devoted weekly to PST, (c) whether the trainees are interested in receiving PST and (d) total time available to practice psychological skills.
4. Before starting the PST programme, objectives of PST should be explained to them which should be easily defined in measurable terms.
5. **Designing PST schedule:** After needs and requirements of the trainees have been known and objectives of psychological skills have been identified, the specific strategies should be devised to achieve the objectives. First of all, the formal meeting may be conducted on someday before the practice session for educating trainees on PST, for example, imagery, anxiety management, attention control, goal setting and so on. Even informal meetings may be arranged to impart information and build rapport. A training schedule should determine when to start the training and for how long the training should continue. The psychologist must teach and inculcate these psychological skills. Hence:
   a. PST should become a regular part of the formal training programme.
   b. Commitment to the programme, such as:
      i. Motivation cannot be injected with a syringe
      ii. Self-confidence cannot be swallowed in tablets form
      iii. Anxiety cannot be flushed from the system with eczema

Evaluating the PST Programme

Evaluation of the PST programme is a very important aspect of PST. There are some ethical considerations, which will help to show the effectiveness of the programme due to the following:

1. Evaluation gives feedback for knowing the effectiveness of the programme, and if the need arises, it may be used for modifying the programme.
2. Evaluation ensures trainees to suggest modifications in the programme to be conducted.
3. Evaluation is the only method to judge the programme objectively to know if the goals are being achieved.

The following are some questions to be answered for assessing the effectiveness of the PST programme:

1. What techniques are needed to know its effectiveness?
2. Has sufficient time been given to practice the psychological skills?
3. How useful is the practice session?
4. How useful is the individual practice on PST?
5. Should the psychologist be available?
6. Is the psychologist knowledgeable, informative and easy to talk with?
7. Should anything be added to or deleted from the programme?
8. What are the major strengths and weaknesses of the programme?

Problems in the PST Programme

The following are some of the common problems being faced in PST:

1. **Lack of conviction:** Many people are not interested in this programme. We will have to convince them that developing psychological skills will bring success to them.
2. **Lack of time:** Some psychologists frequently contend that there are some people who do not have enough time to practise psychological skills. But it is essential that time can be found if psychological skill training is made possible.
3. **Lack of knowledge:** Psychologists usually point out that some people lack specific knowledge about PST. Experience may help them to understand the specific problems they face. Due to the lack of knowledge, PST faced many problems.
4. **Lack of follow-up action:** Psychological skills need to be probed into so that the trainees have learned well enough to use in their event performance. Usually, it is found that there is a lack of follow-up action.

Application of PST

In the modern era of technological advancement, there is a pivotal need to learn and teach psychological skills. It is pertinent in the current times that everyone must possess psychological tools which make this modern life comfortable, pleasurable and worth living. Modern life has become very intricate and is full of strains and stresses, anxiety, frustrations, maladjustments, disgust and grief. Psychologists are trying their best to make human life happy, healthy and prosperous by offering some strategies for coping with the stress of daily life. Psychology is not only confined to study human behaviour, but it also helps to create psychological well-being and human wellness with the research works in the area of mental health and positive psychology.

In every human profession, the productivity of work is desired, and the efficiency of work can be increased by the knowledge of applied principles of human behaviour. The information regarding psychological skills and social competencies is the need of the hour. Of course, these skills are acquired through the exposure of varied types of lifetime experiences. Psychologists working in the area of health psychology, and positive psychology have devised certain techniques which are quite helpful in our daily life. One of these strategies or skills is the skill of imagery, which is considered as a master skill. Besides it, there are many others such as stress management, emotional arousal regulation, managing psychic energy, and psycho-regulative techniques. Others in the list include motivation, goal setting, developing self-confidence, attention and concentration skills, which enhance effectiveness and bring success at every step in our life. Hence, it is necessary that we should learn and imbibe these skills to make them a part of our daily life.

Psychological skills are beneficial in all walks of life, both professional and personal life. These skills play an important role in the fields of education, healthcare, sports, organizations and marketing, police and prison administration as well as in home-care activities. After getting training about these skills, they should be practised in life. For example, imagery is useful for mental rehearsal, managing psychic energy gives more vigour and energy in initiating any activity in life. Of course, motivation is required in the completion of any task and its accomplishment depends upon the goal-setting skill, which is also related to the fulfilment of our objectives and aims of our chalk-out programme as well as achieving the pursuit of excellence. Now, let us consider those areas of life where these skills can be applied:

1. **Education:** This is the priority area of our modern life. It is said that the future of the nation is laid down in the classroom where teachers have a very important role to play. The main objective of modern education is the all-round development of the child, that is, developing a balanced personality. There is an interaction between teachers and students in the classroom, and in order to make teachers most effective, they are taught subjects such as educational psychology, developmental psychology and other allied topics to make them acquainted with the knowledge of psychological principles, theories and systems. If we want to produce effective and role model teachers in our society, they should be taught psychological skills, which are very essential to deal with the students in the classroom. For example, motivational skill is required before the teacher starts teaching the lesson, to create interest in the lesson so that the students may be attracted to the lesson being taught with their full attention and concentration. Similarly, goal-setting skill is needed in the preparation of lesson planning and their monthly schedule of teaching.

It has been observed that many students lack confidence, and usually, they complain about this problem. The reason may be that they do not have interest in studies and their mind wanders to some other activities. They are unable to comprehend and retain the material learnt in their memorization process. With the result, they develop an inferiority complex, become nervous and adopt aggressive behaviour as well. Hence, there is a need to inculcate the feelings of self-confidence, which will create a sense of self-worth, self-esteem and self-concept. Here, the teacher can help the students in developing the self-confidence, which is possible if they have the knack for the self-confidence skill. Besides this, the teacher can also help the students to manage and channelize their psychic energy; otherwise, it may go waste in the anti-social activities. The teacher should also regulate their emotional arousal, which is a natural process in their developmental stage, especially among adolescents with the help of psycho-regulative techniques.

Moreover, time management skill needs to be applied in classroom teaching. The teacher is a group leader in this process of teaching and learning who should have a good command on their language, which is only possible if they possess the communication skill, both verbal and non-verbal. All this will be only possible if the teachers not only have the knowledge of their subject but also possess these psychological skills.

2. **Medical care:** In the field of healthcare, doctors, nurses, physiotherapists and paramedical staff pay a very useful role in society. Besides the knowledge in their own field, that is, biomedical sciences, they also need the knowledge and skills of psychology as they are dealing with human beings. They help to bring a smile on the faces of suffering humanity by curing their illnesses and rehabilitating them in their personal lives. So all these personnel should be taught the knowledge of the psychological skills, which are needed in their professional life. These are the persons who are working day and night for human wellness. They are not only looking after the physical health of human beings but the total health, which includes mental, emotional and social health too. Medical healthcare is a serving profession that is dealing with the sick and unwell patients. So they are more prone to strains and stresses and remain under tension for most of the time. There is a need to educate the medical staff regarding the techniques of stress management as well as psycho-regulative strategies in order to be free from any minor or major mental disorder so that they can serve the humanity in a better way.

   They should be given training in the skills of imagery and goal setting, as they have to rehabilitate their patients with care, especially injury patients. Many of them can be cured with behavioural therapies along with the medical and physiotherapy treatment. Even the physiotherapists should also learn these psychological skills in order to treat their patients in the most effective way. In fact, the area of physiotherapy and nursing is based on the sound principles of psychology.

3. **Sports:** The concept of PST was originated from the area of sports psychology. In fact, sports psychologists have been applying the

psychological skills on the sportspersons to enhance their sports performance. The psychological skills such as managing psychic energy, imagery, goal setting and motivation are being used by the coaches with the help of sports psychologists in order to maintain and sustain their motivation level and to keep their morale high as well as setting their goals for the peak performance and achieving excellence. Sports, especially competitive sport, is laden with anxiety, stress and tension due to insecurity and uncertainty of the outcome of the competition. The sports performance of these competing players has affected adversely because of the mental pressure on them to win only. The athletes who are suffering from some psychological problems can be helped with the skills of psycho-regulative techniques and stress management strategies. These techniques are being applied by the coaches on their sportspersons after learning from the sports psychologists in Western countries but less attention has been paid in this area of sports sciences in India; as a result, the performance of Indian athletes is not at par with those of other countries in international competition. American sports psychologists such as Rainer Martens, Cratty and Singer have conducted much research work on the application of these skills. Imagery is the latest area of research work for the American sports psychologists.

The first author of the book worked as a sports psychologist at Netaji Subhas National Institute of Sports, Patiala, for many years. He has the practical experience of conducting the mental exercises as a part of psychological training when he was associated with the Indian athletics team and Indian women hockey team as official team psychologist. He has been conducting the mental exercises on the national players and found positive results. The nature of the mental exercises is given further below. The objectives of psychological skill training in the field of competitive sports are given in Box 14.1.

These exercises (Box 14.2) will definitely assist in the enhancement of sports performance and reaching excellence/peak performance. If learnt, players can do these exercises on the day of competition either at their place of stay or in the playground

> **Box 14.1:** Objectives of the Psychological Skill Training
>
> 1. To help the players to be mentally fit, alert, tough and well prepared for competition
> 2. To sustain the motivational level of the players and also to increase their morale
> 3. To regulate their emotional arousal during competition
> 4. To alleviate the stresses and strains of the competitive situation and also to lessen the mental pressure and nervousness
> 5. To optimize the competition anxiety and also to update their activation level.
> 6. To increase their concentration ability in the game
> 7. To develop self-confidence and self-image/self-prestige
> 8. To set their winning goals and to give positive feedback and reinforcement

> **Box 14.2:** Programme of Mental Exercises
>
> A programme of mental exercises for 15–20 minutes per session has been chalked out as follows:
>
> 1. Exercises for mental relaxation for 5–7 minutes. To relax physically as well as mentally in Shavasana position taking deep breathing, normal breathing and concentration on their different body parts.
> 2. Autogenic exercises for providing mental toughness and alertness for 5–7 minutes. To bring feelings of heaviness and warmth and to feel preparedness physically and mentally for the competition.
> 3. Visualization exercises as a mental rehearsal for 3–5 minutes. To think and feel that they are in the competition setting and to get ready for competition and also to think mentally about their movement patterns as if they are going to perform in the competition.
> 4. Self-talk for self-confidence for 2–3 minutes regarding winning, best performance and excellence. They will say internally to themselves, 'I can win, I must win, I will have to win today' and also 'I will perform well, I must perform well and I can perform well'.

independently just before the competition. These exercises are meant for mental relaxation, toughness, alertness, rehearsal and also to develop self-confidence as well as to increase the concentration ability.

4. **Business and marketing area:** Now, the concept of PST has become very popular in the area of business and organizational management. In order to increase the productivity of the materials and products, the business leaders have to motivate the workers and labour class so that they may work very hard for their organization and also to achieve the organizational goals. Here, the motivation and goal-setting skills are very much required. For the selection of the personals for the organization and the training of these persons, the knowledge of psychological skills needs to be imparted. Even in the area of marketing, the personals who are working hard for the sale of their products, they need not only to be good salespersons but also be good practical psychologists in dealing with the customers. They have to know the psychology of human beings, in order to be an effective salesman, attracting the customers and convincing them for their products. For this purpose, they should be trained in psychological skills, so that to achieve their targets within schedule timing. Hence, they should learn the skills of time management, communication and goal setting and so on.

5. **Police and prison administration:** In the public sector, the most important departments are the police and prison administration. Police has the responsibility of maintaining law and order in the society as the crime rate is increasing in these days. It is essential for the officers and officials of the police department that they should deal with the law violators psychologically because they are also human beings, but those who have gone socially insane. Of course, they are a headache for the administration, yet it is the function of the welfare state to look after them according to the laws of the nation. Their behaviour has deviated, and they need to be reformed and educated to become good citizens of the nation. So all the police personals should be trained and educated regarding psychological skills which will be useful to them while performing their duties.

Similarly, the prison department is meant to keep watch and ward on those criminals who have been convicted by the courts. The purpose of the modern prison administration is not punitive but reformative. We have to reform those criminals who are spending their days of punishment in the jails and bring the behavioural modification. This purpose will only be achieved if the officers and officials of this department are educated in the psychological knowledge and they should also be trained in psychological skills, which may be helpful to them in performing their duties efficiently.

6. **Homemaking job:** Home caring is a full-time job for housewives. Women who are not working in offices, factories, schools or any other place of work have also an important function to perform at home. They spend their whole day in the household chores which include cooking in the kitchen, cleaning the house, laundry, gardening the lawn, looking after the children and caring for the husband. They are not only looking after the physical needs but also caring for the psychological needs of their family members. Hence, the information regarding psychological skills is very much required for them. They have to care for the educational needs and medical care of their kids. A mother is not only the first teacher of the child but also a good psychologist for her child. So she needs the knowledge regarding psychosocial skills along with the information regarding child psychology. She is not only a housewife but the most affectionate and affable lady in the family, and on her shoulders lie the happiness and prosperity of her family and the society.

So at the end, it may be stated that in these days training of psychological skills has attracted the attention of psychologists, behavioural scientists and educational administrators. Much research work in this area of PST has started now by the researchers to find out the new parameters of psychological skills in the field of positive psychology. But still, not much literature is available which may educate the people in this new area of wide application. So there is a need to write new books by the eminent psychologists and other experts should also devote their time on producing good literature for the benefit of people from all walks of life. Moreover, an attempt may be made by non-government organizations, social organizations or business houses to organize workshops and training courses for short or long term for the employees and other working men and women to acquaint them and keep them abreast with the latest findings in this area. Psychologists are interested in bringing positivity in the behaviour of the people so that humanity may thrive and lead a life full of happiness, health, grace, glory and is worth living.

SUGGESTIONS

After studying all the relevant psychological skills which are very important for our modern lifestyle, it is suggested that the psychologists should conduct more research work on these skills to come out with the empirical findings to know the efficacy of these psychological skills to reach the logical conclusion. They should also think of many more behavioural skills and concepts which are required in our present time, especially in these days of crisis of coronavirus disease (COVID-19), when the people are passing through bad days of isolation and mental pain of cognitive thought. Psychologists can play a useful role in combating this disease by helping people to manage stress and control anxiety and to face disappointment and frustration. They should come out with practical guidelines on how to live with it and defeat the outcome of this disease. They should suggest some mental exercises for making their life comfortable and pleasurable, for example, breathing and relaxation exercises, self-talk, visualization, meditation and yoga. They should organize a short-term workshop and training programme for teaching some of the psychological skills according to the nature of the problem which the people are facing. In this way, we can say that psychology is meant for human well-being and working for human wellness.

CONCLUSION

Training of psychological skills has become one of the important functions for the psychologists. The first step to starting the PST programme is to determine specific goals. The basic steps for starting PST are (a) conduct the initial orientation, (b) evaluate the present psychological skills, (c) teach the basic skills during the practice session, (d) individual counselling, (e) incorporate PST into practice and session plans, (f) monitoring progress and (vii) evaluation of the PST programme.

For the preparation of the PST programme, the activities which are involved are (a) integration of psychological skills, (b) setting performance goals, (c) engineering the environment and (d) on-site preparation. For learning psychological skills, one should (a) use empathy, (b) select another trainee, (c) aggravate the problem and (d) to include PST into trainees' training programme. There are some essentials points for the PST programme which should be followed. Psychological skills learning is an educative system for mental training. Mental training includes the teaching of some positive variables such as positive mental attitude, mental toughness, aggressiveness, self-motivation, self-confidence, character-building, leadership, anxiety management, concentration, competitiveness and communication skills.

Evaluation of the PST programme is very important aspect of PST. There are some ethical considerations which will help to show the effectiveness of the programme. The problems in this programme are (a) lack of conviction, (b) lack of time, (c) lack of knowledge and (d) lack of follow-up action.

Psychological skills are beneficial in all walks of life, both professional and personal life. These skills play an important role in the fields of education, healthcare, sports, organizations and marketing, police and prison administration as well as in home-care activities. After getting training about these skills, they should be practised in life. In these days, training of psychological skills has attracted the attention of psychologists, behavioural scientists and educational administrators. Much research work in this area of PST has started now by the researchers to find out the new parameters of psychological skills in the field of positive psychology.

PST not only has the theoretical implications for human wellness, but it has practical aspects in modern life. The application of these psychological skills is the need of the hour not only in professional life but also in personal life. Teachers, doctors and other medical staff, coaches in the field of sports, industrial workers, organizational personals, the police officer and prison officers need to be trained and educated on some psychological principles which are useful in their professional life, and especially, they should take initiative in learning the psychological skills and behavioural strategies which help them to be the most effective persons to serve the society in a very productive manner.

REFERENCES

Alderfer, C. P. (1969). An empirical test of a new theory of human needs. *Organizational Behavior and Human Performance*, 4(2), 142–175.

Appley, M. H., & Traumbull, R. (1967). *Psychological stress*. Appleton Century Crafts.

Armstrong, J. S. (Ed.). (2001). *Principles of forecasting: A handbook for researchers and practitioners*. Kluwer Academic Publishers.

Aubrey, B. (2010). *Managing your aspirations: Developing personal enterprise in the global workplace*. McGraw-Hill.

Bandura, A. (1977a). Self-efficacy: Toward a unifying theory of behavioral change. *Psychological Review*, 84(2), 191–225.

Bandura, A. (1977b). *Social learning theory*. Prentice Hall.

Bandura, A. (1982). Self-efficacy mechanism in human agency. *American Psychology*, 37(2), 122–147.

Bandura, A. (1986). *Social foundations of thought and action: A social cognitive theory*. Prentice Hall.

Bandura, A. (1997). *Self-efficacy: The exercise of control*. W. H. Freeman and Company.

Barrow, J. (1977). The variables of leadership. A review and conceptual framework. *Academy of Management Review*, 2(2), 231–251.

Bennett, J. G. (1964). *A spiritual psychology*. Hodder & Stoughton.

Benson, H. (1975). *The relaxation response*. William Morrow.

Benson, H., & Proctor, W. (1984). *Beyond the relaxation response*. Berkley Books.

Boutcher, S. H., & Trenske, M. (1990). The effects of sensory deprivation and music on perceived exertion and affect during exercise. *Journal of Sport & Exercise Psychology*, 12(2), 167–176.

Brandell, J. R. (1997). *Theory and practice in clinical social work*. Simon and Schuster, p. 189.

Brockmann, E. N., & Anthony, W. P. (2016). Tacit knowledge and strategic decision making. *Group & Organization Management*, 27(4), 436–455.

Brown, J. D. (1993). Self-esteem and self-evaluation: Feeling is believing. In J. M. Suls (Ed.), *Psychological perspectives on the self, Volume 4: The self in social perspective* (27–58). Lawrence Erlbaum Associates.

Burton, D. (1983). Evaluation of goal setting training on selected cognitions and performance of collegiate swimmers (Unpublished doctoral dissertation). University of Illinois, Urbana.

Burton, D. (1984). Goal setting: A secret to success. *Swimming world, 2*, 25–29.

Burton, D. (1989a). Winning isn't everything: Examining the impact of performance goals on collegiate swimmers' cognitions and performance. *The Sport Psychologist, 3*(2),105–132.

Burton, D. (1989b). Impact of goal specificity and task complexity on basketball skill development. *The Sport Psychologist, 3*(1), 34–37.

Campbell, A., Converse, S. E., & Rodgers, W. L. (1976). *The quality of American life*. Russell Sage Foundation.

Campbell, R. N. (1984). *The new science: Self-esteem psychology*. University Press of America.

Cattell, R. B. (1957). Personality and motivation theory based on structural measurement. In J. L. McCary (Ed.) *Psychology of personality*. Grove Press.

Cattell, R. B. (1965). *The scientific analysis of personality*. Penguin.

Cratty, B. J. (1973a). *Movement behavior and motor learning (3rd Ed)*. Lea & Febiger.

Cratty, B. J. (1973b). *Psychology in contemporary sports*. Prentice Hall.

Csikszentmihalyi, M. (1975). *Beyond boredom and anxiety*. Jossey-Bass Publishers.

Csikszentmihalyi, M. (1982). Towards a psychology of optional experience. In L. Wheeler (Ed.), *Review of personality and social psychology* (volume 3, 13–35). SAGE Publications.

Csikszentmihalyi, M. (1985). Emergent motivation and the evolution of the self, In D. Kleiber & M. Maehr (Eds.), *Advances in motivation and achievement* (Volume 4, 93–119). JAI Press.

Csikszentmihalyi, M. (1990). *Flow: The psychology of optimal experience*. Harper & Row.

Diener, E., & Diener, M. (1995). Cross cultural correlates of life satisfaction and self-esteem. *Journal of Personality and Social Psychology, 68*(4), 653–663.

Diener, E., Suh, E. M., Lucas, R. E., & Smith, H. L. (1999). Subjective well-being: Three decades of progress. *Psychological Bulletin, 125*(2), 276–302.

Duffy, E. (1957). The psychological significance of the concept of 'arousal' and 'activation'. *Psychological Review, 64*(5), 265–275.

Duffy, E. (1962). *Activation and behaviour*. Wiley.

Duval, S., & Wicklund, R. A. (1972). *A theory of objective self awareness*. Academic Press.

Feltz, D. L., & Landers, D. M. (1983). The effects of mental practice on motor skill learning and performance: A meta-analysis. *Journal of Sport Psychology, 5*(1), 25–57.

Feltz, D. L (1988). Self-confidence and sports performance. In K. B. Pandolf (Ed.), *Exercise and sport science reviews* (423–457). Macmillan.

Fiedler, F. (1967). *A theory of leadership effectiveness*. McGraw Hill.

Fredrick, B. L., & Thomson, J. (2002). Positive emotions trigger upward spirals toward emotional well-being. *Psychological Science*, 13(2). https://dx.doi.org/10.1111/1467-9280.00431

Freud, S. (1923). *The ego and the id, XIX* (2nd ed.). Hogarth Press.

Garland, H. (1985). A cognitive mediation theory of task goals and human performance. *Motivation and Emotion*, 9(4), 345–367.

Gould, D., & Krane, V. (1992). The arousal–performance relationship: Current status and future directions, In T. Horn (Ed.) *Advances in sport psychology* (119–141). Human Kinetics.

Gould, D., & Krane, V. (2002). The arousal-athletic performance relationship: Current status and future directions. In T. S. Horn (Ed.), *Advances in sport psychology* (119–142). Human Kinetics.

Hamilton, R. A., Scott, D., & MacDougall, M. P. (2007). Assessing the effectiveness of self-talk interventions on endurance performance. *Journal of Applied Sport Psychology*, 19(2), 226–239.

Haney, C. J. (2004). Stress-management interventions for female athletes: Relaxation and cognitive restructuring. *International Journal of Sports Psychology*, 35(2), 109–118.

Hardy, L., Jones, G., & Gould, D. (1996). *Understanding psychological preparation for sport: Theory and practice of elite performers*. John Wiley & Sons.

Harris, D. V., & Williams, J. M. (1993). Relaxation and energizing techniques for regulation of arousal. In J. M. Williams (Ed.), *Applied sport psychology* (185–199). Mayfield.

Harter, S. (1996). *Historical roots of contemporary issues involving self-concept*. John Wiley & Sons.

Hatzigeorgiadis, A., Nikos, Z., & Theodorakis, Y. (2007). The moderating effects of self-talk content on self-talk functions. *Journal of Applied Sport Psychology*, 19(2), 240–251.

Jackson, S. A. (1992). Athletes in flow: A qualitative investigation of flow states in elite figure skaters. *Journal of Applied Sport Psychology*, 4(2), 161–180.

Jackson, S. A. (1995). Factors influencing the occurrence of flow states in elite athletes. *Journal of Applied Sport Psychology*, 7(2), 138–166.

Jackson, S. A. (1996). Toward a conceptual understanding of the flow experience in elite athletes. *Research Quarterly for Exercise and Sport*, 67(1), 76–90.

Jackson, S. A. (2000). Joy, fun, and flow in sport. In Y. L. Hanin (Ed.) *Emotions in sport* (135–156). Human Kinetics.

Jackson, S. A., & Csikszentmihalyi, M. (1999). *Flow in sports*. Human Kinetics.

Jackson, S. A., & Roberts, G. C. (1992). Positive performance states of athletes: Toward a conceptual understanding of peak performance. *The Sport Psychologist*, 6(2), 156–171.

Jackson, S. A., Kmiecik, J. C., Ford, S. K., & Marsh, H. W. (1998). Psychological correlates of flow in sport. *Journal of Sport & Exercise Psychology*, 20(4), 358–378.

Jacobson, E. (1938). *Progressive relaxation*. University of Chicago Press.

Jain, A. (2018). Development of self through meditation, yoga, values and spirituality. In A. J. Singh and P. Kaur (Eds.). *Understanding the self*. Twenty First Century Publications.129

James, W. (1896). Great men and their environment. In W. James (Ed.), *The will to believe and other essays in popular philosophy* (216–254). Midwest Journal Press.

Jones, G. (1993). The role of performance profiling in cognitive behavioral interventions in sport. *The Sport Psychologists*, 7(2), 160–172. https://doi.org/10.1123/tsp.7.2.160

Jung, C. G. (1933). *Psychological types: Collected works* (Vol. 6). Routledge.

Kahneman, D., & Tversky, A. (Eds.). (2000). *Choices, values, and frames*. Cambridge University Press.

Krahenbuhl, G. S. (1975). Adrenaline, arousal and sport. *Journal of Sports Medicine*, 3(3), 117–121.

Landers, D. M. (1980). The arousal-performance relationship revisited. *Research Quarterly for Exercise and Sport*, 51(1), 77–90.

Landers, D. M., & Boutcher, S. H. (1986). Arousal-performance relationships. In J. M. Williams (Ed.), *Applied sport psychology: Personal growth to peak performance* (163–184). Mayfield.

Landin, D. M. (1994). Questions and answers. *ISSP Newsletter*, p. 20.

Lavey, R. S., & Taylor, C. B. (1985). The nature of relaxation therapy. In S. R. Burchfield (Ed.), *Stress: Psychological and physiological interactions*. Hemisphere.

Lazarus, R. S., & Folkman, S. (1984). *Stress, appraisal and coping*. Springer.

Lewin, K. (1951). *Field theory in social science. Selected theoretical papers*. Harper.

Lindzey, G.E. (1954). *Handbook of Social Psychology: Applied Social Psychology*. Addison-Wesley publishing company, Inc.

Locke, E. A., & Latham, G. P. (1990). *A theory of goal setting and task performance*. Prentice Hall.

Locke, E. A., Shaw, K. N., Saari, L. M., & Latham, G. P. (1981). Goal setting and task performance. *Psychological Bulletin*, 90(1), 125–152.

Loehr, J. E. (1986). *Mental toughness training for sports: Achieving athletic excellence*. Stephen Greene Press.

Luthans, F., & Youssef, C. M. (2004). Human, social, and now positive psychological capital management: Investing in people for competitive advantage. *Organizational Dynamics*, 33(2), 143–160.

Maddux, J., & Lewis, J. (1995). Self-efficacy and adjustment: Basic principles and issues. In J. E. Maddux (Ed.) *Self-efficacy, adaptation, and adjustment: Theory, research and application* (37–68). Plenum Press.

Martens, R. (1976). Competitiveness and Sport. Paper presented at the International Congress of Physical Activity Sciences, Quebec City, Canada.

Martens, R. (1987). *Coaches' guide to sport psychology*. Human Kinetics.

Maslow, A. H. (1943). A theory of human motivation. *Psychological Review, 50*(4), 370–396.

McGrath J. E. (Ed.). (1970). *Social and psychological factors in stress*. Holt Rinehart and Winston.

Miller, S., & Weinberg, R. (1991). Perceptions of psychological momentum and their relationship to performance. *The Sport Psychologist, 5*(3), 211–222.

Morris, T., & Koehn, S (2004). Self-confidence in sport and exercise. In T. Morris & J. Summers (Eds.) *Sport psychology: Theory applications and issues* (2nd ed., 175–209). Wiley.

Murray, H.A. (1938). *Explorations in Psychology*. Oxford University Press.

Muthiah, C. M. (1980). Pre competition psychotonic training. *Athletic Asia, 10*(1), 9–16.

Nideffer, R. (1976). Test of attentional and interpersonal style. *Journal of Personality and Social Psychology, 34*(3), 394–404.

Orlick, T. (1988). *In pursuit of excellence*. Human Kinetics.

Orlick, T. (2000). *In pursuit of excellence: How to win in sport and life through mental training* (3rd ed.). Human Kinetics.

Orlick, T., & Partington, L. (1988). Mental links to excellence. *The Sport Psychologist, 2*(2), 105–130.

Oxendine, J. B. (1970). Emotional arousal and motor performance. *Quest, 13*(1), 23–32.

Oxendine, J. B. (1984). *Psychology of motor learning*. Prentice Hall.

Pavot, W., & Diener, E. (2008). The satisfaction with life scale and the emerging construct of life satisfaction. *The Journal of Positive Psychology, 3*(2), 137–152.

Porter, K. (2003). *The mental athlete: Inner training for peak performance in all sports*. Human Kinetics.

Richardson, A. (1969). Mental practice: A review and discussion. *Research Quarterly, 38*(2), 95–107.

Robertson, S. I. (2001). *Problem solving*. Psychology Press.

Rogers, C. (1951). *Client-centered therapy: Its current practice, implications and theory*. Boston Houghton.

Rogers, C. (1961). *On becoming a person: A therapist's view of psychotherapy*. Houghton Mifflin.

Ryan, R. M., & Deci, E. L. (2000). Self-determination theory and the facilitation of intrinsic motivation, social development, and well-being. *American Psychologist. 55*(1). 68–78.

Ryff, C. (1995). Scales of psychological well-being. University of Wisconsin, Institute on Aging, 2245 Medical Science Center, 1300 University Avenue, Madison, WI 53706.

Schacter, D. L., Gilbert D. T., & Wegner, D. M . (2009). *Psychology* (2nd Ed.). Worth Publishers. pp. 376

Schmidt, R. A. (1982). *Motor control and learning: A behavioral emphasis.* Human Kinetics.

Schultz, J., & Luthe, W. (1969). *Autogenic therapy.* Grune and Stratton.

Selye, H. (1956). *The stress of life.* McGraw-Hill.

Selye, H. (1959). Perspective in stress research. *Perspectives in Biology and Medicine, 2*(4), 403–416.

Selye, H. (1974). *Stress and coping: The Indian experience.* McGraw Hill.

Selye, H. (1982). The stress concept: Past, present and future. In C. L. Cooper (Ed.) *Stress research: Issues for the eighties.* Wiley.

Shepard, R. (1979). Habitual Physical Activity and Quality of Life. *Quest. 48,* 354–365.

Singh, A., & Singh, N. (2012). Psychological wellbeing of the adolescents in relation to their emotional intelligence. In A. Singh (Ed.), *Positive psychology.* Psycho-Information Technologies.

Smith, R, E. (1980). A cognitive-affective approach to stress management training for athletes. In C. H. Nadeau, W. R. Halliwell, K. M. Newell, & G. C. Roberts (Eds.), *Psychology of motor behavior and sport 1979* (54–72). Human Kinetics.

Sonstroem, R. J. (1984). Exercise and self-esteem. *Exercise and Sport Sciences Reviews, 12,* 123–155.

Spielberger, C. D. (Ed.). (1972). *Current trends in theory & research* (Vol. 2). Academic Press.

Suinn, R., & Clayton, R. D. (1980). *Psychology in sports: Method and application.* Burgess Pub.

Vealey, R. S. (1986). Conceptualization of sport-confidence and competitive orientations: Preliminary investigation and instrument development. *Journal of Sport Psychology, 8*(3), 221–246.

Vealey, R. S. (1988). Sport personology: A paradigmatic and methodological analysis. *Journal of Sport and Exercise Psychology, 11*(2), 216–235.

Verma, S. K. (1988). Measurement of positive mental health: Some theoretical and practical consideration. *Indian Journal of Clinical Psychology, 15*(1), 6–11.

Weinberg, R. S. (1988). *The mental advantage: Developing your psychological skills in tennis.* Human Kinetics.

Weinberg, R. S., & Gould, D. (1995). *Foundations of sport and exercise psychology.* Human Kinetics.

Weinberg, R. S., & Gould, D. (1999). *Foundations of sport and exercise psychology.* Human Kinetics.

Weinberg, R. S., & Gould, D. (2003). *Foundations of sport & exercise psychology* (3rd Ed.). Human Kinetics.

Weinberg, R. S., & Gould, D. (2007). *Foundations of sport & exercise psychology* (4th Ed.). Human Kinetics.

Widmeyer, W. N., & Ducharme, K. (1997). Team building through team goal setting. *Journal of Applied Sport Psychology, 9*(1), 61–72.

Williams, J. M. (2003). *Applied sports psychology* (4th Ed.). Mayfield Publications.
Williams, J. M. (2006). *Applied sports psychology* (6th Ed.). Mayfield Publications.
Williams, A. M., & Elliot, D. (1999). Anxiety, expertise, and visual strategy in karate. *Journal of Sport and Exercise Psychology, 21*(4), 362–375.
Wylie, R.C. (1979). *The self-concept: Theory and research on selected topics* (Vol. 2). University of Nebraska.
Wylie, R.C. (1989). *Measures of self-concept.* University of Nebraska.
Zaichowsky, L. D. (1982). Biofeedback for self-regulation of competitive stress. In L. D. Zaichowsky & W. E. Sime (Eds.), *Stress management for sport*. American Alliance for Health, Physical Education, Recreation and Dance.
Zohar, D. & Marshall, I. N. (2000). *Spiritual intelligence: The ultimate intelligence.* Bloomsbury.

ABOUT THE AUTHORS

Agya Jit Singh retired as Head in the Department of Psychology, Punjabi University, Patiala, after serving for 30 years. He holds a masters degree in psychology and education, with M.Litt in educational psychology and PhD in sports psychology. He has an experience of teaching to post-graduate classes in the area of educational psychology as well as measurement and evaluation. He has also worked as a coordinator in the Department of Correspondence Courses in the University for B.Ed. and M.Ed courses for a few years.

He has the privilege of serving in the prestigious international famed institution, that is, Netaji Subhas National Institute of Sports, Patiala, as a sports psychologist for many years. He worked as a team psychologist with Indian athletic team and Indian women's hockey team before Busan Asian Games in 2002 while serving at Netaji Subhas National Institute of Sports, Patiala.

Dr Singh has also worked as principal-cum-director of a few colleges of education for three years after his retirement. He has published more than 200 articles and research papers in different journals and magazines of repute and published 81 books in psychology and education. Much of his work are under publication. He has guided 42 PhD scholars and 30 MPhil research theses and has attended more than 70 national and international conferences and seminars in India and abroad where he had been presenting his research papers. He also attended 5th World Sports Psychology Conference held at Brussels, Belgium, in November 1987 and also visited National Institute of Sports at Paris, France.

He has visited Belgium, France and the USA on academic pursuits. He was in Boston, USA, thrice and collaborated his work with well-known sports psychologists. Senologic International Society honoured him with research award in 2001. He was given 'Lifetime Achievement Award' in sports psychology by the Sports Psychology Association of India at the International Conference of Sports Psychology held at Lakshmibai National University of Physical Education, Gwalior, in 2009. He was also a member of the Senate and Syndicate of Punjabi University during 1990–1992. He was the member of the Finance Committee of the Central University of Punjab, Bathinda. He was honoured with the award of Eminent Psychologist by Praachi Psycho-cultural Research Association at its 10th Annual Conference held at DAV College for Women, Firozpur Cantt, in 2016. Recently, he was awarded Lifetime Achievement Award in psychology by International Telepsychology Association and Senologic International Society (USA) at Panjab University Chandigarh.

Ramneet Kaur has a PhD in biotechnology with postdoctoral research training from Harvard Medical School, Boston, and Emory University, Atlanta, USA, in the field of cancer biology. Currently, she is a faculty in the Biology Department at the University of North Georgia, USA. Dr Kaur also has an academic position at Mercer University, Atlanta. Her research is in the field of triple-negative breast cancer. She has published various research papers in high impact factor scientific journals in the field of cancer. She has contributed many chapters on psychology topics in several books of psychology. Dr Kaur has an interest in an inter-disciplinary relationship of biology with psychology.

INDEX

Abraham Maslow
  need hierarchy model
    aesthetic needs, 94
    need for curiosity, 94
    need for self-fulfilment, 94
alertness, 193
anxiety reduction, 16
anxious-reactive, 146
arousal
  Landers's view, 43
  Martens's view, 43
  regulation, 66
attention, 186
  characteristics of, 187
  factors influencing, 190–191
    information processing, 192
  flexibility
    guidelines for improving, 197
  focus
    types, 188
  internal factors
    abilities, 194
    interests, 194
    mind set, 194
    suggestions, 195
  skills, 197
    decisions, 192
    training programmes, 198
  types of, 189
autogenic technique, 170

breath control, 178
  effects, 175
  initial relaxation training, 171
  principles, 172
  psychological preparation, 174
  six hierarchical stages, 170
  stages, 172
autonomous nervous system, 124–126
autonomy, 26, 96

behavioural approach of leadership, 249
behavioural training, 19
broad external style (assessing), 190
broad internal style (analyzing), 190

challenge
  relationship between skill, 46
Clayton Alderfer
  ERG theory of motivation, 95
communication, 255
  leaders, 256–259
competence, 96
concentration, 214
  attention strategies, 200
  defined, 199
  guidelines for improving ability, 201
  parts, 200
  training, exercise, 201

controllability, 68
  expectation, 70
  motivation, 70
  relaxed attention, 69
  right setting, 69
coping strategies
  eight conceptual categories, 157
  functional categories, 157

decision-making
  ability, 267–269
  defined, 265
  factors influencing problem-solving, 276
  problem-solving, 273–274
  process, 263
    characteristics, 266
    human behaviour, 264
    phases in, 269–272
  skills
    analytical, 267
    behavioural, 267
    conceptual, 267
    directive, 267
  stages in problem-solving, 274–275
democratic leadership, 248
diffidence, 207

effective dealing, 16
  anxiety reduction, 16
  emotional arousal regulation, 16
  mental imagery, 16
  self-talk, 16
effective leadership, 250
efforts, 214
emotional arousal, 120
  concept of, 121–122
  effect on performance, 126–127
  inducing techniques, 131–132
  interactional model, 128–130
  physiological aspects of arousal states, 122–124
  regulation, 16, 130

emotional health
  facets, 36
emotional intelligence (EI), 21
emotionally healthy person
  characteristics, 36
emotional wellness, 23
  definition, 34
  good health, 36
  total health, 37–38
encouraging and rewarding statements, 217
esteem needs, 93
expectation, 70
external imagery, 64
extrinsic motivation, 88

facilitative skills, 15
  effective dealing, 16
  goal setting, 15
  positive attitude, 15
  self-motivation, 15
false overconfidence, 208
flow, 47, 59
  factors to achieve, 52–53
    concentration on task, 52
    confidence and positive feelings, 53
    environmental conditions, 53
    feeling good about performance, 53
    motivation to perform, 52
    optimal arousal, 52
    physical preparation and readiness, 53
    plans and preparation, 52
    positive attitude, 53
  factors which disrupt, 53–54
  optimum psychic energy, 50–51

goals
  defining, 101
  Locke & Latham's definition, 101
  outcome, 102

Index

performance, 102–103
process, 103
smart, 103
types, 102–104
goal setting, 15
defined, 4
designing programme, 107–109
need, 105
performance, 105–107
programme, 214
psychological skills, 100
styles of, 114–117
uses, 117

human wellness, 20
autonomy, 26
concept, 21–22
environmental mastery, 26
factors, 24–27
meaning, 23
need achievement, 24
opportunity for promotion, 25
personal growth, 27
positive interpersonal relations, 25
recognition of work, 25
salary and wages, 25
self-acceptance, 25
self-concept, 27–29
self-esteem, 29–31
sense of purpose in life, 26
social acceptance, 24
utilization of one's abilities and capacities, 24

imagery, 7, 60–62
applied issues, 65–70
concept, 60–63
fundamentals
controllability, 69
vividness, 68
interventions programme, 65
need and importance, 63–64
objectives, 65

rehearsal, 62
tool, 66–67
injury and pain control, 67
planning for event management, 66
self-image manipulation, 67
stress management, 67
types, 64
uses of, 73–75
Imagery Training Programme (ITP), 72–73
developing, 70–72
implementing psychological skills, 7
imagery, 7–9
mental rehearsal, 9
mental toughness, 10
relaxation, 11
self-talk, 9
intellectual wellness, 23
interactional approach leadership, 250
interactional-oriented motivation, 84
internal imagery, 64
intrinsic motivation, 86–87

Jacobson's progressive relaxation
autogenic technique, 170
Jacobson's Progressive relaxation
procedure, 168
technique, 167
job stress
effects, 149
causes, 150
factors, 150
personal problems, 155
physical problems, 154
psychological problems, 155
sources
extra organizational stressors, 153
group stressors, 152
individual stressors, 151
organizational stressors, 152

laissez-faire leadership, 248
leader–follower relationships, 253
leadership, 242
  behaviour, 244–245
  characteristics, 244
  characteristics/traits, 251
  function
    execution, 246
    inspiration, 246
  style, 247–250
  training, 252–253
love and belonging needs, 93

material self, 225
mental capacity, 193
mental imagery, 16
  Richardson's view, 7, 61
mental skills
  types, 60
mental toughness, 10
mindfulness, 31
  comprehensive technique, 33
  concept, 32
  develops present qualities, 33
  evidence-based, 34
  human wellness in, 31–34
  innovation, 34
  part of lifestyle, 34
  potential, 33
momentum, 214
mood words, 217
motivated behavior
  characteristics, 81–82
  functions, 82–84
motivation, 70, 78, 81
  characteristics, 79
  concepts, 84
  extrinsic, 88
  interactional-oriented, 84
  interaction of intrinsic and
    extinction, 88
  intrinsic, 86–87
  nature, 78–79

need hierarchy model, 88–95
Motivation and Personality, 90
motives, 80
  characteristics, 81–82
  functions, 82–84
  physiological, 85
  social, 85–86
  types, 84–86
  views regarding, 81

narrow external style (performing), 190
needs
  esteem, 93
  hierarchy, 90
  love and belonging, 93
  physiological, 92
  safety and security, 93
  social, 93
Nideffer's Two-dimensional model, 189
non-verbal communication, 259–260

occupational stress
  effects, 156
    coping strategies, 156
optimal psychic energy zone, 54, 59
outcome goals, 102

performance, 214
performance goals, 102–103
performance skills, 14
personal-development
  issues and problems, 236
  meditation and yoga, 236
  transformation, 237
    environmental challenges, 237
    experience, 237
    injuries and accidents, 237
physical energy, 41
physical wellness, 23
physiological motives, 85
physiological needs, 92
positive attitude, 15

Index

positive emotions, 214
practice, 70
process goals, 103
progressive muscle relaxation (PMR) technique, 11
psychic energy, 41, 58
  changes due to increased, 45
    behavioural, 46
    physiological, 45
    psychological, 46
  concept, 42
  need and importance, 57–58
  performance relationship, 47–50
  PST, 56
  psychological stress, 46
psychic energy managing, 45
psyching out, 55
psyching up, 55
psychological capital, 44
  concept, 43–45
  efficacy, 44
  hope, 44
  optimism, 44
  resilience, 44
psychological skills, 1, 18, 62, 100
  facilitative skills, 15
  goal setting, 100
  performance skills, 14
  purpose, 20
  application, 289
    health care, 292
    modern, 291–292
    sports psychology, 292
  approach to manage psychic energy, 55
  behavioural training, 6
  business and marketing area, 295
  communication, 3–4
  conflict resolution, 5
  empathy, 5
  essential, 286
  evaluation, 288
  full-time job, 296
  general psychological preparation, 284
    engineer the environment, 285
    goals, 285
    on-site preparation, 285
    psychological skills, 284
  goal setting, 4
  goal-setting skills, 12–14
  implementing, 287
  managing psychic energy, 11
  mental exercises, 294
  objectives, 294
  phases, 16–19
    acquisition, 17
    education, 16
    practice, 17–18
  police and prison administration, 295
  power of imagery, 11
  problem of concentration and self-confidence, 12
  problems, 289
  questionnaire, 283–284
  self-improvement, 5
  steps, 280–283
  through imagery, 67–68
  time management, 6
psycho-regulative techniques, 166
  arousal control, 167
  rationale behind, 167

quality of life, 20

reactional self, 226
relatedness, 96
relaxation response, 11, 69
  Benson's method, 179
relaxation training
  meditation, 182
  yoga, 182

safety and security needs, 93
selective attention, 192

self
  defined, 222
self-acceptance, 229
self-actualization, 93
  defining, 94
self-awareness, 228
self-concept, 27
  characteristics, 29
  human wellness, 27–29
self-confidence, 210
  benefits, 213
  defined, 204
  diffidence, 207
  emotional arousals, 213
  high thinking and leading a simple life, 215
  imagery, 215
  mastery experiences, 212
  optimum, 206
  physical conditioning, 216
  preparation, 216
  qualities, 207
  self-talk, 216
  successful accomplishments, 215
  verbal persuasion, 213
  vicarious experience, 213
  working confidently, 215
Self-determination theory (SDT), 96–97
self-development, 226
  adults, 234
  commitment, control and challenge (3 Cs), 230
  Indian adolescents
    conflicts, 233
    drugs addicted, 232
    parental deprivation, 233
    sex-relationships, 232
    unemployment and under-employment, 232
    value system, 233
  know ourselves, 235
  personal vision, 234
  planning process, 234
  positive attitudes, 230
  positive relationship, 230
  procedures, 234
  record, 234
  reviewing, 234
  self-care, 230
  self-sufficiency, 230
  sense of we feeling, 230
  techniques, strategies, and practices, 239
  yoga, role, 237–238
self-efficacy, 210
  theory, 211
self-esteem
  human wellness, 31
self-motivation, 15
self-talk, 9, 16
  advantages, 218
self-worth, 209
setting goals
  problems in, 109–111
situational approach of leadership, 248
skill acquisition, 65
skill maintenance, 65
smart goals, 103
social motives, 85–86
social needs, 93
social wellness, 23
spiritual wellness, 23
state-oriented motivation, 84
stress, 136
  alarm stage, 136
  biological and psychological coping strategies, 160
  biological sources, 146
  consequences
    mental health and psychological well-being, 148
    performance, 148
    physical health, 148
  demand, 139
  exhaustion stage, 137

external factors, 145
McGrath model
  behavioural consequences, 142
  environmental demand, 142
  events, 141
  perception of demand, 142
  response, 142
nadi shodhan pranayama (anulom vilom), 159
natural equilibrium, 138
non-adaptive, 138
personality
  characteristics, 145
  type, 146
physiological symptoms of, 147
positive and negative
  distress, 141
  eustress, 140
reaction
  behavioural reactions, 144
  cognitive responses, 144
  physiological type, 143
resistance phase, 137
situational causes, 147
types of reactions, 144
workplace, 149
Yoga *asana*, 159
stress management
  behavioural technique, 161
  biofeedback training, 176
  cognitive techniques, 162
  criticism, 163
  delegation techniques, 163
  nourishment, 163
  physiological techniques, 160
stressors, 138, 145
subjective wellness, 21

task-specific statements, 217
trait approach of leadership, 248
trait-oriented motivation, 84
true self, 226

unconditional positive regard (UPR), 28

vividness, 68
  expectation, 70
  motivation, 70
  relaxed attention, 69
  right setting, 69